POSTWAR MARKET
FOR STATE AND LOCAL GOVERNMENT
SECURITIES

NATIONAL BUREAU OF ECONOMIC RESEARCH

Studies in Capital Formation and Financing

Postwar Market
for State and Local
Government Securities

BY ROLAND I. ROBINSON

A STUDY BY THE
NATIONAL BUREAU OF ECONOMIC RESEARCH

PUBLISHED BY
PRINCETON UNIVERSITY PRESS, PRINCETON
1960

Printed in the United States of America
by Princeton University Press, Princeton, New Jersey

RELATION OF THE DIRECTORS

TO THE WORK AND PUBLICATIONS

OF THE NATIONAL BUREAU OF ECONOMIC RESEARCH

1. The object of the National Bureau of Economic Research is to ascertain and to present to the public important economic facts and their interpretation in a scientific and impartial manner. The Board of Directors is charged with the responsibility of ensuring that the work of the National Bureau is carried on in strict conformity with this object.

2. To this end the Board of Directors shall appoint one or more Directors of Research.

3. The Director or Directors of Research shall submit to the members of the Board, or to its Executive Committee, for their formal adoption, all specific proposals concerning researches to be instituted.

4. No report shall be published until the Director or Directors of Research shall have submitted to the Board a summary drawing attention to the character of the data and their utilization in the report, the nature and treatment of the problems involved, the main conclusions, and such other information as in their opinion would serve to determine the suitability of the report for publication in accordance with the principles of the National Bureau.

5. A copy of any manuscript proposed for publication shall also be submitted to each member of the Board. For each manuscript to be so submitted a special committee shall be appointed by the President, or at his designation by the Executive Director, consisting of three Directors selected as nearly as may be one from each general division of the Board. The names of the special manuscript committee shall be stated to each Director when the summary and report described in paragraph (4) are sent to him. It shall be the duty of each member of the committee to read the manuscript. If each member of the special committee signifies his approval within thirty days, the manuscript may be published. If each member of the special committee has not signified his approval within thirty days of the transmittal of the report and manuscript, the Director of Research shall then notify each member of the Board, requesting approval or disapproval of publication, and thirty additional days shall be granted for this purpose. The manuscript shall then not be published unless at least a majority of the entire Board and a two-thirds majority of those members of the Board who shall have voted on the proposal within the time fixed for the receipt of votes on the publication proposed shall have approved.

6. No manuscript may be published, though approved by each member of the special committee, until forty-five days have elapsed from the transmittal of the summary and report. The interval is allowed for the receipt of any memorandum of dissent or reservation, together with a brief statement of his reasons, that any member may wish to express; and such memorandum of dissent or reservation shall be published with the manuscript if he so desires. Publication does not, however, imply that each member of the Board has read the manuscript, or that either members of the Board in general, or of the special committee, have passed upon its validity in every detail.

7. A copy of this resolution shall, unless otherwise determined by the Board, be printed in each copy of every National Bureau book.

(Resolution adopted October 25, 1926
and revised February 6, 1933 and February 24, 1941)

This report is one emerging from an investigation of postwar capital market developments in the United States aided by a grant to the National Bureau from the Life Insurance Association of America. The Association is not, however, the author, publisher, or proprietor of this publication, and is not to be understood as approving or disapproving by virtue of its grant any of the statements made or views expressed herein.

FOREWORD

THIS study of the market for state and local government securities during the postwar decade is the first major product of the National Bureau's Postwar Capital Market Study to be published. Like companion studies of the markets for Treasury securities, corporate securities and loans, and residential mortgages, this volume provides an analytical description of one of the main sectors of the American capital market as it operated during the postwar decade. Each of the monographs is a self-contained piece of research that, we hope, will make a contribution to study of the sector of the capital market with which it deals. All the monographs use the common statistical framework of the flow-of-funds-through-the-capital-markets statements and of national and sectoral balance sheets, both of which are described in more detail in other reports of the Postwar Capital Market Study. Because of the necessity of starting these monographs and the statistical work on some basic aspects of the capital market (flow of funds, saving, investment, wealth and balance sheets) at approximately the same time in 1956, when the Postwar Capital Market Study was initiated, it was not possible to use the same set of statistical data and the same approach in all of the monographs, even if such uniformity had been regarded as desirable. But the differences are not great.

Robinson's monograph cannot be reduced to a few simple or startling conclusions: it is a careful and realistic description and analysis of the operation of one important sector of the American capital market, the results of which cannot be boiled down into a few paragraphs without losing most of the study's value and significance. It may, however, not be amiss to explain briefly the reasons for a few limitations of the study which many readers will soon notice.

First, the statistical material used ends almost always with the year 1956 and consideration of events occurring after that date is rare. However, the fact that the study does not take specific account of developments during the last three years is in this case not a serious drawback. What has happened since 1956 has been by and large a continuation of what is described in the study. Indeed, the evidence of the last three years, which could not be anticipated when the study was written, provides a good way of checking the relevance of the analysis. I have the impression that on the basis of this test Robinson's study is in all essentials as much up-to-date now as it was when he completed the draft of his manuscript in 1957.

There is another reason why stopping at 1956—or possibly one year later—appears justified. As a result of an expansion of the statistical activities of the Investment Bankers Association of America, we now have considerably more detailed information on several important aspects of the market for state and local government securities, particularly the amounts, character, and price of offerings, than was available during the first postwar decade. Our information is still sadly deficient on a few other aspects, primarily the volume of trading, dealers' inventories, and gross purchases and sales by the main investor groups. These gaps need to be filled before a really satisfactory analysis of the market for tax-exempt securities will be possible. It is probable, however, that when the job of analyzing the market for state and local government securities needs to be done again in a few years, the body of statistical data on which that analysis can be based will be much broader than that available to Robinson, hard as he tried to supplement the insufficient material at hand with *ad hoc* inquiries.

Second, some readers may wish the author had found it possible to devote more time and space to analysis of the relation of the interest rates on tax-exempt securities to those on other types of debt securities. These readers should realize, however, that on many of these points Robinson's study contains more information and goes further in the analysis of the material than the available literature. Moreover, the Bureau hopes to devote a special study to the analysis of interest rates in the United States, a study not limited to the postwar period or to one sector of the market. The advantage of studying the long-term record and the need to allow for the pronounced interdependence of interest rates on different types of capital market investments in any case rule out thorough analysis of interest rate developments in one sector of the capital market over the period of one decade only.

Third, some readers will feel that certain aspects of the study, primarily the relation between net purchases and sales by various investor groups, interest rate differentials and income tax rates would lend themselves well to a more elaborate statistical or econometric treatment. We believe that the present study opens the way for such an approach to the problem. This, it is fairly evident, would have to be conceived and executed on a broad scale. An econometric treatment of the postwar market for state and local government securities isolated from complementary study of other connecting sectors of the capital market and from examination of other periods might easily do more harm than good by giving the impression of a definiteness and precision of results that actually does not exist.

While the primary purpose of this study, as of the other parts of the Postwar Capital Market Study, is the quantitatively founded description and analysis of the operation of one sector of the American capital market during the first postwar decade, consideration was unavoidable of one problem of public policy—exemption of the interest from state and local government securities from federal income tax. Robinson shows that the price state and local government borrowers have received for the tax exemption privilege, measured by the differential in net yields between tax-exempt securities and taxable securities of similar character and quality, has declined sharply during the postwar decade; and is now at an unprecedentedly low level compared to the rates of income tax payable on otherwise comparable taxable securities. At the very least, Robinson has made it impossible for us to ignore any longer the question of whether the tax-exemption privilege is being granted without an adequate *quid pro quo*. Robinson's presentation ends with 1956; since that time the devaluation of the tax-exemption privilege has proceeded further.

In conformity with the Bureau's general policy, Robinson raises questions but makes no suggestions regarding policy. Similarly, Robinson, without taking a position himself, adduces enough material to make it doubtful whether the tax-exemption privilege of state and local government securities rests on anything except a grant by Congress in the income tax law, so that what Congress has given, Congress can take away. Whether this is so must of course remain primarily a question for constitutional lawyers to decide. If the decision should be in the direction to which Robinson's discussion in Chapter 1 points, the policies to be adopted with regard to the tax exemption of state and local government securities will be a purely political and economic matter freed from the supposed fetters of a constitutional mandate.

In that situation, careful consideration certainly would have to be given, both from a political and economic point of view, to two possible ways of dealing with the tax-exemption privilege: its abolition by Congressional action, limited for reasons of equity to future issues of state and government securities; and an offer by the federal government to pay a subsidy to future issuers of state and local government securities, a subsidy the exact size of which would have to be carefully determined. Robinson presents data which show that the federal government could offer most issuers of state and local government securities more than they now save by issuing their obligations in tax-exempt form, and yet leave the Treasury with a net increase in income. These conditions may change, and buyers may again have to pay more for the tax-exemption privilege—in the form of substantially lower rates—than they do now. But if the basic demand-supply situation in the market for tax-exempt securities is as Robinson outlines it, such a change is not highly probable.

RAYMOND W. GOLDSMITH
Director, Postwar Capital
Market Study

PREFACE

THIS study is a part of the National Bureau's inquiry into the capital markets of the United States. The central purpose of this inquiry has been to use the gross flows of funds within the capital markets derived from the extensive financial data compiled by Dr. Goldsmith in his study of saving as a tool for analysis of the market process. In addition to this central project, however, it was necessary to examine in detail the institutional characteristics of various sectors of the market. This report is a study of one of these sectors.

The tendency of economists to focus their attention mainly on the fiscal policies and operations of the federal government has led them to neglect, relatively, the financial problems of state and local governments. This sector has nevertheless been of mounting importance during the postwar era. Current state and local government receipts and expenditures grew, but the pressure on these governments to make long-deferred capital improvements caused state and local government capital expenditures to grow even more rapidly. Capital outlays, in turn, led to more borrowing. This inquiry thus was made during a period of rapid development in the market for state and local government tax-exempt obligations.

The major problem isolated in this inquiry is the erosion of tax exemption as means of supporting state and local government financing. The problem has grown more acute during the past few years and in many ways this study should be considered an interim report on the factors that accounted for this sizable erosion.

All of the exploratory work and most of the drafting underlying this report were completed during the year 1955-1956 when I was on leave from Northwestern University. During that year I was greatly helped by Justine Rodriguez and Jack Farkas, both of whom were then on the National Bureau staff. Morris Mendelson supplied invaluable assistance both in construction of the statistical foundation and later in the process of integrating these statistics into the general flow-of-funds material prepared in connection with the capital markets inquiry. My debt to him is very large. Revising and polishing of this study has been done mainly in spare time while working in the Division of Research and Statis-

tics at the Board of Governors of the Federal Reserve. I am grate-
ful to Ralph A. Young, Director of that Division, for his encour-
agement in completing this task.

An inquiry into a market organization must depend on the
willingness of those intimately acquainted with the institutional
arrangements of the market to talk freely and frankly; bare statistics cannot convey the kind of knowledge an investigator needs.
Interviews for the purpose of exploring the matter were arranged
for me by Mr. George Wanders, editor of *The Bond Buyer*. The
list of respondents was long but special mention must be made
of those who not only submitted patiently to the interview process
but subsequently gave me written comments on the manuscript or
made supplementary responses to the special questions addressed
to them. Mr. John Linen, who recently retired from the Chase
Manhattan Bank; Mr. Cushman McGee of R. W. Pressprich &
Company; Mr. Neal Fulkerson of the Bankers Trust Company,
and Mr. Harry Severson, a financial consultant on the market,
all gave me a great deal of time and help. Mr. Norris Johnson of
the First National City Bank of New York gave parts of the manuscript a very helpful reading. Frank Morris of the Investment
Bankers Association contributed more to this project than indicated by the many footnote references to his work in this field.
Professor Harry G. Guthmann read the entire manuscript and
gave me particularly helpful suggestions on the use of tax-exempt
securities by investors.

The National Bureau organization was of invaluable aid. I received early counsel from Solomon Fabricant, William J. Carson,
and Geoffrey H. Moore. The staff reading given my manuscript
by Raymond Goldsmith, W. Braddock Hickman, Geoffrey Moore,
Morris Mendelson, and C. Harry Kahn is gratefully acknowledged.
The debt to Geoffrey Moore and Harry Kahn is particularly great.
Moore opened up an important line of development for Chapter
6 and Kahn undertook the quantitative research that made application of this idea possible. In addition I am indebted to Professor Lawrence H. Seltzer and to Laszlo Ecker-Racz for a number
of helpful suggestions. The directors of the Bureau who read the
manuscript—Professor Walter Heller, Albert J. Hettinger, Jr., and
Percival F. Brundage—not only fulfilled their basic judicial role
but gave me some useful ideas for further improvement.

Acknowledgment should also be made to the Advisory Committee on the Study of the Postwar Capital Market, which assisted in drafting plans for this investigation. Members of the Committee were: W. A. Clarke, George T. Conklin, Jr., W. Braddock Hickman, Norris O. Johnson, Arnold R. LaForce, Aubrey G. Lanston, Robert P. Mayo, Roger F. Murray, James J. O'Leary, Winfield W. Riefler, Robert V. Roosa, R. J. Saulnier, William H. Steiner, Donald B. Woodward, and Eugene C. Zorn, Jr.

The specific debt to Raymond Goldsmith acknowledged above fails to represent my full obligation to him. It was he who gave a considerable amount of direction to the project in its beginning, who helped mold rough ideas into operational research plans, who read innumerable drafts constructively, and finally who constantly rekindled my enthusiasm when it tended to flag. My debt to him is more than I can express adequately here.

The charts were drawn by H. Irving Forman with his usual competence. The style of the manuscript was inestimably improved by Cornelius J. Dwyer. Miss Anita Perrin managed, in ways I do not understand, to assemble a presentable manuscript from the scribbled scraps of paper that I presented to her.

Each of these persons, in his own way, helped me to eliminate or moderate many flaws that were in the original manuscript. But flaws remain. These are my undivided responsibility.

ROLAND I. ROBINSON

Washington, D.C.
March 13, 1959

CONTENTS

TABLES

CHARTS

POSTWAR MARKET

FOR STATE AND LOCAL GOVERNMENT

SECURITIES

SUMMARY AND CONCLUSIONS

THE postwar market for state and local government securities accounted for approximately one-seventh to one-ninth of the gross volume of long-term funds (including real estate mortgages) raised through the capital markets. If measured on a net basis—new issues less retirement—the importance of this market was somewhat greater: between one-fifth and one-eighth of the net flow of funds into long-term uses. The relatively greater importance of net over gross state and local government capital financing is accounted for by the fact that the average maturity of state and local government securities marketed has been fairly long and the amount of refunding or repayment prior to maturity is less than in other segments of the capital market.

The unique feature of the market for state and local government securities, the one that sets it apart from other segments of the capital market, is that interest income from these securities is exempt from federal income taxes. The federal government stopped granting this privilege to investors on its own securities in 1941. Since then state and local governments have had a new-issue monopoly of this privilege. The other characteristics that influence this market, such as quality of securities and maturity distribution of offerings, are also encountered in other sectors of the capital market.

The exemption of state and local government securities from the taxation of the federal government originated in the constitutional division of sovereignty in the United States. Some constitutional lawyers, including a number of specialized municipal bond attorneys, feel that the doctrine of reciprocal immunity between the states and the federal government first stated in *McCulloch v. Maryland* in 1819 would make a federal tax on interest income from state and local government obligations unconstitutional. Many others, apparently including a majority of academic and federal government lawyers, feel that the passage of the 16th Amendment removed this bar and that thereafter the federal government could have taxed the income from state and local government obligations. Since Congress explicitly exempted taxation of such income by statute in 1913, that is where the matter has since rested. In effect, the issue has not been adjudicated.

3

The popular defense of tax exemption is that it helps state and local governments finance meritorious capital expenditures: schools, roads, sewers, waterworks, and the like. Thus tax exemption has a powerful political appeal. At present the possibility that the exemption could be erased from the statute books seems remote. But viewed as a problem in economics rather than politics, this exemption seems to have become an increasingly ineffectual aid to state and local government finance. A rational investor will not accept a lower yield from a state and local government security unless it is offset by a more than equal tax savings. Since this comparison must stand the scrutiny of the marginal investor, intramarginal holders necessarily have tax savings considerably greater than the reduction of borrowing costs to state and local government. This margin may be viewed as a kind of "investors' surplus."

Over the five years from 1951 to 1955, state and local governments saved on interest cost at a rate averaging less than three-quarters of one per cent by virtue of tax exemption. During the same period, the federal government lost annually on reduced taxes an amount equal to about two per cent of the tax-exempt bonds sold. The amount at issue would, at a rough guess, be a sum in excess of half a billion dollars at present levels of interest rates. This amount is suggested by multiplying the one per cent differential by the outstanding debt of state and local governments which is now in excess of fifty billions of dollars. The revenue foregone by the federal government as a result of this exemption can be viewed as a way of aiding state and local governments to improve educational plants, build roads, and make other kinds of state and local government capital outlays. This indirect subsidy, however, has clearly become a quite inefficient one. It has helped state and local government finance only moderately but has cost the federal government substantial amounts. Furthermore, it has helped the most severely pressed local governmental units the least. This was particularly true in the case of lower-grade obligations where the need of subsidy or help may be particularly great. In other words, the toll roads, rapidly growing school districts, and expanding municipalities apparently gained less from tax exemption by way of reduced borrowing cost than the cities and states where borrowing needs were less pressing. The subsidy element in tax exemption has not been correlated with need.

It has been suggested that in the absence of tax exemption smaller local governmental units might have to pay a rate of interest even higher than that paid by corporations of comparable size and credit quality. (Corporate interest costs, fully subject to income taxes, have been used for comparative purposes at several points in this study.) This possibility exists and cannot be denied. Nevertheless it does not seem likely. In the 1920's when tax exemption was worth far less than now, smaller local governmental units apparently were able to borrow at rates below those applying to comparable smaller corporations. Rates for both were high but not excessively high for local government. Size probably affects the credit quality of local government less adversely than it does the credit quality of corporations. The logic of credit analysis supports this assumption.

The two principal causes for the reduced efficiency of tax exemption as a borrowing aid are: first, the demand for funds by state and local governments increased enormously. Almost all borrowers increased their demands on the capital markets but none have had a more sustained impact than state and local governments. Second, the number of investors combining tax exposure and a natural investment interest in these obligations failed to expand equally and very likely shrank relatively. As a result of these two factors, yields on state and local government securities increased sharply, relative to other yields as well as absolutely.

STATE AND LOCAL GOVERNMENT DEMAND FOR FUNDS

During the postwar decade, 1946-1955, state and local governmental units borrowed increasingly large amounts. In the early postwar years, the backlog of deferred public construction was large. In addition, these governmental units have been called on to furnish a growing volume of services. Shifts in the housing and location of population combined with sustained prosperity have contributed to this situation. Still another factor was that public construction costs increased faster than the general price level. The high birth rate and rising incomes not only pushed families into the suburbs; they also led to enlarged demands for school and recreational facilities. The increased automotive population would have been even more crowded without added roads. To allow traffic on the roads a chance to move meant off-street parking facilities. And thus the chain of causation has run.

The immediate circumstance explaining most state and local government borrowing in the postwar decade has been some kind of governmental capital outlay. Borrowing, at least on a long-term basis, to finance deficits in current expenditures over current receipts has been rare. States borrowed rather large amounts for veterans' bonuses, but aside from this case noncapital financing accounted for only a small fraction of the postwar total.

State and local government capital expenditures have not been subject to any evident cyclical influence since World War II. They appear to have been unaffected by any of the three modest dips in business activity. This experience suggests that the basic demand for the services of these facilities is not geared closely to short-term income fluctuations. Furthermore, the planning and execution of these works has such a massive momentum that it is not likely to be disturbed by short-term business fluctuations. This has probably also been true in earlier periods, although during the Great Depression state and local government capital expenditures were drastically cut.

Indeed, it can be said that the borrowing by state and local government to finance capital expenditures has recently had more of a countercyclical than a cyclical character. State and local governments, sensitive to the level of interest rates, tend to defer financing in periods of tight money markets and to hasten to the market when interest rates decline. Since financing is undertaken well in advance of the actual capital expenditures, a prolonged period of tight money markets would have to elapse before this influence succeeded in much dislocation of the time pattern of state and local government capital expenditures. Ultimately, however, this influence seems to be felt.

Most state and local government capital expenditures are for a type of facility that is not directly revenue-producing. Free roads and school buildings and other public structures still dominate state and local government capital expenditures. However, an increasing proportion of the capital outlays of state and local governments are for revenue-producing facilities: toll roads and bridges, sewer and water systems, and sometimes such projects as ferryboat systems, intra-urban transportation systems, public parking facilities, and occasionally even facilities to attract new industrial ventures to a locality. Projects of this sort are frequently financed, not on the basis of the full faith and credit of the sponsoring state and local governmental unit, but rather on the basis of the revenue that these projects promise to produce. A later portion of this summary will mention a few of the other factors lying back of revenue bond financing. The influence of business conditions on the ability of these facilities to produce revenue, and therefore to service their bonds, is still largely untested.

SIZE OF THE MARKET: THE INVESTORS

Although the demand for funds has been formidable and insistent, the number of investors interested in this market has not kept pace. Only a limited number of institutional investors are able to take full advantage of the privilege of tax exemption. Price level fluctuations have convinced many individual investors that purchasing power preservation is more important than preservation of fixed-dollar after-tax income.

The composition of investor participation in the market for state and local government securities during the postwar decade changed largely because of the shifting value of tax exemption to various investors. Some investors are tax-exempt *per se*: nonprofit institutions, and qualified pension funds. Such investors obviously have no reason to accept a lower yield for the privilege of tax exemption. Life insurance companies are taxed according to a gross investment income formula which gives them only modest use of the privilege of tax exemption.[1] Commercial banks and fire and casualty insurance companies (both stock and mutual) are taxed at the full corporate rate on net marginal investment income; tax exemption is valuable to them and they are, as might be expected, leading buyers of such securities. Individuals vary; income level,

---

[1] In 1959, after this manuscript had been sent to the printer, Congress changed the formula by which life insurance companies compute their federal income tax liabilities. The new tax provisions are so complex that their effects are still being disputed by industry tax experts. The investment advantage of tax-exempt securities under this new legislation appears to be particularly ambiguous. The complexity of the law is so great that some industry representatives believe that it may be changed again soon. Accordingly, no effort has been made to analyze the new tax provisions for life insurance companies at this stage. Later references to the income taxation of life insurance companies are, however, made obsolete by this event.

7

ownership of equities or direct ownership of a business, access to investment outlets such as oil royalties or rental real estate account for these basic differences. Some individual investors are aggressive builders of wealth; tax-exempt securities hold little appeal for them since capital gains are likely to be their goal. The rate of capital gain accrual they seek is likely to be quite a bit in excess of prevailing yields on all fixed interest obligations whether or not tax-exempt. Aggressive investors are also likely to demand portfolio mobility. They shy away from many tax-exempt obligations because of their limited marketability. Investors with relatively high incomes who aim mainly at capital conservation are the principal individual buyers of tax-exempt obligations. One of the most significant bits of evidence of a declining interest of individual investors in this market is the smaller proportion of tax-exempt securities in large estates.

The changes in ownership of state and local government securities during the postwar period reflected each of these influences. During the early years of the decade, life insurance companies were active sellers of the state and local government obligations they had accumulated when yields were higher and commercial banks were avid buyers. Individuals were relatively neutral. Until the closing year of the decade commercial banks were important buyers of new issues; they were deterred only by interludes of monetary tightness. Fire and casualty insurance companies bought rather more common stocks than tax-exempt securities during the early part of the decade; but in the later part, when equity prices were quite high, they put more of their newly accruing funds into tax-exempt securities. The shift from equities to tax exempts also appears to have been true of personal trusts administered by corporate fiduciaries. Individuals bought tax-exempt securities directly whenever the yields on them approached fully taxed yields but withdrew from the market when the margin widened. The direct market to individuals seemed to show viability primarily when tax-exempt yields were close to the yields on comparable fully taxed securities.

Investors have been broadly logical in their treatment of the privilege of tax exemption. But in their treatment of risk they have by no means been so clearly rational. The market seems to require high premiums to assume even moderate degrees of credit risk.

While the credit of some state and local government units is not beyond reproach, the general quality of such credit is high. "Intermediate-grade" Baa or A securities are of respectable quality. They simply do not have the wide margin above reasonable standards possessed by very high-grade securities.

Presumably this emphasis on quality reflects the character of the investors who buy tax exempts. They are not the aggressive and capital-gains maximizing type; they are conservative and cautious. This is true of the institutions that invest in this market as well as of the individuals who use it. As a result, intermediate or lower-grade tax-exempt securities are less benefited by tax exemption than the high-grade ones. Endowing the financing of toll roads, bridges, tunnels, ferries, and other revenue-producing projects with the privilege of tax exemption has thus proved to be a rather barren subsidy; many investors have gained rather materially from the privilege, but these projects have not retained a respectable proportion of this amount by virtue of their ability to offer this privilege to the market. The most impressive demonstration of this fact is that quite a few toll-road bonds have been bought by life insurance companies which are subject to a 6½ per cent marginal rate of taxation on income.

THE MARKETING OF NEW STATE AND LOCAL GOVERNMENT ISSUES

The marketing of new-issue state and local government securities cuts across both the capital and money markets. The marketing institutions include investment banking institutions and a number of commercial banks. These institutions are organized to compete in public bidding to acquire these issues and to resell them to investors. Many high-grade state and local governments raise capital at a marketing cost of less than 1 per cent; most of them achieve a cost of less than 1½ per cent. Only in periods of capital market tension do marketing costs go much higher. Lower-grade and longer-term obligations meet somewhat higher costs, anywhere from 2 to 3 per cent. Only rarely does one encounter a cost for marketing capital issues in excess of 4 per cent, and then generally for marginal projects based on revenue financing.

The marketing institutions constitute a refined and sensitive system. The underwriters do not seem to discriminate against governmental units in any clearly irrational way. In fact it can be said that the market is remarkably adaptive to the many complexities of state and local government finance; that the marketing institutions, in most cases, tend to have a constructive influence on the financial policies of governmental units; at the same time they help to educate and persuade investors to accept the peculiar and the unusual types of securities that grow out of the exigencies of such finance.

We could find no evidence that these marketing institutions were other than neutral with respect to the pricing process—with one possible exception. That exception grows out of the inventory practices of dealers. By the nature of this market dealers are forced to take net long positions. Short positions are rare and dangerous. Because dealers' inventories may be a source of loss to the investment banking community, the short-term price record of this market is often erratic. This factor may also help to explain the frequent and wide price fluctuation of state and local government securities.

Nothing found indicated that the existing organization of the marketing institutions has an enduring influence on the level of tax-exempt yields. The ultimates of price and yield determination are clearly a combination of the demands for funds, of investor supply of them, and of Federal Reserve policy. The dealer community sometimes seems to have a mild low-rate bias: dealers bid actively, and are happier when yields are declining because they gain more than they lose from movement in this direction. But this is mostly sentiment; there is no evidence that they have enough ultimate economic power to give much effect to such an influence.

The personnel of this market are thoroughly sophisticated and aware of the several elements of irrationality mentioned at various stages of this study. But, being realists, they accept the existence of these irrational factors and allow for them. They bid for new issues on the basis of what they believe investors will pay for them. If investors will pay more for the bonds of a midwestern city that is an infrequent borrower than for PHA contract Housing Authority bonds supported by a federal government contract to service the debt, investment bankers reflect this preference in their bidding actions, even though they believe such an investor judgment to be partly irrational.

THE SECONDARY MARKET IN TAX-EXEMPT SECURITIES

The degree of marketability of state and local government obligations is disputed. Defenders of this market claim that these obligations are reasonably marketable, but critics of it do not agree. Evidence is hard to marshal, but the facts collected in this study suggest that the time required to market any appreciable volume of these securities is considerable (unless the owner is willing to cut prices drastically) and that the marketing cost in the secondary market is higher than in the new issues market.

The principal quantitative conclusion reached with respect to the secondary market is that it apparently parallels closely the new issues market as respects yields but moves conversely as respects volume. Unlike corporate securities, the obligations of state and local governments do not go through a "seasoning" process. The only systematic comparison of new-issue and secondary market yields possible is one based on a very short time series of new-issue yields prepared by the Investment Bankers Association. No clear difference in yield between securities offered in the new issues market and those offered in the secondary market could be detected in this short-term comparison. Revenue obligations based on projects under construction and for which there is no operating experience are an exception to this rule. But such revenue obligations, as we shall find, are more like corporate obligations than like full-faith-and-credit obligations of states and local governments.

When the new issues market is dormant, the secondary market takes on life and vitality. Investors seek to meet their portfolio needs in this market and dealers actively seek offerings. When the supply of new issues is ample, the secondary market tends to become less active.

The one great exception to this rule was the development of tax "swaps" near the end of the postwar decade. The tax rules applying to commercial banks permit them to deduct the security losses from current income in computing tax liability. On the other hand, they continue to have the privilege of treating capital gains on a preferred tax basis. As a result, commercial banks engage in extensive tax "swaps," booking losses in tax years of declining prices on the securities they sell.

PRICING THE PRIVILEGE OF TAX EXEMPTION

When in 1941 the federal government elected to make the income from its own obligations taxable, it left tax exemption to be exploited by state and local governments. With a monopoly of this privilege for subsequent new issues, the yields on state and local government obligations were driven down to a very low level in the postwar period. In 1946 the computed yield on 20-year Aaa state bonds went to 0.9 per cent; the *Blue List* of that period showed offerings of 30- to 40-year obligations at 1 per cent yields and even less. By the fall of 1957, the yield on a comparable obligation was about three and one-half times as high.

In retrospect, 1946 yields were at an absurdly low level. They were only about two-fifths of the yields on fully taxable high-grade obligations; the other three-fifths was the premium paid for tax exemption. If this premium seems high in retrospect, it might have seemed even higher in prospect. In the 1920's and 1930's when securities of the federal government generally offered partial tax exemption (and in some cases complete tax exemption), the value of the privilege was generally modest. Even though tax rates in 1946 were well above the levels of the 1920's and 1930's, many were confidently expecting tax reductions. In other words, the high premium paid for tax exemption at the beginning of the postwar decade should not be viewed as normal, but rather as a special circumstance that happened to prevail at the time our formal analysis begins.

As the postwar decade advanced, the fear of a shortage of tax-exempt obligations diminished and finally vanished. The premium on such obligations accordingly shrank. This was not a steady trend; it came in spurts and was reversed at least once. In 1948 when a tax cut was being debated at length in Congress, the premium shrank; tax-exempt securities declined in price more than other securities. Their recovery in 1949 was parallel only to that of taxable obligations (and possibly less than that). In late 1950 the fear of taxes induced by the involvement in Korea brought about a reversal and the prices of tax-exempt obligations moved contrary to other security prices. But this was a short-lived move; it was reversed in early 1951.

Starting in 1951 and reaching a climax in 1953, the money markets experienced their first real tightness in two decades. The prices of tax-exempt securities dropped greatly. But the significant fact was that they dropped more than those of fully taxable obligations of about the same credit quality. This experience suggested that state and local government security yields were unusually sensitive to Federal Reserve credit policy.

This impression was deepened in 1954 when, in money markets made easy by Federal Reserve policy, the prices of state and local government securities recovered somewhat more than those of taxable obligations. In 1955, 1956, and early 1957, when money market conditions tightened, the prices of state and local government obligations again went down more than those of comparable taxable securities.

In a technical market sense, this sensitiveness of state and local government obligations might be explained largely by commercial bank investment policy. Commercial banks bought tax-exempt securities actively when loan demand was modest but reduced their purchases (or even sold) when loan demand became urgent. While this fact may be a plausible explanation of the greater short-term sensitivity of the state and local government security market, the more fundamental reason seems to be that the proportion of investors having rational tax reasons for being interested in this market has remained constant or even declined while the demand for funds has been broadening. State and local governments have had to bargain away an increasing proportion of the advantage of tax exemption to investors.

The yield differential between high-quality state and local government securities and those of intermediate quality continued to be relatively wide. They ended the decade just about as far apart as when it started. On the other hand, the differential between grades of corporate obligations narrowed. It can be argued that the absolute credit quality of "intermediate" corporations improved considerably during this decade. But in many ways the same thing could be said of local governmental units. The shifts of population and the demands for public services strained the finances of many governmental units. At the same time the fundamental economic situation of many of these governmental units probably improved. It is hard to support the view that corporate credit has improved so much more than state and local government credit as indicated by the changes in these yield differentials.

The more convincing explanation seems to be that the principal investors in state and local government obligations tend to be temperamentally conservative. Risk-takers find little in this market to attract them. Thus the differential between the highest grade securities and those of intermediate grades is not a reflection of a rational judgment of risk, but an expression of investor preference. The price for finding risk-bearers for investment in tax-exempt obligations appears to be much higher than any actuarial valuation that might be put on the risk.

Offering scales on tax-exempt obligations are a measure, of a sort, of maturity-yield interest rate differentials. They might be thought of as yield curves. The evidence collected in this study showed that the shape of the maturity-yield functions for state and local government serial offerings often varied from the shape of the similar function for U.S. Treasury obligations or other fully taxable securities.

Neither the shape of these curves nor their variations from the more conventional yield curves seemed to square with the principal interest rate hypotheses. Liquidity preference certainly could not explain it since the spread between early and intermediate maturity tax-exempt obligations has often exceeded that of U.S. Treasury obligations, whereas the liquidity preference hypothesis would lead one to expect the opposite relationship. The forecasting hypotheses as an explanation of maturity-yield relationships also fails to square with observed differences. Past differentials have been poor harbingers of later yield changes. The most reasonable explanation, a purely institutional rather than theoretical one, is that this market is highly segmented. Investors have strongly held maturity preferences. The relative participation of various investor groups fluctuates and seems more often than not to furnish the most reasonable explanation of shifts in the maturity-yield relationship.

The prices of state and local governmental obligations have been somewhat more variable than those of other securities, both in frequency of price changes and in the range of price movements.

This volatility apparently has been due to the fact that state and local government obligations are influenced both by changes in the general levels of interest rates and by the changing yield discount of the privilege of tax exemption. Compounding two factors of variability (which sometimes coincide and sometimes do not) makes them more volatile than is true of those securities which are influenced by just one of these factors.

Estimates of the reduction in cost of borrowing by state and local government compared with the loss of revenue by the federal government suggested that soon after World War II most of the advantage of reduced borrowing costs was being retained by state and local government borrowers while investors obtained relatively little advantage from the purchase of tax-exempt securities. The amount of new-issue borrowing was small in this period and most of the advantage of low yields accrued to investors who sold out their holdings in the secondary market. Life insurance companies were important sellers at this juncture. As the decade wore on, however, the reduction in the cost of borrowing grew relatively smaller when compared with the loss of revenue by the federal government. This was particularly true during years of heavy state and local government borrowing. Although the estimation of both these magnitudes is necessarily crude, it seems quite clear that the revenue lost by the federal government was two to three times the reduction of borrowing costs. The differential between revenue lost and borrowing cost reduction was particularly great in the case of lower-grade obligations. The problem, therefore, was that those state and local government units most in need of good borrowing terms were least able to make full use of the privilege of tax exemption.

Although the differential widened over the decade and therefore suggests a trend, this is probably an unwarranted conclusion. Prior to World War II state and local government obligations did not have a monopoly on tax exemption so the experience then cannot be used to lengthen our historical perspective. On the other hand, it seems quite safe to conclude that in periods of heavy borrowing most of the advantage of tax exemption must be passed along to investors and relatively little of it can be retained by state and local governments. In other words, an average of the annual figures weighted by the volume of financing in each year is considerably below a simple average of the annual figures. In fairness, it should be made clear that the erosion of the benefits of tax exemption may have been partly due to the fact that changes in tax law during the decade opened up other means by which investors could minimize tax liability.

While tax exemption can be viewed as a boon to state and local governments, it is not an unmixed advantage. Because so many investors have no logical reason for investing in tax-exempt securities, the market is necessarily smaller than for fully taxed obligations, and, furthermore, it is more erratic. The relatively small savings in borrowing costs netted by state and local governments must be offset against the fact that they must finance in a more confined and less stable market.

Those who feel that tax exemption is an important factor in reducing state and local government borrowing costs may be giving too little weight to the intrinsically high quality of these credits. While there have occasionally been defaults on these obligations, most of them were cured without great delay. Ultimate losses on these obligations have been small and rare. State and local government credit would deserve a high credit standing apart from tax exemption and would deserve relatively low interest rates.

THE MARKET FOR REVENUE OBLIGATIONS

Citizens, acting through their state and local governments, apparently believe that some governmental activities should be self-financing and self-supporting. Revenue financing is an expression of this belief. The special authorities established by states to operate harbors, bridges, toll roads, and the like exemplify such circumstances. The market for revenue obligations is much more like the corporate bond market than that for full-faith-and-credit obligations of state and local governments. First, a much larger proportion of them are in term rather than serial form. Second, a larger proportion of them are handled as negotiated deals rather than by public competitive bidding. Third, investors usually judge the quality of a security by its ability to earn income.

Revenue financing has also been used to escape the debt limits imbedded in state constitutions and financing statutes. When the political obstacles to the removal of debt limits are great, revenue obligations have been used in circumstances where full-faith and general credit obligations would ordinarily be appropriate. One state has a constitutional debt limit which has, in effect, required it to do all of its borrowing in revenue form. School districts and other special-purpose districts have sometimes been unable to borrow and so have had to arrange complex lease contracts or other devices so as to establish the financial foundation on which a revenue financing project could be undertaken. Whenever financing is supported only by a pledge of revenue, it costs more than it would if based on a pledge of full-faith and general credit. This penalty is often material.

Although all commercial banks may purchase revenue state and local government obligations, members of the Federal Reserve cannot participate in the underwriting of them. For this and other reasons they frequently do not take an active interest in this market even as investors. Commercial banks which are members of the Federal Reserve System have recently been seeking legislation to permit them to underwrite revenue obligations.

Revenue bonds have attracted somewhat different investors than those that buy full-faith and general credit obligations. Although individuals constitute the larger part of the market for these securities, there is a general feeling that it is a different group of individuals from the one that purchases full-faith and general credit obligations. The revenue bonds used to finance toll roads and other quasi-speculative ventures have unquestionably attracted individuals of somewhat more aggressive character than those that typically buy full-faith and general credit tax-exempt obligations.

CHAPTER 1

Problems of the Market for State and Local Government Securities

PURELY on the basis of size, the market for state and local government securities deserves respectful attention. During the postwar decade, the securities offered by these governmental units have accounted for more than one-fifth of the gross volume of new securities publicly offered. If federal offerings are omitted from this total, the proportion accounted for by state and local governments has been about one-third of the volume of new cash offerings in the public security markets. If the volume of state and local government borrowing is compared with a total that includes real estate financing and private placement, the proportions are, of course, somewhat more moderate: from one-seventh to one-ninth of the gross volume of new long-term financing. Clearly, the amount of funds taken by state and local government is a respectably large part of the total, no matter how measured.

The importance of state and local government security marketings, however, involves matters other than quantitative size. State and local government finance has acquired a fairly special public significance in the postwar period. In the first place, the number of services demanded of government has shown no signs of diminishing and in many ways has tended to grow. For example, most plans for educational improvement would involve a direct drain on state and local government finance. Very often they involve the kind of expenditures that imply capital market financing.

The managers of state and local government finance appear to have felt that borrowing in the later postwar capital markets was unusually difficult and costly. Those who have recently achieved an age appropriate for responsible administration of public finance have, indeed, had no experience with high interest rates. The 1930's were a period of generally low interest rates. In the immediate postwar period there was a considerable differential between state and local government interest costs and those of other borrowers. These combined facts may have accustomed the managers to very low interest rates. Later in the postwar period, when interest costs were rising, those of state and local governments went up even more. Though the interest costs of such funds remain low by historical standards, they nevertheless are considerably higher than the very low levels reached in the immediate postwar period: roughly a trebling. One of the principal problems of this inquiry, therefore, will be to seek out the reasons for the relative as well as the absolute increase in the cost of money to state and local governments and the rationale of state and local government financial managers in resisting such cost increases.

Not only has state and local government financing been of significance from the demand side of the capital market; it has presented some quite special characteristics on the supply side of the market. The supply of funds by investors for these securities has been conditioned by a complex structure of investment policies. In the first place, state and local government issues now have a virtual monopoly of tax exemption of interest income. Likewise, these obligations are generally of high credit quality. Thus, these obligations appeal to those parts of the market desiring conservative investment outlets and valuing tax exemption materially. But when rates have been adjusted to these two facts of high quality and tax exemption, they are generally too low to attract funds from investors who are willing to be aggressive and who do not put a high value on the tax-exemption feature.

Other important postwar changes also took place on the supply side of the capital markets. In the first postwar years, many investors shared the widespread view that deflation might again in peacetime become the dominant economic problem it had been during the 1930's. Safety of principal seems to have been emphasized at least briefly in the early postwar period. Later this fear disappeared and, in time, it came to be replaced by a far more optimistic view, one that put emphasis on a general expectation of growth and prosperity. Even later, the expectations of investors were even further modified toward the belief, somewhat cynical in its overtones, that secular inflation was inevitable.

This cycle of expectations had the tendency of inducing an investor predisposition toward the securities of state and local governments in the early part of the postwar decade and away from them in its later portion. It is hard to make more than a rough and general assessment of these expectations in quantitative terms. It is clear, however, that the investment policies of trustees, for example, underwent shifts of the general nature described here.

Still one other general change in the pattern of investor expectations appears to have taken place. In the early postwar decade, it appears that investors expected tax rates to be considerably reduced without much delay. For a brief period, there was some actual realization of these expectations. During the period of the Korean hostilities, tax rates went up again. Some investors, however, apparently viewed this reversal as a quite temporary one. The outcome of the presidential election in 1952, which was regarded as a conservative victory, gave at least temporary support to this belief. As time wore on, these expectations were considerably modified. The nature of international developments ultimately led most investors to the sober conclusion that sizable tax reductions were quite unlikely.

Expectations with respect to future tax rates apparently have been paralleled by other kinds of expectations: those with respect to the supply of tax-exempt obligations. When the federal government removed the privilege of tax exemption from its own securities, starting in 1941, it was not initially clear that this would be a permanent break in policy. With the passage of years, however, it has become quite clear that the federal government has gained considerably by this policy. With the present size of the public debt, the amount that could have been saved by lower borrowing costs would have been negligible. On the other hand, the amount of tax revenues foregone would have been considerable. At present, there is no expectation that the federal government will reverse its position with respect to the taxation of interest income from its own obligations. Therefore, expectations with respect to the supply of tax-exempt securities are virtually coterminous with expectations with respect to the supply of state and local government obligations. Because tax exemption was a clear monopoly of new state and local government securities only in the postwar decade, and because this feature has a long and somewhat controversial history, this story needs review before we embark on other aspects of the study.

LEGAL FOUNDATION OF THE EXEMPTION OF INTEREST ON STATE AND LOCAL GOVERNMENT OBLIGATIONS FROM FEDERAL TAXATION[1]

Interest income from state and local government securities has been exempt from income taxation by the federal government by statute since 1913, the year in which the Sixteenth (income tax) Amendment was ratified. In the absence of circumstances that make a test of constitutionality possible, the present legal situation is not entirely clear.

The first form in which the issue arose was in the state taxation of a federal instrumentality rather than the reverse. The note issuing power of the second Bank of the United States was subjected to a very special tax by the State of Maryland. In the famous case *McCulloch v. Maryland*,[2] this tax was declared unconstitutional. Although the decision seemed to be aimed at the discriminatory nature of the tax, it is often cited as the origin of the doctrine of the reciprocal immunity. This doctrine in its simplest form was that the states could not abridge the powers of the federal government nor the federal government the power of a state by taxation. Whether this power extended to a nondiscriminatory tax was not made clear since *McCulloch v. Maryland* specifically permitted state taxation of real estate property owned by the Bank of the United States if levied in a nondiscriminatory fashion. Recent decisions suggest that the courts would not invoke the doctrine of reciprocal immunity unless a tax could be shown to be a "tangible or certain economic burden" on the government or instrumentality being taxed. *Esso Standard Oil v. Evans et al.* 345 U.S. 495 (1953) and *Mayo v. U.S.* 319 U.S. 441 (1942). Later in this study, state and local government borrowing costs are shown to be reduced only moderately by virtue of tax exemption; removing this exemption would not be very burdensome.

During the Civil War, the federal government imposed an income tax that covered both interest on state obligations and the salaries of state employees. However, in 1870 the federal income

[1] The material for this section has been drawn from two sources: Lucille Derrick's *Exemption of Security Interest from Income Taxes in the United States*, October 1946, Vol. xix, No. 4, part 2, of the *Journal of Business* (The University of Chicago Press), Chapter iii, pp. 6-37; second, an unpublished manuscript by George E. Lent on the "Origin and Survival of Tax-Exempt Securities."

[2] 4 Wheat 316 (1819).

tax on salaries of state employees was invalidated.[3] The income tax levied during the Civil War lapsed but, largely as the result of Populist pressure, an income tax was reenacted in 1894. Bowing in the direction of *Collector v. Day*, this act specifically exempted salaries of state employees but just as specifically included interest received from state and local government obligations. This tax was declared unconstitutional in the following year. Unfortunately, the initial decision was followed by a rehearing; although the two decisions reached the same final opinion they stressed somewhat different logic and therefore leave some ambiguity.[4] The first decision emphasized the doctrine of reciprocal immunity. Those who go back to the first decision of *Pollack v. Farmers Loan and Trust Company* tend to believe a federal tax on the incomes from state and local government securities unconstitutional. Under the rehearing of the case, however, the decision was based primarily on the lack of direct apportionment in the assessment of this income tax. Since the 16th Amendment specifically gave the federal government power of a tax income without direct apportionment, those going back to the rehearing of *Pollack v. Farmers Loan and Trust Company* would tend now to believe a tax on state-paid interest to be constitutional. The 16th Amendment, which became effective in 1913, provided that: "the Congress shall have power to lay and collect taxes on incomes, from whatever source derived, without apportionment among the several states, and without regard to any census or enumeration." The effect of this amendment on the taxation of interest income from state and local government securities has never been tested. After the amendment had been adopted, there was some controversy as to this point, but the initial tax legislation enacted under this constitutional authority specifically exempted both the salaries of state and local officials and the income from state and local bonds from federal income taxation. Later this exemption for the taxation of the salaries of state

---

[3] *Collector v. Day* 11 Wall 113 (1870). The relevance of this case to the general problem of the power of the federal government to tax state salaries may be doubted. A Massachusetts judge was the subject of this case and the supreme court, in declaring the tax invalid, said that it "fell upon the right of the state to administer justice through the courts." Later, the courts permitted federal taxation of the salaries of state employees including judges. *Helvering v. Gerhardt* 306 U.S. 466.

[4] In the cases of *Pollack v. Farmers Loan and Trust Company* 157 U.S. 429 (1895) and rehearing 158 U.S. 601 (1895).

and local government officials was rescinded and the constitutionality of such a tax was upheld.[5] The exemption of income from state and local government bonds, however, was never removed from the statutes, thus the absence of a court test.

At present, legal opinion as to this constitutional issue remains divided. Some of the law firms specializing in the delivery of opinions on municipal bonds include a phrase in their opinion to the effect that federal taxation of the interest income from such obligations by the federal government would be unconstitutional without the consent of the issuing state or local government. Other firms content themselves with simply the opinion that the obligations are exempt from federal income taxation "under existing legislation."

The Treasury Department, in an effort to obtain a ruling on the constitutional question despite the independent statutory exemption, brought suit against several bondholders of the Port of New York Authority for payment of income taxes on interest received from bonds issued by that Authority. The primary ground of the suit was that the Authority did not constitute a state or local government. It appears, however, that the Treasury Department was hoping that it might get some clue as to the basic constitutional situation into the public record in the settlement of this case. The tax court ruled against the federal government on the statutory issue but left the constitutional issue open. The Treasury Department thereupon appealed. The Circuit Court of Appeals for the Second Circuit handed down a split decision (*Commissioner of Internal Revenue v. Shamberg's Estate*, 144 Federal Reporter, 2nd Series 998 [1944]).

The majority ruled the Port Authority to be a governmental instrumentality and therefore exempt. But none of the judges went beyond the statute to the constitutional question that the Treasury Department sought to have adjudicated.

The authority of the federal government to include state and local government securities in the assessment of estate taxes has been upheld as constitutional.[6] Likewise, the assessment of capital

---

[5] *Helvering v. Gerhardt* (Port of N.Y. Authority) 306 U.S. 466. States may also tax the income of federal employees. *Graves v. O'Keefe* 306 U.S. 466; 59 S. Ct. 595.
[6] *Greiner v. Llewellyn*, 258 U.S. 384; 42 S. Ct. 324; 66 L. ed. 676 (1922).

gains taxes on transactions in state and local government securities has been upheld.[7]

In 1938, the Department of Justice prepared a long (219 pages) legal study of the constitutionality of federal taxation of the income from state and local obligations.[8] They believe it to be clearly constitutional and said so in quite emphatic language. In the same year, the attorney generals of several states prepared a consolidated answer debating the constitutionality of such a tax. Since both sides might be considered parties at interest, a neutral observer can do no more than look toward academic opinion on this point. To the extent that law review articles may be used as evidence, it appears that this opinion is slightly balanced toward the side of believing such a tax constitutional. This opinion, however, tends to be held by legal authorities otherwise identified with "liberal" positions. So-called conservatives tend to be less certain. The only judgment that a nonlegal observer can safely venture is that adjudication of the issue probably would depend on the make-up of the Supreme Court at the time of decision.

As a practical matter, the two governmental authorities exempt income from each other's securities from taxation: states, the income from federal obligations; and the federal government, the income from state and local government obligations. Each level of government treats its own securities as it sees fit. Most states exempt the interest on their obligations and those of local governmental units in their jurisdiction from taxation, but do not exempt the interest income of the obligations of other states and their subsidiary units. During World War I the federal government offered many complex versions of partial and complete exemption from its own income taxes of the interest income from its securities. Prior to 1941 most securities of the federal government enjoyed exemption from so-called "normal" taxes; a few of them enjoyed complete exemption. The basis of exemption was usually the security itself, but sometimes exemption depended on the tax status of the holder or the amount of his holdings. For example, prior to 1941, income on the first $5,000 of holdings of savings bonds was exempt from taxation but holdings in excess of such amounts were taxed. When the future need for large bor-

---

[7] *Willunts v. Bunn*, 282 U.S. 216; 51 S. Ct. 125; 75 L. ed. 304 (1931).

[8] *Taxation of Government Bondholders and Employees*; Department of Justice, 1938.

rowing became likely in early 1941 the federal government made interest income from all of its future issues fully subject to its own income taxes. Subsequent events have justified the wisdom of this step. All secretaries of the Treasury, from Mr. Mellon through Mr. Morgenthau, advocated the removal of the exemption on both federal and state and local government securities. When the federal government removed exemption from its own securities, it had to take this step unilaterally. In retrospect, it is hard to picture the courage as well as foresight that this action required.[9]

THE SUPPORT OF PUBLIC INVESTMENT BY TAX-EXEMPT FINANCING

Few kinds of investment, public or private, are as closely geared to and dependent upon external financing as state and local government capital outlays. State and local governmental units that are large enough to have continuous capital expenditure programs can sometimes finance these outlays on a pay-as-you-go basis. This is true of road construction by some state governments and true of larger water and sewerage systems, and even of school construction, by some larger cities. But when the needs for capital improvements bunch, as was characteristic of the postwar period, borrowing is required. Thus the state of the market for state and local government securities may be a determining influence on the rate of capital expenditures by such governmental units.

In the 1946-1955 decade, state and local governments are estimated by the National Income Division of the Department of Commerce to have spent $50.8 billions on new capital construction. During this same decade the gross long-term borrowing of state and local government amounted to $38.7 billions; a modest fraction of this was for veterans' bonuses or other noncapital purposes. With allowance for this factor, it appears that about two-thirds of the capital outlays of state and local government were initially financed by borrowing. Debt repayment, however, is a form of saving. Over the decade as a whole, state and local government saving in this and other forms financed one-half of their capital outlays. While this later fraction is of interest when one tries to balance the income and capital accounts of the decade, the former

[9] H. C. Murphy, *National Debt in War and Transition* (McGraw-Hill, 1950), pp. 31-34.

fraction is the one that measures the strategic role of the capital markets in initiating capital expenditures.

COMPARISON OF THE STATE AND LOCAL GOVERNMENT SECURITY
MARKET WITH OTHER SECTORS OF THE CAPITAL MARKETS

For general orientation, it may be useful to start with some relatively simple comparisons of the market for state and local government securities with the other principal capital markets.

The securities of state and local governments are similar to those of the federal government in several respects. All Treasury securities and a large majority of state and local government obligations[10] depend ultimately on the power of the issuing government to tax and to collect the taxes due it. State and local government obligations have, in practice, high credit quality.

But it would be unwise to push the analogy of state and local government credit to that of federal government credit too far. In terms of institutional structure, the market for state and local government obligations is much closer to that of corporate bonds than to the market for Treasury securities. Treasury obligations are traded mainly by commercial banks and a small group of specialized dealers. State and local government obligations are underwritten by banks and by the great investment banking firms, but a large number of small dealers also operate in the state and local government market. The secondary market for state and local government obligations is more like the secondary market for corporate bonds than the Treasury security market.

The pairing in marketing institutions, however, is not the same as the pairing of securities in investors' portfolios. It would be much more common to find Treasury bonds and corporate bonds paired by life insurance or pension fund investors; the tax position and investment outlook is similar. On the other hand, state and local government obligations are more likely to be paired by individual investors or casualty insurance companies with holdings of corporate equities. Individuals who seek tax exemptions are often the

[10] The principal exceptions are state and local government revenue obligations which are not based on the "full faith and credit" of such governmental units as are "general obligations" but are secured only by specially designated revenues. Because revenue bonds have different market characteristics they will be dealt with separately in Chapter 7; many of our comments prior to that time will apply principally to the market for "full faith and credit" obligations.

27

less aggressive, more conservative investors, much like commercial banks.[11]

In most respects the market for state and local government securities is quite different from the market for mortgages. But these two markets share one important characteristic: a considerable fraction of each is still quite local in character. While the fraction is larger in the mortgage market, this survey indicates that a sizable part of the market for state and local government securities is also essentially local in nature, and is thus insulated from some of the influences of central capital markets.

COMPETITIVE BIDDING IN STATE AND LOCAL MARKET

Public competitive bidding is almost universal in the initial sale of full faith and general credit state and local government obligations. The mechanics of competitive bidding have required some agile management of the investment banking machinery. The units in which state and local government securities are offered on the market are often quite small. Syndicate managers, therefore, must develop economical and efficient operational organizations in order to file an adequate number of bids without incurring considerable expense. While the investment banking machinery has not yet had to adopt true mass production techniques, the circumstances surrounding the purchase of state and local government obligations raise related operating problems. The competitive bidding requirement has, in fact, led to quite a bit of active bidding for the choice types of obligations and has led to the formulation of a continuity of bidding and buying groups.

Although competitive bidding remains dominant in the offering of full faith and credit obligations, negotiated financings seem to be becoming more frequent in the offering of revenue obligations. This may mean that the greater continuity of contact between underwriter and the financing body has been found to have distinct advantages for this type of financing.

LEGAL RESTRICTIONS ON BORROWING AND BORROWING PRACTICES

State and local government borrowing is hedged about by many constitutional and statutory restrictions. The complexity of many

[11] J. Keith Butters, Lawrence E. Thompson, and Lynn L. Bollinger, *Effects of Taxation: Investments by Individuals* (Graduate School of Business, Harvard, 1953), Chapters II and XI.

bond issues grows out of the necessity of complying with these restrictions. The harness of legal restrictions appears to be more and more binding as one goes down the size scale of local governmental units. This raises an important question: Have all types, sizes, and locations of state and local governmental units been able to get fair and equitable access to this market? Asked differently: does the market discriminate against some governmental units in an arbitrary or capricious way? The impersonal rule of the market has sometimes been challenged in business finance; for example, small business is thought by some to suffer from discriminatory practices. Are similar circumstances encountered by the financial managers of small municipal and local government units?

DOES TAX EXEMPTION HANDICAP OTHER BORROWERS?

The existence of tax exemption is sometimes thought to attract a flow of investment funds in the capital markets to the detriment of other borrowers. More specifically, it has been averred that tax-exempt financing by state and local government works to decrease the supply of funds available to business. This question was the subject of an extended and detailed Congressional inquiry as early as 1922. In the first three months of that year the House Ways and Means Committee held hearings on the subject and later sponsored a joint resolution which would have removed the privilege of tax exemption from state and local government financing. This was passed by the House in early 1923 but it died in the Senate under the pressure of state and local governments.[12] It is significant that there appears to have been a fairly real conviction on the part of many witnesses, including many from the financial community, that tax exemption limited the supply of funds available for private finance.

The issue was revived against a considerably different economic background in 1939 at hearings before another Congressional committee.[13] This time the emphasis was less on the disadvantage of tax exemption to business financing, and much more on the way

---

[12] The economist for the House Committee, C. O. Hardy, recounts the story in his *Tax-Exempt Securities and the Surtax* (Macmillan, 1926). Chapter 2 is most directly relevant to this story, but fragments of it appear in some of the later discussion.

[13] 76th Congress, 1st Session, Hearings before the Special Committee on Taxation of Governmental Securities and Salaries.

tax exemption thwarted the effects of progressive income taxation. Much the same point was repeated at the TNEC hearings and reproduced in the staff monographs produced in this inquiry.[14]

HOW GREAT IS THE ADVANTAGE TO BORROWERS OF TAX EXEMPTION?

The financial managers of state and local governmental units probably are disposed, after experience during the postwar decade, to belittle the significance of the question we have just raised. The one they would like to have answered is: How much, if any, does tax exemption help in reducing state and local governmental borrowing costs?

During the postwar decade, the advantages of tax exemption passed largely from borrowers to investors. In the early postwar months, the yields on tax-exempt securities were only about four-ninths of those prevailing on fully taxable high-grade obligations. In other words, the market was discounting a marginal tax rate of close to 55 per cent. Since the volume of funds available for market investment by investors in such a tax bracket was small, just about all of the advantage of tax exemption was being retained by state and local government borrowers.

This changed greatly during the postwar decade, at the end of which the larger share, by far, was being taken by investors. State and local governments were able to retain very little. This made tax exemption a quite ineffectual subsidy. It cost the federal government a considerable amount but gave borrowing state and local governments little advantage. The fragments of evidence that explain this development appear in several places in this inquiry: in the study of investors who buy the obligations and in the inquiry into differential interest rate developments.

One related factor must be singled out for special attention: the quality of state and local government credit. If all levels of government gain equally from tax exemption, the form of subsidy has some measure of equity even if it be an ineffectual subsidy. But if the gain is uneven, then a still different kind of question is raised. Evidence developed later suggests that only the better quality governmental borrowers retain a significant portion of the subsidy implicit in tax exemption.

14 TNEC Monograph No. 20, pp. 189-199.

STRATEGIC PRACTICES OF THIS MARKET

This market is one in which strategy plays a vital part. The skill of municipal finance officers is partly a skill of strategy and timing. The skill of underwriters is one of tactics and strategy. The skill of investment managers for the principal institutional investors that buy tax exempts is partly a skill of timing: picking the times to hold off and wait for better yields, deciding when to "buy the market" boldly. The secondary market in state and local government securities is honeycombed with institutions of strategic significance: for example, a limited number of brokers do nothing but act as agents for recognized dealers, a kind of informational shield between buyer and seller. (The principal stock in trade of these brokers is knowledge of the markets, a record of speedy executions, and an iron reputation for concealing the identity of their principals—their capital is often nothing but office rent and a switchboard.)

METHOD OF INVESTIGATION

The character of this investigation, its limits as well as its ambitions, were set by the nature of the larger project of which this study is one part. This study is one of three market studies, the other two of which deal with the market for corporate securities and the market for nonfarm mortgages. These three market studies, in turn, are part of a general study of postwar capital markets. This parent project is, in turn, related to two earlier projects: the Study of Saving,[15] conducted by Raymond W. Goldsmith, and the Study of Capital Formation and Financing, headed by Simon Kuznets.[16] The study of postwar capital markets is being built upon a social accounting foundation: an application of the flow-of-funds technique to an analysis of capital markets.[17] While simplified versions of the sources-and-uses technique have been variously applied before, this system attempts to tie together nonfinancial as well as

[15] National Bureau of Economic Research; published in three volumes by Princeton University Press, 1955 and 1956.

[16] Only part of the studies growing out of this project had been published at the time this was written. Further work is reported in the Thirty-ninth Annual Report of the National Bureau (May 1959).

[17] The intellectual origin of this technique is detailed in Morris Copeland's *Moneyflows in the United States*, published by the National Bureau in 1952. The *Flow of Funds in the United States*, published by the Federal Reserve Board in 1955, extends the figures and the period covered.

financial factors as causal elements in the system of capital market determination. Against this larger frame of reference, a study of the state and local government security market should emphasize the points at which this market ties to other markets, the extent to which it creates influences that spread to other capital market sectors, and the degree to which this market is influenced by events in other sectors. The questions posed in the preceding section should cluster about such general framework of economic considerations.

THE PROBLEM OF DATA

The market for state and local government securities is not illuminated by an adequate amount of systematic public information. One reason is that this is an unregulated market. Public regulation tends to increase the amount of systematic and reliable data available. For example, the regulation of larger public offerings of corporate securities has led to the filing of registration statements and the publication of prospectuses that contain data of considerable interest and unquestioned reliability. The same cannot be said of many state and local government security sales. So-called official statements are sometimes issued in the sale of state and local government revenue obligations. These statements look like prospectuses, they are printed by the firms that print prospectuses, and they follow the same general typographical and organizational style. But the information contained in them is far less comprehensive. A security analyst or economic investigator usually does not find in them the wealth of detail that he can count on in looking at corporate registration statements and prospectuses. Such information as is shown probably is reliable, but the penalties for misstatements or concealment of relevant information are by no means as severe.

The lack of data is further aggravated by the fact that the market for state and local government securities is an over-the-counter market. Our knowledge of these markets is quite limited. The Wharton School survey of over-the-counter securities markets[18] is the only comprehensive and systematic study of this subject. Unfortunately this study is less revealing with respect to the market

[18] Irwin Friend, G. Wright Hoffman, Willis J. Winn, Morris Hamburg, and Stanley Schor, *Over-the-Counter Securities Markets* (McGraw-Hill, 1958).

32

for state and local government obligations than with respect to other over-the-counter securities markets. The reason is an eloquent commentary on the understandable reluctance of businesses (or individuals) to reveal themselves except under the pressure of law or public opinion. The responses to the questionnaire underlying that survey were far more comprehensive for the registered brokers and dealers than for the exempt ones who limit their activities to governmental securities.[19] While the registered brokers and dealers account for quite a large fraction of the market for state and local government securities, the exempt dealers, particularly the dealer departments of commercial banks, appear to do an even greater part of the total business. The margins of error of estimates relating to the state and local government security market (and Treasury security market) are thus far greater than for the estimates relating to corporate bond or stock activities.

SOURCES OF QUANTITATIVE MARKET DATA

State and local government finance has been the subject of much economic research, but no investigation appears to have dealt with the marketing of the securities of these governmental units. About the only research material having a direct bearing on the subject of markets are the estimates of ownership, the principal published one being by Lent.[20] An estimate by Menderhausen of the ownership of various types of assets by size of estate can be used to ascertain the relative importance of state and local government security ownership at various income levels.[21] But this is only indirect evidence about the nature of the markets.

Direct evidence about the functioning of the state and local government security market can be found only in trade publications. The principal ones are: the *Bond Buyer* (the word *"Daily"* is added to the daily edition of this publication), the *Blue List of Current Municipal Offerings* (more commonly known by the first two words of its title), the *Investment Dealers Digest,* and several investors services, such as Moody's and Standard & Poor's.

19 *Ibid.,* Appendix A, "Activity on Over-the-Counter Markets."
20 "The Ownership of Tax-Exempt Securities, 1913-1953," Occasional Paper 47 (National Bureau, 1955). Goldsmith's *Study of Saving* presents estimates of individual ownership by size of estate (Vol. III, Table E-53).
21 *Study of Saving,* Vol. III, Part III.

The (Daily) *Bond Buyer* is best known to statisticians as the compiler of weekly and monthly figures of "municipal"[22] bond sales. These figures of public offerings have become the principal source of such data and are widely quoted; they are also used by the Securities Exchange Commission in its statistics of public security offerings. In addition the *Bond Buyer* compiles:

a. Two indexes of municipal bond yields

b. An estimate of the 30-day visible supply of securities (securities for which a public sale is scheduled within the next 30 days)

c. Transactions in major (underwriting) accounts, including purchases during the week, and amounts unsold at the end of the week (usually Thursday) from which the amounts sold out of major accounts can be estimated

d. A monthly series of bond sales approved in municipal elections.

The *Bond Buyer* also carries two regular features which explain much of its use in the trade: a detailed record of leading proposed bond sales, including details on previous sales of the governmental unit announcing the new sale; advertisement of these sales in official form; and a record of individual "Municipal Bond Sales, in Detail," including a listing of unsuccessful bidders and the prices of terms they offered as well as the price paid by the successful bidder. Other tabulations, mainly of narrow interest to underwriters as such, are also published.

The *Blue List of Current Municipal Offerings* is a record of the bonds being offered for sale by virtually every state and local government security dealer of consequence. The *Blue List* thus becomes a daily record of the inventory of securities *being offered for sale*. The last four words of the preceding sentence deserve some emphasis. The *Blue List* total is widely quoted as representing dealers' inventories of state and local government obligations. But there is a great deal of speculation in the trade as to the degree of understatement of *Blue List* figures. Our investigation did not give us an insight of sufficient accuracy to permit an estimate of the amount of understatement. Evidence was found, however, indicating that ownership of state and local government securities by nonbank dealers in state and local government securities is probably con-

---

22 The word "municipal" is still widely used in the trade to embrace all classes of state and local government obligations.

34

siderably greater than the amounts they offer in the *Blue List*. The difference, however, is not necessarily securities temporarily withheld from the market but sometimes represents securities held in investment accounts. When dealing with the matter of market strategy, we shall discuss the actions of dealers in showing or concealing their inventory position.

A new source of statistical and analytical data has recently appeared and has come to be of considerable use in appraisal of the state and local government security market. The *Investment Bankers Association of America* has inaugurated a detailed study of new offerings and publishes a monthly statistical survey of these offerings and a quarterly analytical summary. This new source was used extensively in this report particularly in connection with an analysis of the financings deferred because of tight money markets presented in Chapter 2.

The *Investment Dealers Digest* publishes the concessions offered by the major accounts to NASD members who are not members of the buying groups, and frequently presents a rather frank discussion of the sales experience of the leading individual accounts, including comments about the institutional character of buying interest in individual issues, something that is not regularly reported elsewhere.

Moody's Investors Service publishes ratings of the leading issues being offered for sale and compiles weekly and monthly estimates of yields on state and local government securities by security ratings. The published ratings of this service have vast market influence, and its more detailed and confidential analyses of the leading issues being offered for sale carry considerable weight both with underwriting firms and investors. *Standard Statistics-Poor's* also maintains a rating service, as does *Fitch*. *Standard Statistics-Poor's* ratings seem to have an appreciable market influence. *Dun and Bradstreet* does not publish security ratings but prepares analyses of the financial standing of various state and local governmental units and indirectly of the various securities they issue. They cover fewer issues than reached by the rating agencies, but their influence appears to be substantial in the cases they analyze. *Standard Statistics* and *Dow-Jones* both publish weekly indexes of municipal bond yields; the latter also published an index of revenue bond yields until February 1957.

NONQUANTITATIVE EVIDENCE

In the absence of more formal and comprehensive sources of market data a considerable amount of reliance had to be placed on the opinions of persons who were close to this market. Many were interviewed: the managers of municipal bond syndicates in the great investment banking houses, the managers of municipal bond departments in commercial banks (both dealer and non-dealer banks), the specialized brokers who act only for dealers, the investment managers for institutional investors who buy tax-exempt obligations, and finally the editors of the principal trade publications.

Research by interview can be enormously educational for the interviewer. But the faithful transmission of what he finds involves many dangerous steps. An effort was made to conduct these interviews in a reasonably systematic way: to have standard questions that could be used many times. But in the end it was found that the most illuminating fragments of interviews came, not from following such a systematic procedure but from pursuing what often started out as an incidental issue or a side comment. The footnotes of conversation thus often proved more illuminating than the text. One of the reportorial problems has been that of giving generalized expression to facts that were shown this interviewer in confidence. The standards of documentation and reproducibility of research reporting becomes strained under these circumstances. And still, to assume blandly that this evidence did not exist would have amounted to suppression of valuable data. The compromise followed was that of reporting only those opinions which were expressed by two or more persons, and to seek confirmation of most facts, opinions, or ideas from several sources. But to preserve anonymity, the following pages report many opinions without acknowledging their sources. This was necessary. To make this doubtful practice acceptable we have tried to assume the role of being an honest reporter as well as an inquiring economist.

CHAPTER 2

The Demand for Funds by State and Local Governments

SUMMARY

The usual reason that state and local governmental units borrow in the capital markets is to finance lumpy capital expenditures. On some occasions since World War II state governments have borrowed to pay soldiers' bonuses. In a very few instances cities and local governmental units have borrowed to meet budgetary deficits. But since the Great Depression such use of their borrowing powers has been rare; the dominant reason sending financial managers of governmental units to the capital markets is to cover a planned capital expenditure.

State and local governments usually feel bound by the strong tradition for an annually balanced current budget and are sometimes so bound by law. On the other hand, borrowing for capital purposes is widely sanctioned. In many states it is easier for a local government to get tax power to cover debt service than to make capital outlays directly.[1] An added reason for borrowing, however, is that many governmental units find it almost impossible to save in advance for capital expenditures; if they try to do so the pressure for tax reductions becomes irresistible. There are exceptions, of course; during World War II many state and local government units accumulated liquid reserves which in effect financed some early postwar capital expenditures. Nevertheless, the financing of capital expenditures out of accumulated funds is otherwise quite rare.

In many ways the circumstances that cause state and local governments to borrow are not unlike those which cause private corporations to borrow. There are, however, great differences in the

[1] The publication *Horizons for Modern Pennsylvania Local Government*, put out by the Associated Institutes of Government of Pennsylvania Universities, November 1957, Vol. IV, No. 10, reports, "In 1957 the General Assembly of the Commonwealth of Pennsylvania passed legislation which permitted certain cities and townships to establish reserves for future capital expenditures. Two years earlier similar power had been given to boroughs. This authority made it possible for a local governmental unit to put itself on a pay-as-you-go basis for capital expenditures."

37

kind of financing policies and financing limits that control the operations of the state and local governments and those which control corporate operations. Corporate capital expenditures are clearly limited by some sort of earnings or gross profits test. This test is not applied with the same rigor to state and local government expenditures except in the case of revenue financed projects. The limits on state and local government borrowing are more likely to be either constitutional or statutory limits than earnings limits. As a result, the financing policies of the managers of state and local government affairs really do not have any close analogy to those of corporate financial management.

The character of borrowing varies by level of governmental unit. For example, state governments frequently have such large budgets and such detailed financial plans that they can plan and schedule capital expenditures to correspond roughly to the expected stream of tax receipts. This is particularly true for expenditures such as roads which may be tied to receipts from gasoline taxes. At the other extreme, very small governmental units are likely to find capital expenditures much more lumpy and therefore more dependent on financing by borrowing. The proportion of capital expenditures at local levels that is financed by borrowing is considerably larger than the proportion of capital expenditures at state level that is so financed.[2]

Since borrowing tends to be for capital expenditures, the time profile of state and local government borrowing is likely to lead the timing of their capital expenditures. State and local government capital expenditures do not seem to be influenced by minor cyclical fluctuations. Such expenditures, however, were clearly curbed during the Great Depression. While they have not yet achieved a true counter-cyclical character, state and local government capital expenditures do not appear to have been retarded during the three minor postwar recessions, and may have been stimulated in 1954.

Though state and local government capital *expenditures* do not conform except to very broad cyclical influences, the *financing* of them appears to be somewhat more sensitive to short-term cyclical

[2] R. W. Goldsmith, *A Study of Saving in the United States* (Princeton University Press for National Bureau of Economic Research, 1955), Vol. I, Tables G-4-6, and 15.

influences. State and local governments traditionally arrange financing fully before making any capital expenditures; in other words, financing leads outlays. As a result, financing might also be expected to show little cyclical influence. This does not seem to be the case. Among the financing limits that are put on state and local governments, there is frequently a limit on the rate of interest that may be paid. These limits, combined with a natural desire to minimize financing costs, cause state and local governments to be particularly coy in attempting to time their market offerings advantageously. It would be inappropriate to contrast the financing policies of state and local governments with those of private corporations in this regard, but it is possible that state and local governments are more sensitive to interest rate fluctuations than are corporate financial managers. In any event, quite a bit of latitude is used by state and local government managers in timing their offerings to the capital markets. As a result, the pattern of state and local government financing is quite erratic and highly variable over the short-run, even though not conforming to any clearly recognized minor cyclical pattern.

The ultimate limit on the demands for funds by state and local governments is a combination of the demand of their citizens for capital expenditures and the ability of these units to service debt. The first of these factors eludes measurement, but the second is subject to fairly clear and explicit statistical testing. The ability of state and local governments to service debt is basically their ability to collect taxes. This is in turn a limit that is determined not merely by the value of assessed property but also by the tolerated level of tax rates.

The structure of this chapter will follow the sequence of topics introduced in this summary in analyzing the demand for funds. It will consider first the relationship of capital expenditures to financing. Then it will examine the financing policies of state and local government financial managers. Following this, differences in financial policies and financial practices by level of government will be analyzed. Next the timing of borrowing, both in terms of its cyclical content and its short-term variability, will be examined. Finally, the ability to service debt and the relationship of this ability to the demand for funds will be reviewed.

CAPITAL EXPENDITURE IS THE PRIME CAUSE OF MOST
STATE AND LOCAL GOVERNMENT BORROWING

A modest portion of state and local government capital expenditure is covered out of current receipts—roughly one-third in 1955.
The remainder is financed by borrowing. Such borrowing accounted
for the major share of state and local government borrowing—in
the postwar decade about eight-ninths of it. Evidence on this point
is found in the Federal Reserve purpose classification for new long-
term issues. This tabulation, summarized in Table 1, shows that

TABLE 1

Long-term State and Local Government Borrowing,
by Purpose, 1946-1955

Purpose of Issue	Millions of Dollars	Percentage Distribution
Schools	7,863	19.9
Highways	6,821	17.3
Sewer and water	4,494	11.4
Residential building	2,868	7.3
Veterans' aid	2,865	7.2
Miscellaneous public service enterprises	2,000	5.1
Bridge and tunnel	1,607	4.1
Hospitals and institutions	700	1.8
Port and airport	680	1.7
Recreation	308	.8
Industrial building	106	.3
Other	2,780	7.0
"Unidentified," i.e., under $500,000	4,998	12.7
Total new capital	38,090	96.6
Total refunding	1,341	3.4
Grand total	39,430	100.0

Source: Summarized from Federal Reserve Board unpublished mimeograph
tabulation of state and local government security offerings by purpose.

refunding and veterans, bonus issues accounted for only about one-
ninth of the identifiable types of borrowing during the postwar
decade; the remainder was to finance capital outlays. As nearly
as can be estimated, only a modest fraction of these capital outlays

was for land and existing structure; most was for new construction. Furthermore, it appears that most construction was on a contract basis: force account construction (that which is done by regular government employees) apparently is rather less frequently financed by market borrowing. An exception in some states is highway construction. Other examples are hard to find. Annual figures for purpose of borrowing are shown in Table 2 in dollars; the percentage array of these figures is made in Table 3.

The relationship of state and local government borrowing to the capital expenditures of these governmental units during the postwar decade is tested in Table 4. In this table the borrowing for veterans' aid (bonuses) and for refunding has been omitted; the remainder can be treated as a reasonably close estimate of borrowing for true capital expenditures.

Anticipatory borrowing apparently has been common during the postwar period. The low rates prevailing during much of this decade, particularly on tax-exempt borrowing, had the effect of stimulating borrowing of funds not immediately needed. State and local government units could borrow with tax-exempt obligations and turn about and invest the proceeds in Treasury securities which were taxable obligations to many other holders. Since state and local governments are tax-exempt institutions *per se,* they used the privilege of tax exemption on their own issues to help to solve their liquidity problems.

Table 4 shows that the proportion of new construction expenditures to borrowing in the same year declined regularly from 1946 through 1951, the ratio dropping from a level of over 70 per cent to under 50 per cent. This is contrary to what one would expect. Both the amounts of capital expenditure and of borrowing were increasing rapidly; if the timing of their increases were not parallel, then a quite different construction should be put on the figures. This evidence more properly suggests that borrowing is usually undertaken somewhat in advance of the period of construction. The practice of completing financing before starting construction is general in revenue-supported projects. Buyers want to be assured that the project can be finished and prefer advance guarantee of costs to the full extent possible. When short-term interest rates on Treasury obligations are fairly high, the cost of such conservatism is negligible.

TABLE 2

Long-term State and Local Government Borrowing, by Purpose, Annually, 1946-1956

(millions of dollars)

Purpose of Issue	1946	1947	1948	1949	1950	1951	1952	1953	1954	1955	1956
New capital–total	1,047	2,311	2,798	2,896	3,579	3,188	4,093	5,473	6,788	5,911	5,383
Schools	194	205	412	524	709	582	967	1,319	1,432	1,516	1,455
Highways	140	128	237	351	451	478	777	1,336	1,680	1,241	650
Residential building	9	70	148	203	123	361	423	506	456	570	258
Hospitals & institutions	8	34	35	47	96	135	38	133	77	98	62
Sewer & water	154	222	314	400	487	464	419	647	674	712	752
Miscellaneous public service	27	253	124	145	131	176	223	156	596	169	646
Recreation	11	22	29	37	34	8	24	44	58	40	41
Bridge & tunnel	27	74	186	169	59	102	161	251	456	121	48
Port & airport	67	47	107	67	68	26	60	48	88	102	137
Veterans' aid	39	672	643	263	635	41	100	140	162	169	110
Industrial building	....	....	....	1	81	5	5	7	1	4	11
Other	89	166	214	240	218	201	283	344	533	490	575
Unidentified	282	418	348	449	487	608	613	542	576	680	638
Refunding total	155	42	192	107	114	90	314	82	180	65	63
Total	1,202	2,354	2,989	3,003	3,694	3,278	4,407	5,555	6,969	5,976	5,446

Source: Same as Table 1.

TABLE 3

Long-term State and Local Government Borrowing, by Purpose, Annually, 1946-1956

(per cent distribution)

Purpose of Issue	1946	1947	1948	1949	1950	1951	1952	1953	1954	1955	1956
New capital-total	87.1	98.2	93.6	96.4	96.9	97.2	92.9	98.5	97.4	98.9	98.8
Schools	16.1	8.7	13.8	17.5	19.2	17.8	22.0	23.7	20.5	25.4	26.7
Highways	11.7	5.4	7.9	11.7	12.2	14.6	17.6	24.0	24.1	20.8	11.9
Residential building	0.8	3.0	4.9	6.8	3.3	11.0	9.6	9.1	6.5	9.5	4.7
Hospitals & institutions	0.6	1.4	1.2	1.6	2.6	4.1	0.8	2.4	1.1	1.6	1.1
Sewer & water	12.8	9.4	10.5	13.3	13.2	14.2	9.5	11.6	9.7	11.9	13.8
Miscellaneous public service	2.2	10.7	4.1	4.8	3.6	5.4	5.1	2.8	8.6	2.8	11.9
Recreation	0.9	0.9	1.0	1.2	0.9	0.2	0.5	0.8	0.8	0.7	0.7
Bridge & tunnel	2.3	3.1	6.2	5.6	1.6	3.1	3.7	4.5	6.5	2.0	0.9
Port & airport	5.6	2.0	3.6	2.2	1.8	0.8	1.4	0.9	1.3	1.7	2.5
Veterans' aid	3.2	28.6	21.5	8.8	17.2	1.3	2.3	2.5	2.3	2.8	2.0
Industrial building	....	....	....	0.0	2.2	0.1	0.1	0.1	0.0	0.1	0.2
Other	7.4	7.1	7.1	8.0	5.9	6.1	6.4	6.2	7.6	8.2	10.6
Unidentified	23.4	17.8	11.6	14.8	13.2	18.5	13.9	9.8	8.3	11.4	11.7
Refunding total	12.8	1.8	6.4	3.6	3.1	2.7	7.1	1.5	2.6	1.1	1.1
Total	100.0	100.0	100.0	100.0	100.0	100.0	100.0	100.0	100.0	100.0	100.0

Source: Calculated from Table 2.

43

TABLE 4

Borrowing for Capital Expenditure Compared with New
Construction Outlays of State and Local Governments, 1946-1956

	Borrowing for Capital Expenditure	New Construction[a]	Total Expenditures	Proportion of col. 1 to col. 2	Proportion of Previous Year to Current Year	New Construction as a Proportion of Total Expenditures
	Millions of dollars			Per cent		
1946	1,010	1,431	11,133	70.6		12.8
1947	1,639	2,482	14,513	66.0	40.6	17.1
1948	2,155	3,638	17,902	59.2	45.0	20.3
1949	2,626	4,917	20,393	53.4	44.0	24.1
1950	2,944	5,375	22,638	54.8	49.0	23.7
1951	3,147	6,436	23,902	48.9	46.0	26.9
1952	3,996	6,715	25,486	59.5	47.0	26.3
1953	5,336	7,243	27,165	73.8	55.2	26.6
1954	6,626	8,477	30,070	78.2	62.9	28.2
1955	5,742	9,161	32,718	62.7	72.3	28.0
1956	5,274	10,044	35,483	52.7	57.0	28.2

[a] Includes purchases from business.
Source: Col. 1: same source as col. 1 of Table 1: "new capital" minus "veterans' aid." Col
2 and 3: *National Income Supplement, 1954,* Table 9, pp. 172-73, for 1946-53. Figures for 19
to 1956 from National Income Division, Department of Commerce; annual estimates in *Surv*
of Current Business. Cols. 4, 5, and 6: computed.

If the long-term borrowing of each year is compared with the
new construction outlays of the following year, as is done in column 5 of Table 4, the results follow a quite different pattern than
that in column 4. They show a fairly steady level from 1947
through 1952 and thereafter increase fairly sharply. The presumption that borrowing anticipates new construction expenditures by
about one year is not entirely unreasonable. On some types of
projects, such as toll roads and bridges, the period of anticipation
is clearly much longer than one year. On other and smaller types
of construction projects the degree of anticipation may be less than
one year.

The time pattern of the increases in the borrowing ratio shown in column 5 is consistent with other well-known facts of state and local government finance. In the early postwar period the liquid assets accumulated during the war, combined with the high receipts of these governmental units due to excellent business conditions, made it possible to cover the cost of more than a half of new construction out of current revenues. But during the later years of the decade, expenditures for new construction mounted faster than total expenditures.

The proportion of new construction financed by borrowing is not, of course, a converse measure of the degree of state and local government saving. New borrowing is generally in serial form and the repayment of debt by state and local government has usually been in excess of the rate at which state and local government assets should be depreciated.[3] Furthermore, allowances for force account construction are in addition to the contract construction figures in Table 4. Census estimated such force account construction to have been $615 millions in 1954.[4]

Although state and local government capital expenditures seem to have burgeoned in the postwar period, they were about the same proportion of total state and local government expenditures as in the 1920's. Measured as a fraction of national product, however, total state and local government expenditures have tended to become slightly larger.[5] If allowance were made for the expenditures financed by federal grants but for essentially state and local government purposes, the tendency for these expenditures to grow might be more evident.

[3] But not by particularly comfortable margins. Goldsmith's *Study of Saving* shows the depreciation on original cost basis for state and local government depreciable assets combined to have been $1,538 million in 1949. Depreciation on a replacement cost basis was figured to be $2,836 million, or about 85 per cent higher. Table 4 suggests that about one-half of state and local government capital outlay is financed by borrowing. These figures suggest that depreciation on an original cost basis for assets acquired by borrowing was about 0.8 billions of dollars, or 1.4 billions on a replacement cost basis. The probable retirement of long-term debt in 1949 was just about equal to the larger of these two figures. See Tables GI and 13, pages 1045 and 1063, Vol. I.

[4] *Summary of Governmental Finances in 1954*, Table 15 (Government Division of the Bureau of the Census).

[5] Some forecast that the proportion may grow further. See "The Expanding Role of State and Local Governments in the National Economy," *Monthly Review*, Federal Reserve Bank of New York, June 1957; also see the Severson estimates in *State and Local Government at the Crossroads*, National Committee for Municipal Bonds, January 1958.

BORROWING POLICIES OF STATE AND
LOCAL GOVERNMENTAL UNITS

Law and tradition control much of the borrowing process; the margin left for policy determination by finance officers is modest. But some of these factors are of considerable importance in terms of market strategy.

The timing of offerings is one of the subjects left, in part, to administrative policy. Many full faith and general credit offerings, however, leave the finance officer relatively little latitude. If the public demand for the projects involved is considerable, there is not much public sympathy with waiting because "the market is temporarily weak." Public administrators have some latitude; they can vary the time of announcement and can even reject all bids if they find them unacceptable. But the margin of maneuver is not much more than a few months. The officers in charge of financing public authority projects usually exercise somewhat greater latitude in selecting offering dates.

The maturity of most public offerings is also administratively determined. Observation of new offerings announcements suggests that terminal maturities of 20, 25, and 30 years now dominate the serial offerings. A few run longer; this is sometimes true of PHA contract housing authorities bonds. A few issues, usually state bonds, are limited to maturities of as short as 10 or 15 years. Term bond issues based on the revenue of specific projects are generally issued with initial maturity of 30 or 40 years usually qualified by some kinds of call provisions. Some underwriters report that the maturity of new offerings has been stretched out in recent years somewhat beyond those prevailing in the 1920's or 1930's. They suggest that 15- and 20-year terminal maturities were dominant then. This view, however, is not universally held.

State and local government security maturities are sometimes geared to the life of the asset being financed, as is usually done in business finance, but the practice seems to be less general.[6] It is more common to find that maturity has been tied to some estimate of revenues. For example, most water and sewer issues, whether revenue or based on full faith and credit, appear to be given a

---

[6] For example, railroad equipment trust obligations are given a modal life of about 15 years because this is a conservative estimate of the economic life of equipment. Right-of-way bonds, on the other hand, have very long maturities.

maturity so that anticipated receipts cover the serial maturities and interest requirements comfortably. As a result such maturities are often put at about 30 years. But water and sewer systems are not fashion-determined projects; no technological obsolescence of them is in prospect; and they seem to remain operative for many decades and even for centuries. The other side is illustrated by school building bonds. Before 1940, issues of such obligations usually had a terminal maturity of 20 years and many issues still observe that limit. But there has been a tendency for school bond maturities to be stretched out to 30 and even 40 years. This appears to be particularly true of the school building issues of authorities or corporations such as are used in Pennsylvania, Indiana, and Kentucky because of restrictive debt limits. Here the relation between the final maturity and length of economic life of the underlying asset may be the opposite of that observed for water and sewer bonds. Public school buildings less than 40 years old and even less than 30 years old are already being called obsolete. Will some of the bonds now being sold outlive the school buildings the construction of which they finance?

The market itself has variable preferences with respect to the length of the terminal maturities. Sophisticated finance officers are reported to adjust their offerings to such changes in market tolerance, but the practice is far from common. One notable exception to this rule is the Public Housing Administration; it has become very sensitive to the state of the market and its tolerance of terminal maturities.[7] Twice it has changed the maturities of its offerings to meet current market conditions.

The apparent elongation of maturities in recent state and local government offerings may be explained by factors parallel to the factors that account for the lengthening of mortgage maturities. Lenders have developed an increased tolerance to them; borrowers have discovered the greater freedom it gives them. As a result, borrowers less often put an equal dollar amount in each maturity than they did formerly; they lighten maturities in the early years and concentrate them in later years. In periods such as 1955 and 1956 when commercial banks are reluctant buyers, underwriters welcome such schedules of maturities.

---

[7] *8th Annual Report,* Housing and Home Finance Agency (1954); PHA section; p. 365.

During recent years the maturities of many issues seem to have been stretched out a bit from earlier standards on the excuse that the longer issues were callable. The privilege of calling a serial issue usually becomes effective only after about a decade, and customarily in the reverse order of maturity. In many cases where taxes have been pledged for the service of a callable bond issue, it is likely that the securities with the longest maturities will be retired before the intermediate maturities. The practice of calling in reverse order of maturity was adopted initially to permit state and local governments to get fully out of debt in advance of the final maturity. This sometimes leads to what is known in the trade as a "humpbacked" offering scale: yields of the longest bonds may be below those of the intermediate maturities.

A recent buying practice of underwriters has blocked such calls, apparently quite inadvertently. In most sales, buyers are permitted to name the coupon structure. Because of the conventional municipal form of interest cost computation, underwriters sometimes put absurdly low coupons on the final maturity such as 1/10th of one per cent.[8] When this is done, the governmental unit must jump the hurdle of calling (usually at quite a bit above par) a security that, on a market yield basis, is worth much less than par. The advantage of the call privilege to borrowers can be reduced considerably by this practice.[9]

Short-term credit is used in state and local government financial management but in a rather restrained way at present. Excessive use of it appears to have led to difficulties in the past and so it is avoided. Furthermore, if short-term credit exceeds expected tax receipts, refunding of this debt can be embarrassing. Commercial banks often are hesitant to refund short-term credit with more short-term credit. Some investors are reluctant to buy long-term obligations where they fear the management of short-term debt has been unsound. Whether this fear has any substance in fact or not, it appears to be genuinely held. The Public Housing Administration is one of

[8] The reasons for this odd practice are explained in Appendix B.

[9] This was clearly true of two $30 million issues of California school bonds, one in November 1955 and the other in March 1956; also a City of Louisville issue marketed in April 1956. In all three cases, the existence of low terminal coupons (1/4 of one per cent on the two California issues and 1/10 of one per cent on the Louisville issue) skimmed off a large part of the potential advantage of call. It is not clear that state and municipal finance officers are as yet fully aware of this result.

the few public bodies to make extensive use of short-term credit. It has guided the local housing authorities into a program of using short-term notes for projects under construction.[10] This agency follows closely the fluctuations in interest rates and often uses short-term credit in an effort to wait for relatively favorable long-term rates. These PHA short-term notes often account for almost half of the total of short-term state and local government credit outstanding. Table 5 tells the story of infrequent resort to short-term financing in the postwar decade.

TABLE 5

Long-term and Short-term State and Local Government Debt
(Interest Bearing), Year-ends, 1945-1956

	Total	Short-term (Maturity of One Year or Less When Issued)	Long-term	Ratio of Short to Long-term (per cent)
		(*M i l l i o n s o f d o l l a r s*)		
1945	18,946	353	18,593	1.9
1946	18,523	454	18,069	2.5
1947	20,032	551	19,481	2.8
1948	22,328	625	21,703	2.9
1949	24,802	781	24,021	3.3
1950	28,069	932	27,137	3.4
1951	30,518	919	29,599	3.1
1952	33,711	1,194	32,517	3.7
1953	37,456	1,645	35,811	4.6
1954	41,873	1,847	40,026	4.6
1955	45,593	1,579	44,014	3.6
1956	49,041	1,527	47,514	3.2

Source: Table A-1.

LEGAL RESTRAINTS ON STATE AND LOCAL GOVERNMENT BORROWING

State and local governments borrowed heavily during the postwar period primarily because of a mounting demand for public capital improvements. Population growth has increased the demand

[10] *8th Annual Report* cited above, pp. 364-65.

for new housing and public services. But while population, particularly at the lower age levels, has been growing, its location has also been shifting. Rural families have been moving to the city, and city population has been moving from urban to suburban areas. Some cities and one Federal Agency have been attempting to counter the blight of urban centers by improved housing (slum clearance), improved public facilities such as streets and parks, and better sanitary systems. Almost every one of these developments compound the need for public capital expenditures: sewer and water systems, schools, roads, hospitals, public housing authority projects, parks, and the like.

Then, too, the automobile is a great multiplier of public expenditures: drivers want better roads (and will sometimes pay tolls for the use of such roads), they also want better parking facilities whether on-street or off-street. And better roads should not be identified merely with the dramatic through highways; the demand is also for better local roads and side streets. The extension of housing in areas of increasing radii around the hubs of great cities—made possible by the automobile—means the building of entirely new sets of streets and roads. Automobile registration doubled in the postwar period.

This strong and insistent public demand often encounters the obstacle that our forefathers frequently put rigid limits on the power to tax and to borrow in state constitutions or into the statutes creating local governmental units. The demand for public services that require borrowing often comes in conflict with the legal limitations on such borrowing. For reasons that a political scientist but not an economist might try to explain, this conflict has not been met head-on. Much legal ingenuity has been devoted to finding ways, other than by a direct constitutional change or statutory revision of circumventing the effect of law without breaking it. This is a complex business at best. It takes an exceptional amount of legal skill to tread such a narrow and devious path. Not that such acts should be thought of as involving a moral breech: indeed the lawyer who finds some way to finance the construction of school buildings so evidently needed by a growing population in spite of a constitutional debt limit that seems at first glance to make this impracticable, doubtless feels that he is doing a public service. But the fact remains that the market for state and local government securities is complicated by the existence of a great deal of borrowing that, while legal, has had to be tailored into a pattern of legality by considerable indirection.

Investors in state and local government obligations are understandably sensitive to the pitfalls of this complicated legal foundation. Investment bankers and public officials are similarly disposed. As a result, virtually every step of this business is guided or sanctioned by legal advisers. Prudent public officials or bodies do not initiate or announce their intention to borrow until they have the advice of counsel. Investment bankers retain counsel and clear all questionable matters with them. All bids and all sales are conditioned upon the delivery of legal opinions by firms of repute; the point is of such consequence that it appears in the advertising of almost every new issue. In fact, investors appear to discriminate among law firms; an opinion from a well-known firm is to be preferred to one from a more obscure firm. A copy of this approving opinion is attached to every bond as it is issued. In the secondary market, the sale of a bond without a copy of the original opinion ("ex opinion") is awkward and sometimes impossible. Even with all of these safeguards, it is not always possible to be certain that legal obstacles will not delay bond sales or the delivery of bonds after the sales have taken place. Taxpayer suits are given respectful hearing by the courts.[11] While some investors do not seem to worry about the legal problems that might complicate their portfolio operations, many do; the necessary caution involved takes time and adds to the complexity of this business.

The legal restrictions on the borrowing power of individual state and local government units are sometimes reflected in the market by the appearance of novel types of governmental organization. For example, states sometimes create or establish new authorities which have the power to borrow, and sometimes to tax, in such a fashion that the offspring can do what the parent body cannot. Judging the credit quality of many state and local government

11 For example, the biggest issue of state and local government obligations ever sold—the $415 million issue of Illinois Toll Road bonds—came to market in October 1955 and had been all sold by the formal offering date. But delivery was delayed for about two months by taxpayer suits, a matter of considerable inconvenience to the firms handling the deal and not without some influence on the prices of both state and local government obligations and Treasury obligations during the period of delay.

obligations naturally means that one must look beyond these forms and see the economic and political realities that underlie them—assuming counsel confirms the fact that these devices can stand the test of adjudication.[12]

The existence of such a harness of legal restrictions explains partially the widespread requirement that bonds be sold by competitive bidding. Originally competitive bidding was required in the sale of state and local government obligations to avoid the connivance of politicians and investment bankers. The protection of self-interest that might be expected to police direct negotiation in the marketing of corporate obligations does not prevail in public finance. The market's valuation of some of the more complexly devised state and local governments is so uncertain that competitive bidding may be needed to protect innocent public finance officers. Without such a guide, the arrangement of a fair price by negotiation might be often disputed and uncertain. As a result, competitive bidding is accepted without much debate even though many underwriters resist the practice in the field of corporate finance. It is significant that lately the rule of competitive bidding has been broken with increasing frequency. The major exceptions have occurred in the case of the new authorities that borrow on the basis of the revenue expected from the projects they sponsor. The laws creating the new authorities operating revenue projects have not always required competitive bidding; a number of these bodies have negotiated their financing without public bidding.

Competitive bidding doubtless explains some of the characteristics of the market for this group of securities. The process of getting out an announcement or invitation to bid, and the interval that must be allowed for bidding groups to organize, takes quite a bit of time. The public officials or finance officers of state and local government units try to anticipate market conditions but this cannot be done as adroitly as is possible in negotiated financing; the time of the sale may come when dealer inventories are high and the bids are bound

[12] Not always as clear as might be expected. For example, B. U. Ratchford has argued quite persuasively that certain types of (and possibly most) revenue bonds are not tax-exempt. See "Revenue Bonds and Tax Immunity" in the *National Tax Journal*, March 1954, Vol. vii, No. 1. Any decision confirming Ratchford's view would have a devastating impact on the market for such obligations; in fact a suit challenging the existing immunity would have wide market repercussions even if the general view were that it had little chance of succeeding. The market is sensitive to threats, no matter how remote.

to be unfavorable. Until shortly before the sale a finance officer can call off the sale without creating ill will; this is done occasionally. Once the sale is held, finance officers are reluctant to reject all bids even if they consider none of them very good. The leaders of organized bidding groups—managers of syndicates and other investment bankers—condemn such an action as having wasted their time and money in organizing groups and preparing bids. For these reasons all bids are seldom rejected. Frequently the price at the time of reoffering is higher than the best bid rejected. The unwieldy mechanics of competitive bidding may have the unintended result of building up inventories when the market is generally recognized as being weak. This sort of involuntary expansion of dealer inventories may account in part for the erratic character of this market, dealt with more fully in Chapter 6.

STATE AND LOCAL GOVERNMENT BORROWING
AT VARIOUS LEVELS

States and local governmental units that borrow vary widely both in size and in character; they are so various that they make for a complex market. No other open capital market covers such a wide range of borrowers. Corporations whose securities are traded in the public markets, particularly the organized exchanges, usually are the larger ones. The market for corporate bonds is relatively homogeneous as to size and character of corporate issues. The market for residential mortgages on single family dwellings is almost uniformly one of small borrowers; it is keyed to and organized around that situation. This is not true of state and local government finance. Some states and a few cities borrow in such large amounts that they can be compared only with the most massive corporations. At the other extreme, many tiny units of local government often have to borrow.

While such diversity might have been expected to have resulted in cost penalties for the small, obscure, and unfamiliar type of governmental organization, some cost-of-financing estimates presented in Chapter 4 suggest that such penalties attach only to very small units. Those large enough to offer their bonds on the national market, though relatively small, show no evidence of suffering any sort of size penalty. The principal marketing institutions have shown considerable skill and adaptability in handling the securities of smaller units and of conducting educational campaigns to create markets for unfamiliar types of obligations such as school authority bonds. However, one should not overstress the point. State and local government has paid a price for having a heterogeneous and complex organization.

Virtually every kind of state and local governmental unit is a potential borrower on the new issues securities markets. State governments head the list, cities and towns of all sizes and varieties enter this market; so do school districts and other special purpose districts, counties, townships, boroughs, parishes, as well as specially created authorities. The number of potential borrowers is vast; the Bureau of the Census reported the number of state and local government units to be over 102,000 in 1957.[13] Of the total that might borrow, roughly 15,000 to 20,000 units have exercised this privilege. Some have borrowed many times. The number of outstanding issues is probably at least 25,000 and it may be larger.[14]

Distribution of this borrowing activity by level of governmental unit may be measured by the debt outstanding or by the gross volume of new offerings. Unfortunately, data for the two classifications come from different agencies and so the results are not entirely comparable. The classification of debt outstanding is taken from figures estimated by the Bureau of the Census,[15] while the classification of the type of new issues put on the market comes from the Federal Reserve tabulation already cited.[16] The outstanding debt of state and local governmental units based on Bureau of the Census data is shown in the first column of Table 6, and the gross amount of long-term debt issued in the postwar period in column 3. Differences in classification, where not reconcilable, are indicated by the offset arrangement of the table.

Coincidence accounts for the fact that the amount outstanding in 1954 should have been so near to the gross amount of new financing during the decade. State governments account for about

[13] "Governments in the United States in 1957," Bureau of the Census.
[14] On January 1, 1955, 2,810 outstanding issues covering a somewhat smaller number of issuers had been rated by *Moody's Investors Service*. In 1950, Moody's estimated that 20,100 issues were outstanding. The number of issues to which new ratings are assigned by Moody's each year runs from one-sixth to one-tenth of the number of long-term offerings listed by the *Bond Buyer*. Since this source misses some of the smaller issues, an estimate of 25,000 issues now outstanding seems more reasonable. Friend, et al., *Over-the-Counter Securities Markets*, Table 2-4, p. 54.
[15] *Survey of Governmental Finances in 1954*, Tables 18 and 19.
[16] See source note for Table 1.

TABLE 6

Long-term State and Local Government Debt:
Amount Outstanding in 1954 and New Issues, 1946-1955

Governmental Unit[a]	Amount Outstanding, 1954 (in millions)	(per cent)	New Issues, 1946-1955 (in millions)	(per cent)
State	9,317	25.3	9,637	24.4
County	2,624	7.1	2,549	6.5
Township	782	2.1		
City (municipality)	13,892	37.6	8,750	22.2
School district	5,827	15.8	4,820	12.2
Special district (special authority)	4,455	12.1	8,555	21.7
"Unidentified," i.e., under $500,000			5,119	13.0
Total	36,898	100.0	39,430	100.0

a Federal reserve classification, where different, in parentheses.
Source: Col. 1: summary of governmental finances, 1954, Bureau of the Census, Table 18. Col. 2: computed. Col. 3: summary based on Federal Reserve Board unpublished mimeograph tabulation of "Long-term Security Offerings of State and Local Governments by Issuing Authority." Col. 4: computed.

a quarter of the total in each case. If the amount that is reported as "unidentified" in the Federal Reserve classification is roughly divided between school districts and smaller municipalities (where most of it probably belongs), it is evident that city borrowing is the most important single segment. When the market labels all state and local government obligations "municipals" it is almost more literal than figurative. School districts are set apart when they are identifiable as such, but it is known that in many areas the finance of public schools cannot be separated from city finance. Special district financing, a rapidly growing part of the total, is the other principal kind of state and local government unit.

CYCLICAL INFLUENCES ON THE TIMING OF STATE AND LOCAL GOVERNMENT BORROWING

The only available annual series of state and local government capital expenditures is the one provided by the national income estimates of the U.S. Department of Commerce. These estimates are available back to 1929. This annual series suggests that while the capital expenditures of state and local government may be curbed by a massive depression such as the one suffered from 1929 to 1933, they were very little affected by the fairly sharp downturn between 1937 and 1938 and they were not discernibly affected by the mild postwar dips in 1949, in 1953-1954 and in 1957. On the other hand, there is no evidence that state and local government capital expenditures tend to be countercyclical; a more correct statement would be that they are insensitive to moderate changes in business activity, though responsive to drastic ones.

Strategic elements in the timing of borrowing. Even though state and local government capital expenditures appear to be insensitive to moderate cyclical influences, the borrowing to finance them appears to be sensitive to a number of short-run market influences of a countercyclical nature. This is made possible by latitude in the timing of borrowing already mentioned. The latitude financial managers have in the timing of their market actions may explain this erratic quality. They try to delay financing when conditions appear unfavorable but then hurry to the market when conditions improve. As Chart 1 shows, seasonally adjusted state and local government borrowings for the postwar period show an increase in the 1949 downturn and at the 1953-1954 downturn and again near the end of 1957. On the other hand, in the periods of peak private business activity, borrowing seems to have been reduced. To the extent that state and local government financial managers use their timing latitude successfully, they have been a true countercyclical influence in the market.

There are limits to their capacity to play this role. While state and local government financial managers can temporarily withdraw from active capital markets and avoid high interest rates, sooner or later they are forced to overcome their reluctance and to enter the market for needed funds. In other words, there is some evidence that there is a cyclical character to state and local government borrowing of a very short period and relatively moderate amplitude which is related to the state of the capital markets but not related to somewhat broader business developments.

Interest elasticity of demand for funds. State and local governmental units have faced sharply increased costs of raising funds in the postwar period. The issue of interest cost has become a political

CHART 1

State and Local Government Securities
Sold by Public Offering, Monthly at Annual Rates, 1946-1957

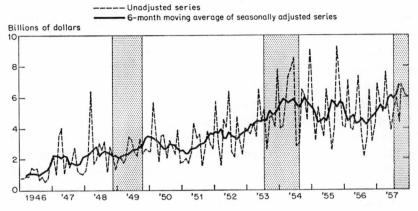

- - - - - Unadjusted series
———— 6-month moving average of seasonally adjusted series

Note: Shaded areas represent business cycle contractions and unshaded areas, expansions, according to National Bureau of Economic Research reference cycle dates.

Source: *Bond Buyer*; seasonal adjustment by Shishkin method.

issue of consequence. The Federal Reserve has been charged with responsibility for impeding the construction of school buildings and sanitary facilities. In periods of tight money no bids have been received for some issues[17] and in other cases all bids have been rejected as being unreasonably high. These circumstances illustrate the economic question being discussed here: the degree of interest elasticity in state and local governmental demands for funds. In practical terms, did the episodes of unsuccessful or abortive financing result only in short deferment, or has tight money sometimes produced a true and lasting reduction in the volume of financing?

Evidence in the next few paragraphs suggests that the first circumstance is nearer reality than the second one. Many of the issues for which bids were rejected or for which no bids were received were later reoffered successfully. Even when remarketing has not been attempted, capital projects have sometimes been financed in other ways. For example, in quite a few states the funds accruing

[17] This is more often than not accounted for by an unrealistic interest rate limitation in the invitation to bid.

in public retirement funds are normally invested in taxable obligations. But under stress these funds have been used to buy tax-exempt issues that had been unsuccessfully offered on the market. The burden of higher interest cost is thus either put on the beneficiaries of these retirement systems or deferred for the governmental units concerned if the retirement benefits are guaranteed.

Experience during periods of tight money markets. It may be said that in the postwar period to date tight money markets have occurred only in 1952-1953 and again in 1955-1957. During both periods an appreciable number of state and local government issues that had been planned or announced for offering were either deferred or offered unsuccessfully. Pickering has estimated that in the second quarter of 1953 the volume of such issues was about $300 million.[18] He also found considerable evidence of deferral in late 1952 and the first quarter of 1953. In general, however, most of the financing deferred appears to have reached the market later.

A similar estimate was prepared by Morris for the 9-month period July 1956 to March 1957. He estimated deferred financing in that period to have been $539 million.[19] It appeared that a majority of the issues were only deferred but had not been abandoned. Deferment, of course, performs an economic function.

One point on which these two investigators agree is that the enduring effect of higher interest rates is more evident in revenue obligations than in the case of general obligations. Pickering pointed out that the coverage of debt service in the case of revenue obligations was often relatively modest so that the changes in interest costs could have wiped out what would otherwise have been considered an acceptable margin of coverage by most prudent investors. Experience subsequent to the Pickering memorandum illustrates this point very well. In 1954, 40-year bonds for a planned toll road with estimated safety margin acceptable to investors could have been sold at a yield of around $3\frac{1}{4}$ per cent. No such issues were brought to the market in late 1956, but the prices on toll road bonds in the secondary market indicated that comparable obligations would have had to bear about a $4\frac{3}{4}$ or

[18] This estimate appears in an unpublished Federal Reserve manuscript, "Effects of Credit and Monetary Policy Since Mid-1952 on State and Local Government Financing and Construction Activity," by Richard C. Pickering, dated April 18, 1955.

[19] By Frank E. Morris in the IBA *Statistical Bulletin*, April 1957, No. 3, pp. 1-4.

even a 5 per cent coupon. The resulting increase in debt service cost would amount to about a fifth. In other words, a project for which the engineers had estimated a coverage of debt service of 1.5 times—apparently acceptable to many investors—when an interest rate of $3\frac{1}{4}$ per cent is assumed, would have found itself with a coverage of only 1.2 times if an interest cost of $4\frac{3}{4}$ per cent had to be expected. Such a coverage is usually thought to be too small by most investors.

Experience in periods of ease. While there have been several episodes of easy credit in the postwar periods, the only one studied with any intensity was Pickering's study of the year 1954.[20] His conclusions, while quite tentative, suggested that the large volume of issues in the year 1954 was partly due to the moderately lower rates.[21] Many projects were made feasible by the rates then prevailing which would have been marginal at much higher rates. Unlike deferments during periods of credit tension, the volume of general obligations that were made feasible by lower interest costs cannot be estimated by objective tests. As already indicated, this can be done in a general way for many revenue obligations, though there are exceptions. For example, the elasticity of demand for the services of sewers and sanitary systems probably is far less than for toll roads. The illustration used above is not applicable to all types of revenue obligations. It is not at all impossible, however, that as much as one-tenth of the offerings in 1954 were generated by the favorable terms then available. The amount might be larger. Similar evidence might be uncovered if the year 1958 were to be scrutinized.

THE ABILITY OF STATE AND LOCAL GOVERNMENTAL UNITS TO SERVICE DEBT

Except for revenue obligations (which will be separately treated in Chapter 7) the ability of state and local governments to service their obligations is based on their ability to tax. This rule is qualified by a few exceptions but they are unimportant and can be neglected.

The ability to tax is better measured in terms of the practical

[20] Memorandum cited above in note 18.
[21] The same observation could have been made of the first half of 1958.

limits than of the legal limits on its exercise. Tax revolts are not unknown in the United States and in a few cases debt defaults apparently resulted from these revolts. Defaults on state and local government obligations in the 1930's suggest that local governments, while sensible of the rights of creditors, are even more sensitive to the pressure of their own electorates. Public bodies will default in an extremity before they will put intolerable burdens on their citizens. State and local government taxes at the end of the postwar decade were about the same proportion of personal income as in 1939. Some margin for increased taxing therefore probably exists. But residents of some rapidly growing suburban towns appear to feel that the margin is not too remote. At present levels of taxation, debt service of all forms of state and local government units accounts for about one-tenth of tax revenues or slightly more. But such an average may conceal considerable dispersion. The distribution of debt service among individual governmental units is what counts. For example: annual debt service appears to be only about one-twentieth of annual state tax revenues; indeed the whole debt of states is less than one-year's tax receipts. In the case of local government, debt service appears to require between one-sixth and one-seventh of tax receipts. The total debt of these units is almost three times their annual tax receipts. The most significant fact is that the ratios of debt service and of debt to taxes appear to be growing at all levels of state and local government.

The critical point is an intangible one: How willing are state and local government electorates to tax themselves? Almost every full-faith and general credit obligation outstanding is supported by adequate assessed value and adequate income—if debt payment is put high in the list of preferences by the citizens of the government owing it. State and local taxes are frequently quite regressive. Most of the citizens who vote for bond issues also pay some of the taxes that retire them, but they may not be conscious of the commitment for tax increases that such borrowing implies. A simple illustration will make the point clear. Toll road traffic studies suggest that the demand for toll road services, particularly by commercial users, is quite elastic. If all roads were paid for on a "pay-as-you-use" basis, it is almost certain that our national demand for highways (and maybe automobiles) would shrink. People—even though they pay the same ultimate cost—seem more willing to vote bond issues for free road than to pay for toll roads.[22]

Not only are there differences between states and local governments, but there are great differences *among* states and *among* local governmental units in their debt burdens and their ability to service them. This is shown in the following series of three charts. Chart 2 ranks the per capita debts of states in 1955. The states which have high debts by this test are not necessarily those which have been growing rapidly; indeed, rank correlation of debt and growth was only .11.[23] Chart 3 shows a similar array of the cities. Both charts demonstrate the vast disparity in individual governmental units with respect to indebtedness.

When we examine differential borrowing costs in Chapter 6 we shall find that, all other credit factors being equal, those states and cities which borrow sparingly tend to get premium treatment by the market; those which borrow heavily, even if of good credit quality, have to pay a penalty for the frequency of their resort to the market. Some differences in debt among governmental units, particularly among states, are accounted for by differences in the level at which various governmental functions are provided.

Differences in income levels might be expected to account for the diversity in debt levels. If this test could be applied to city and suburban debts, the results would be of great interest; some significant results might be found. But the only data available to us for test were for states. As a preliminary very simple test, the effect of income differences was tested by comparing debt to personal income. The results are shown in Chart 4. While some of the extreme differences are ironed out by this adjustment, more remain than were suppressed. The conclusion remains inescapable: differences among states and among local governmental units are great. Averages are of little use in measuring the ability of state and local government to service debt. This could be tested only by a kind of case study, something far outside the aims (and resources) of this project.

One factor complicating a relative judgment of credit at the state

[22] The Highway Act of 1956 is ample demonstration of this assertion. Traffic engineers could not conceivably find enough highway locations on which the amounts of expenditure contemplated by this act could be spent for self-supporting toll roads.

[23] Debt per capita as against relative population changes, 1950-1955.

CHART 2

State Government Debt per Capita, by States

(Net debt at end of fiscal 1955)

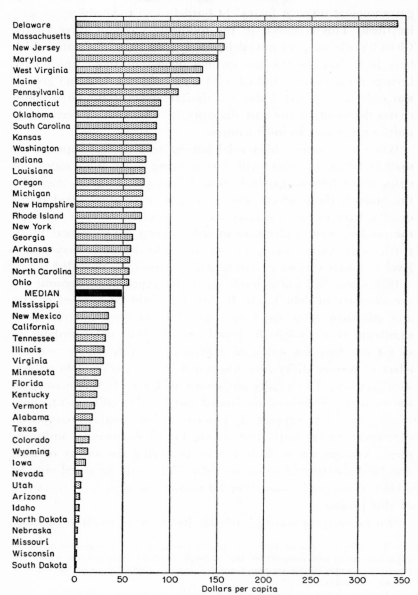

CHART 3

City Government Debt per Capita, in Major Cities

(Net debt at end of fiscal 1954)

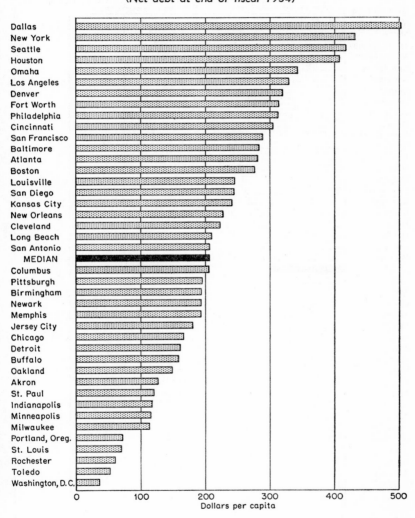

Dollars per capita

CHART 4

Ratio of State Government Debt (Gross) per Capita to Personal Income per Capita

(Gross debt—personal income for year 1954)

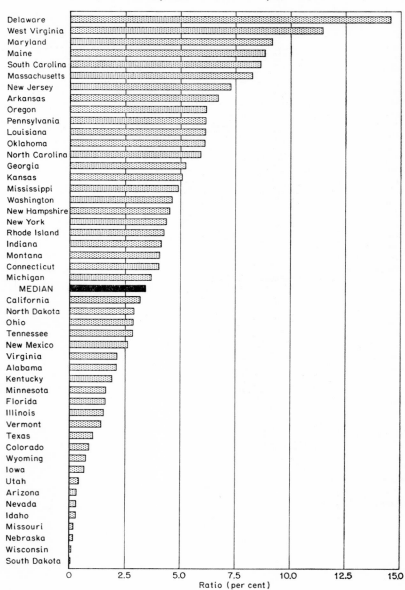

Ratio (per cent)

level and at the local level is grants-in-aid. In modern times (possibly in all times, if the record of history were open to us) large central governments often come to the aid of smaller constituent governmental units. The federal government aids states and local governments to perform their traditional functions, such as the state-aid highway construction program. State governments aid their constituent local units, and so on. For example, the Pennsylvania system of financing school buildings by special authorities seems to be quite dependent upon a system of state aid to schools. Many other examples could be found. Some feel that the volume of downstream grants-in-aid is likely to increase.

The combination of great diversity in the concentration of debt and of a rising level of borrowing during the postwar decade might lead to the expectation of some deterioration in the quality of new offerings. Such does not appear to have been the case. As Table 7 shows, the quality of the new offerings rated by Moody's appears to have been about as high near the end of the decade as at the beginning.[24] This increase in the quality of securities offered is, however, not evidence of an improvement of state and local government credit. Rather, it means that governmental units with the highest credit ratings were infrequent borrowers in the early postwar period but have since entered the markets to an increasing extent. The fact that the amount of debt outstanding has increased tends to reduce at least slightly the quality of the total outstanding. But the growth of debt has been almost matched by the growth in income and so sustenance of a high rating for state and local government obligations is reasonable—if income continues to be high.

[24] The new Housing Authority bonds with PHA contracts (virtually amounting to a federal government guarantee) which have been offered since 1951 are rated Aaa and tend to improve the average quality. But even exclusion of these issues, an alternative shown in the lower part of the table, would not change the conclusion greatly.

TABLE 7

Percentage Distribution of State and Local Bonds Rated by
Moody's Investors Service, by Rating Group, 1945-1955

			RATING		
	Aaa	*Aa*	*A*	*Baa*	*Ba* *B* *Caa*
1945	4.2	16.2	46.1	27.0	6.4
1946	7.6	22.7	47.6	19.2	2.8
1947	16.4	50.2	20.2	11.6	1.4
1948	33.9ᵃ	23.2	31.2	10.5	1.1
1949	9.4	30.2	38.3	20.1	2.0
1950	12.6	41.2	32.6	12.0	1.5
1951	27.0	31.4	28.6	11.6	1.5
1952	23.5	21.2	42.5	10.6	2.1
1953	24.4	31.9	32.1	11.0	.6
1954	22.4	27.0	38.1	11.0	1.5
1955	22.2	29.6	35.0	12.2	1.0

*Without housing authority loans
guaranteed by the PHA*

1951	15.0	36.5	33.2	13.4	1.8
1952	10.1	25.0	50.0	12.5	2.4
1953	13.0	36.7	36.9	12.7	.6
1954	13.3	30.2	42.6	12.3	1.6
1955	11.2	33.8	39.9	13.9	1.1

ᵃ Due to $500 million of bonus bonds: $300 million in
New York (2 issues), $200 million in Ohio both Aaa.

Source: Listings of individual issues in weekly bond
service of Moody's Investors Service. These ratings are
sometimes revised and listed in the annual *Moody's Investors Manual of Governments*. No allowance was made
for the effect of such revisions. Revenue obligations were
included, where rated; but obligations based on revenue
from projects without operating experience are generally
not rated.

CHAPTER 3

The Supply of Funds by Investors in State and Local Government Obligations

SUMMARY

One principal feature sets state and local government securities apart from other capital market obligations: exemption of the interest return from the income taxation of the federal government, and usually exemption from income taxation by the state of issue.[1] As a result most of the state and local government securities privately held are held by persons or institutions which are subject to high federal income taxation. As would be expected, few are held by institutional investors which are tax-exempt as such. Individuals are the most important holders; later in this chapter we shall review evidence suggesting that most of the state and local government securities held by individuals are owned by upper-income bracket investors—as would be expected. Commercial banks are the most important institutional investors; they are subject to corporate income taxes at the standard rates. Fire and casualty insurance companies are next in size of holding. Both types of companies in this field pay the standard corporate tax rate on marginal investment income with certain exceptions.[2] Life insurance companies are the only important investing institutions which buy state and local government obligations in appreciable volume though partly sheltered from federal income taxes. Life insurance companies are taxed according to a quite special formula. While life insurance companies enjoy only moderate tax advantages from owning tax-exempt securities at present, they may consider themselves prudent to hold some tax exempts as a protection against the pos-

---

[1] It is frequently forgotten that interest income from state and local government obligations is quite generally taxed fully by states themselves in states other than that of issue. In 1952, 31 of the 34 states having a corporate income tax taxed the income from securities issued by other states; 16 taxed the income from the obligations of the home states. In the same year 30 of the 33 states having a personal income tax taxed the income from securities issued by public bodies in other states; 8 taxed those of the home state.

[2] Under the Revenue Code of 1954, certain mutual insurance companies pay a normal tax of 25 per cent rather than the usual 30 per cent and accordingly, when the 22 per cent surtax is allowed for, have a marginal tax rate of 47 per cent rather than 52 per cent.

sibility of future changes in tax laws. Since many toll road and other revenue bonds yield about as much as could be secured on fully taxed securities, they have the opportunity to store up a reserve of tax exemption for the future without suffering impairment of income in the present. A mild revival of mutual savings bank interest in these securities seems to have started after 1951 when the tax laws were changed so that some mutual savings banks became subject to corporate income taxation. The only group of investors—other than state and local governments themselves—clearly free of income tax liabilities are the fraternal societies. Their holdings have dropped from a small to a smaller part of the total amount privately held. State and local governments themselves are important investors in their own securities. Their holdings are material and they are sometimes important market factors, but the incentive lying back of this is generally a parochial one.

The purpose of this chapter is to examine the investment practices and policies of each of the principal investors in state and local government obligations: why they buy them, their policies with respect to maturity and quality, and the alternative uses of funds that each type of investor might make. This examination is necessary because each of the principal classes of investors has a quite different investment problem. Consequently, the timing of their purchases has varied greatly. In some periods individuals have dominated the market; in others, banks have taken the leading role and casualty insurance companies have also been increasingly important. The participation of life insurance companies has been quite irregular.

No other market seems to have experienced such pronounced and frequent changes in customers. The sharp fluctuations in the securities absorbed by the various groups are shown in Table 8. This table is limited to "private" acquisitions. No group shows a really stable record; the nearest approach to stability is found in the record of fire and casualty companies. The participation of commercial banks is shown to have varied from as little as 3 per cent to as much as 63 per cent of net increases in private holdings.

It is quite likely that the sharp and frequent shifting in the participation of various investors in the market for state and local government securities has given it some of the price volatility noted

Year	Commercial Banks (1)	Mutual Savings Banks (2)	Life Insurance Companies (3)	Fire and Casualty Insurance Companies (4)	Fraternal Societies (5)	Nonbank Security Dealers (6)	Miscellaneous Financial Institutions (7)	Nonfinancial Corporations (Except Dealers) (8)	Residual (Mainly Individuals) (9)	Total Private Acquisitions (10)
				Amount in millions of dollars						
1946	425	−30	−108	−12	6	40	−2	2	−254	67
1947	881	2	−5	78	−5	−97	2	36	510	1,402
1948	385	6	263	229	4	24	1	52	1,120	2,084
1949	887	15	180	284	−5	−15	1	51	650	2,048
1950	1,570	2	100	316	−16	118	20	68	539	2,717
1951	1,080	59	18	304	−1	14	5	52	459	1,990
1952	991	178	−17	423	3	−156	3	65	1,141	2,631
1953	632	82	145	748	−11	202	6	91	1,853	3,748
1954	1,765	193	548	783	10	+70	19	219	800	4,407
1955	112	37	192	793	21	+100	32	250	1,795	3,832
1956	203	32	235	721	0	−100	15	75	1,796	2,977
				Percentage						
1946a										
1947	62.8	−0.1	−0.4	5.6	−0.4	−6.9	0.1	2.6	36.4	100.0
1948	18.5	0.3	12.6	11.0	0.2	1.2	....	2.5	53.7	100.0
1949	43.3	0.7	8.8	13.9	−0.2	−0.7	....	2.5	31.7	100.0
1950	57.8	0.1	3.7	11.6	−0.6	4.3	0.7	2.5	19.8	100.0
1951	54.3	3.0	0.9	15.3	−0.1	0.7	0.3	2.6	23.1	100.0
1952	37.7	6.8	−0.6	16.1	0.1	−5.9	0.1	2.5	43.4	100.0
1953	16.9	2.2	3.9	20.0	−0.3	5.4	0.2	2.4	49.4	100.0
1954	40.0	4.4	12.4	17.8	0.2	−3.0	0.4	5.0	19.6	100.0
1955	3.4	1.1	5.8	23.8	0.6	....	1.0	7.5	56.9	100.0
1956	6.8	1.1	7.9	24.3	....	−6.7	0.5	2.5	63.8	100.0

a Because the total is so small, the percentage distribution is not analytically significant.

Source: Dollar amounts, first differences of Table A-3; percentages computed from dollar amounts.

in Chapter 6. The "offering scales"[3] for state and local government securities which are presented in that chapter vary in slope and shape from the yield curves of either corporate bonds or Treasury securities because of the shifting composition of the market. The greater range of price fluctuation for state and local government securities, noted in Chapter 6, is probably related to this market characteristic. After this examination of the position of the various groups of investors, the chapter will conclude with some generalizing comments.

THE MARKET FOR STATE AND LOCAL GOVERNMENT OBLIGATIONS AMONG INDIVIDUALS

At the opening of the postwar decade, individuals held slightly more than 60 per cent of the state and local government obligations privately owned. By mid-1952 this fraction had been reduced to about 45 per cent. But at the end of the decade this fraction was starting once more to rise. Of the net increase in privately held state and local government obligations during the postwar decade, about 35 per cent was absorbed by individuals. This story may be read from Table 9.[4] Even more notable is the evident fact that individual acquisitions have varied greatly from year to year. Individual holdings declined through the end of 1946. In 1947, however, individuals increased their purchases sufficiently to account for three-eighths of the net gain in 1947. In 1948 they accounted for more than half. In the three years, 1949 through 1951, individuals acquired only about a quarter of the gain in private holdings. In 1952 and even more in 1953, with sharply higher interest rates, individuals accounted for almost four-ninths of the increase in private holdings. This proportion fell to about one-fifth in 1954 when money markets were eased and banks bid prices up. When money market conditions were reversed in 1955 and 1956, individuals again became the dominant factor in the market, accounting for five-sixths of the increase in private holdings.

This evidence suggests that participation in this market by indi-

---

[3] For a definition, see Chapter 4.

[4] This table should be interpreted with considerable care. As explained in Appendix A, Column 1 is derived as a residual from other figures more directly reported. Although the results should be reasonably accurate, they are subject to some systematic biases such as the reporting of holdings on a book-value rather than a par-value basis.

TABLE 9

Holdings of State and Local Government Securities by
Individuals, Annually, 1945-1955

(dollar amounts in millions)

Year End	Amount Held (1)	Total Privately Held (per cent) (2)	Annual Change in Amount Held (3)	Individuals' Acquisitions as a Proportion of Change in Total Privately Held (per cent) (4)
1945	9,559	61.3		a
1946	9,316	59.4	−243	(neg.)
1947	9,814	57.5	498	35.5
1948	10,872	56.7	1,058	50.7
1949	11,522	54.3	650	31.7
1950	12,072	50.5	550	20.3
1951	12,502	48.2	430	21.6
1952	13,645	47.8	1,143	44.7
1953	15,459	47.9	1,814	48.4
1954	16,253	44.3	794	18.0
1955	18,001	45.0	1,748	52.5
1956	19,752	45.8	1,751	59.0

a Total amount privately held declined.

Source: Col. 1: Table A-3, col. 10; Col. 2: Table A-4, col. 10; Cols.
3 and 4: computed from Table A-3.

viduals has had a jerky quality; in some years they have been the
leading buyers, in others they have dropped back in rank. The
principal effort of this section will be to appraise various purported
explanations of this irregularity in individual participation.

The individuals who own state and local government securities
are primarily those with higher incomes; presumption and logic
support this fact. But in order to appraise the size and character
of this market, we need reasonably precise answers to such questions as: At what level of income do such holdings become a significant part of portfolios? What are the investment alternatives
open to those who can advantageously invest in tax-exempt securities? What is the nature of income and saving at the level of income or among the groups that purchase tax-exempt securities?

For example, is proprietary income important in accounting for this demand? If so, the irregularity of proprietary income might account for the irregularity of individual demand. A knowledge of the relationship between wealth and income at the upper levels of each would help to mark out the margins of this market. Those who have high incomes but little wealth seldom start to build a portfolio by buying tax-exempt securities. Those of considerable wealth but modest income (nonincome producing wealth can account for such a case) have little reason to seek tax exemption of income. A man of wealth who is aggressively pushing the development of his own business might have little to spare for investment in tax-exempt form.

As might be expected, our knowledge of these various points is fragmentary. The fragments yield some interesting conclusions, but they fall short of telling the full story. Of necessity, our review of this evidence will have something of the episodic nature that marks its origins. The principal sources consulted and used in this part of the inquiry include:

1. Lent's study[5] of tax-exempt security ownership includes an examination of the concentration of individual ownership by size of income and also by concentration of such ownership in estates by size of estate. Lent also directed some attention to the problem of income concentrated in upper-income shares. He found that two-thirds of the state and local government securities held by individuals in 1940 were held by the upper one per cent income group.[6]

2. Atkinson's study[7] of financial asset ownership includes estimates of the income received from tax-exempt obligations and of the principal value of these obligations in the sample of tax returns covered by this study.

Atkinson's 1949 sample of Wisconsin taxpayers showed that those having an income of $50,000 or more held 2.3 per cent of their financial assets in state and local government securities. The holdings of such securities in this income group accounted for 38 per cent of the total of such securities, the holdings of which were implied by the tax returns.

[5] George E. Lent, *The Ownership of Tax-Exempt Securities, 1913-1953*, Occasional Paper 47, National Bureau, 1955.

[6] *Ibid.*, p. 116.

[7] Thomas R. Atkinson, *The Pattern of Financial Asset Ownership: Wisconsin Individuals, 1949* (Princeton University Press for National Bureau, 1956).

Those having an income of $25,000 to $50,000 held 1.2 per cent of their financial assets in state and local obligations and accounted for 22 per cent of total implied holdings.

Those with incomes of less than $25,000 held less than one-half of 1 per cent of their financial assets in state and local government securities but nevertheless accounted for 40 per cent of the total holdings implied. In this income range, there is no further evidence that the proportion of state and local government securities held is related to size of income; except for the very smallest income size group the others held close to one-half of 1 per cent of their financial assets in this form.

3. Mendershausen estimated the amounts of financial assets held by living persons.[8] This estimate was based on the estate tax returns for the year 1944. Mendershausen estimated that 90 per cent or more of the state and local government securities held by individuals in 1944 were held by individuals who would have been required to file an estate tax return if they had died in that year. Comparison with an earlier study by C. O. Hardy based on similar data suggests that the degree of concentration in ownership had increased from the 1920's to 1944. Robert Lampman has carried the Mendershausen estimates forward in an unpublished National Bureau study but his material was not ready for use in time for inclusion in this study.

4. A Harvard team studied, by intensive interview, the investment preferences and policies of about 750 wealthy individuals.[9] The interviews were made in 1949. Butters-Thompson-Bollinger found the proportion of state and local government securities in the 1949 portfolios of those interviewed to be (Table A-13, p. 468):

Income (thousands of $)	Per cent of Portfolio	Wealth (thousands of $)	Per cent of Portfolio
Under - $ 7.5	*	Under - $ 25	*
7.5 to 12.5	1	25 to 50	*
12.5 to 25.0	2	50 to 100	1
25.0 to 50.0	2	100 to 250	1
50.0 to 100.0	4	250 to 500	2
100.0 and over	7	500 to 1,000	3
		1,000 and over	5

* Less than one-half of one per cent.

[8] Goldsmith, *Study of Saving*, Vol. III, p. 361.

[9] J. Keith Butters, Lawrence E. Thompson, and Lynn L. Bollinger, *Effects of Taxation: Investments by Individuals* (Harvard Business School, 1953).

These findings confirm the major point that holdings of tax-exempt state and local government securities are concentrated among those with high incomes and usually considerable wealth. But they also show that such holdings are not confined to upper income groups. Furthermore the various studies tend to confirm one another, though minor differences may be found. Lent concluded that two-thirds of such individual holdings are to be found in the upper 1 per cent of the income scale.[10] The pattern of Wisconsin holdings estimated by Atkinson suggested a slightly lower degree of concentration. The two do not necessarily conflict; Wisconsin experience might differ from the national average. Mendershausen's evidence suggested that in the year 1944 most tax-exempt securities were held by those with estates which would have been liable for an estate tax. This evidence suggests more concentration than indicated by any of the three other sources.

Since the Butters-Thompson-Bollinger evidence was collected by interviews with a limited group of individuals selected for their wealth, it cannot be used to estimate aggregates. But within the income and wealth categories covered by Butters-Thompson-Bollinger in 1949, the proportions of state and local government securities found was quite consistent with those found in Atkinson. The last two are the only ones that give us postwar evidence. Both of them suggest that ownership of tax exempts, though concentrated in upper income groups, is not confined to them.

The Mendershausen study also presented a comparison of the unadjusted holdings of state and local government securities in the estates filing estate tax returns for a number of years. The degree of variation among years in the proportions shown by these comparative figures is considerable. It suggests that single-date evidence may be almost unreliable. Three of the four studies we use here are single-date inquiries. Lent is the only one whose evidence was not tied to the facts of a single year, and his evidence relates only to aggregate holdings. Relative holdings appear in Table 10. These values are reproduced in Chart 5.

As this chart shows, the proportion of tax-exempt securities in big estates has been declining. There are, however, some year-to-year variations that seem to reflect fluctuations in common stock prices. For example, 1929 shows a low proportion of tax-exempt

[10] *Op.cit.*, p. 116.

TABLE 10

State and Municipal Bonds as a Percentage of Gross Taxable Estates

(current values)

	1922	1929	1939	1944	1946	1950	1955
	(per cent)						
Grand total	3.3	4.4	6.1	5.7	3.9	3.3	2.7
Nontaxable	1.7	1.7	1.1	2.0	0.8	0.6	0.4
By size of net estate:							
(thousands of dollars)							
Under 100	1.1	1.2	1.8	0.9	0.6	0.5	0.2
100-200	1.4	1.7	3.1	1.6	1.0	1.0	0.4
200-300	1.7	2.4	3.6	2.3	1.4	1.8	0.9
300-500	3.0	3.0	6.2	4.0	3.2	3.4	1.7
500-1,000	4.6	3.6	8.9	5.4	4.1	5.4	3.6
1,000-2,000	5.0	4.6	12.5	12.8	8.4	7.9	6.6
2,000-5,000	7.9	7.7	16.5	13.3	14.6	9.6	10.5
5,000 and over	12.0	9.7	14.5	22.7	18.0	18.5	8.1

Source: 1922-46: From *Study of Saving*, Vol. III, Tables E-21 to E-25. 1950: From *Statistics of Income*, 1949, Part 1, p. 324 to p. 328. 1955: From *Statistics of Income*, 1955, Estate Tax Collections, Table 4, p. 16.

securities; presumably a reciprocal of the high equity prices. The reverse is true of 1939. Although common stock prices were advancing during the 1950's, this does not seem to be a fully adequate explanation of the smaller proportion of tax-exempt securities in big estates. Large investors appear to have been convinced that the attractions of capital gains far outweighed those of tax exemption. In fact, the extreme right-hand portions of several of the curves in Chart 5 turn down, suggesting that tax exemption is used more by middle-to-large investors than by the very largest investors. This is particularly true in years of high equity prices.

Lent's and Atkinson's evidence suggest that some holders of state and local government obligations—a majority by number of holders, but a minority by amount—have relatively modest incomes and therefore take only partial advantage of tax exemption. Mendershausen's estimate minimizes the size of this group and an examination of the slope to the curves in Chart 5 would lead to the same conclusions. The Butters-Thompson-Bollinger interviews cannot be used to prepare aggregate estimates. The apparent conflict

CHART 5

State and Municipal Bonds as a Percentage of Gross Taxable Estates

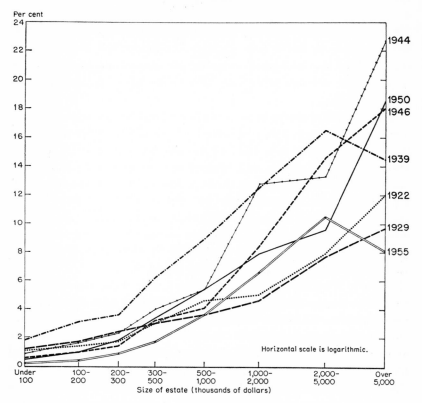

of their evidence with that in other studies may be reconcilable. Both Lent and Atkinson used size distributions of income; Mendershausen's estimates are based on a size distribution of estates or wealth. An estimate of marginal tax rates applying to the holders of tax-exempt securities, prepared by Harry Kahn of the staff of the National Bureau of Economic Research and fully described in the source notes to Table 27, supports the Mendershausen results rather more than those of Lent or Atkinson.

From year to year, the income of a person is likely to vary considerably more than his wealth; this must be particularly true of wealthy individuals who depend on dividends and capital gains for an appreciable part of their income. Thus the reports of any one year might show some holders of state and local government securities receiving incomes that did not put much of a premium on tax exemption. But over the full life cycle of these investors, employment of funds in this way might have been entirely rational. Wealth is less likely to vary than income (although market values will fluctuate in fairly wide swings). Therefore the evidence that state and local government securities are rare in smaller portfolios is consistent not only with such facts as we have but also with investment logic.

Although tax-exempt securities are held mainly by upper income and wealth groups, the proportion of assets in upper income or upper wealth portfolios held in tax-exempt securities is modest. Respondents to the Harvard interviews with wealth of $1 million or more held 5 per cent of their portfolios in tax exempts. The estate tax evidence (Table 10 and Chart 5) shows that, in the years covered, tax exempts averaged from 10 to 25 per cent of estates of $5 million or more; with a median not far from 15 per cent. At the $1 million to $2 million level, the range of the averages was from 5 to 13 per cent. Since these ratios are considerably above the Harvard response, it appears that there may be a difference between the portfolios of living persons and the estates of the deceased. Another possibility is that the respondents to the Harvard interviews may have included an unusual proportion of alumni who had profited by the investment example of Harvard University itself and concentrated on equities.

Some clues in the Butters-Thompson-Bollinger interviews furnish convincing reasons why the ratios of tax-exempt securities in large portfolios may be small. An upper income individual is often relatively little concerned with the production of current cash income; capital gains are far more desirable. Persons of wealth who are aggressively trying to increase their estate further have relatively little use for tax-exempt obligations; they want assets that furnish them with opportunities for capital gains. It is only wealthy investors who were intent on capital preservation for the sake of income production that are interested in tax exemption. The comments reproduced from the interviews showed that aggressive investors treated tax exempts almost with contempt; the return was too low.

Wealth-conserving conservative investors were the ones who

bought tax exempts. This point is of considerable importance; while portfolio shifts can account for part of the market for state and local government securities, the rate of saving of those who are interested in the purchase of tax-exempt securities must be an important limit on the amount of such securities that individuals can absorb from the market year after year. Our knowledge of life-cycle income and saving is still unfortunately limited. But common sense suggests that the rate of saving of those who are still attempting aggressively to build estates is probably higher (save in depression years) than those who have settled down to the process of capital and income preservation. Furthermore, tax-exempt securities are not the only or even the major means for minimizing the tax burden on upper-income individuals. Investments in oil royalties, in income-producing real estate, in various foreign ventures, and even in life insurance have much the same final effects.

A variety of special provisions and exceptions to the individual income tax have been created so that larger income receivers can minimize their tax liabilities by means other than buying tax-exempt securities. Among such features are: conversion of ordinary income to capital gains, depreciation and depletion allowances, income splitting, and rather generous gift provisions (particularly on securities with unrealized capital gains), all of which permit considerable minimizing of potential tax liabilities. Because of these possibilities, investment in tax-exempt securities has lost some of its appeal for upper income individuals. Estimates of the erosion of the tax base have been made by Heller and by Pechman.[11]

The managers of trust accounts are important buyers of these securities. Unpublished estimates by Goldsmith, Shapiro, and Mendelson suggest that about half of the tax-exempt securities bought by individuals are acquired for them by trustees, usually corporate fiduciaries. The investment policies of professional trustees for trust accounts differ greatly from those for individuals. The habits, traditions, and mores of trust investment put much more emphasis on conservatism and capital preservation. It is quite likely that for a given level of income and a given tax position, trust accounts of which individuals are beneficiaries are more likely to use tax-

[11] Walter W. Heller, "Limitations of the Federal Individual Income Tax," *The Journal of Finance*, May 1952, Vol. vii, No. 2, and Joseph A. Pechman, "Erosion of the Individual Income Tax," *National Tax Journal*, March 1957, Vol. x, No. 1.

exempt obligations as an investment medium than would be true of individuals themselves.

When the beneficial interest in a trust estate is divided between a life tenant and a remainderman, the trustee has a problem in equitable treatment of both. The life tenant is entitled to income, the remainderman to principal. Since trust law frequently does not require and frequently may not even allow amortization of premiums unless specifically allowed for in the trust contract, the trustee is forced to seek securities selling near par, where coupon and yield are nearly equivalent. This gives rise to some of the prejudice against both high coupon (premium) and low coupon (discount) obligations mentioned in Chapter 6.

This circumstance is sometimes reversed. If the remainderman is also a trustee (or joint trustee) of the estate, and if the life tenant is his mother he may deliberately invest some of the funds in high-coupon tax-exempt securities. When the coupon is not amortized this amounts to a mild kind of capital consumption. It is a way of persuading mothers who are not very knowledgeable about finance to consume capital without being aware that they are doing so. It was even reported that some individuals deliberately buy high-coupon tax exempts for their own portfolios as a means of engaging in some mild capital consumption, a pleasant deception. The tax rules do not require individuals to amortize the income from premium securities; there would be no point to such a requirement.

The irregularity in time of individual acquisitions of state and local government securities suggests that they are not primarily bought out of current saving but are acquired by portfolio rearrangement. The market potential, over the short run at least, is much more a matter of relative yields than current savings. When yields are attractive, portfolios will be shifted into tax-exempt form. At the quite low yields of 1946, individuals reduced their holdings; when yields became more attractive in 1948, they bought more actively. The heavy acquisitions by individuals in 1953 and 1955 took place when money markets were tight and banks were not buying. To bring out individual buying, yields had to go up considerably. The level of equity prices is also doubtless a market factor of considerable significance. When individuals are bullish on equities, their tax-exempt security buying suffers, but when the equity outlook grows dim, tax-exempt buying by individuals becomes more important.

It would seem logical that to induce individuals to buy on a substantial scale the yields available to investors would have to compare favorably with those available on fully taxed sources of interest or dividend income. The levels of income of those individuals who hold most of the tax-exempt securities is such as to put them in quite high tax brackets. The Harvard survey suggested that most of the holdings were among those with annual incomes of $50,000 or more. In 1949, when that survey was made, the marginal rate of federal income taxation for this minimum was 59 per cent. Even at $25,000 annual income—certainly the lower level according to both the Atkinson and Harvard study for an appreciable degree of concentration—the marginal rate was 38 per cent. It seems likely, therefore, that individuals do not make close or precise comparisons as do institutional investors; their judgments are more general. But they also look toward the longer-term advantage; longer-term judgments are necessarily even less precise. No one could ever make a close choice between the hope for capital gains and the certainty of federal income tax exemption.

Individuals not in higher income brackets who nevertheless own tax-exempt securities are still to be accounted for; our knowledge of them is limited. We do know that many very small issues are marketed locally and that these issues sometimes yield almost as much as fully taxed security incomes. A local investor with little expert investment knowledge and considerable mistrust of the central capital markets may be quite willing to invest in local municipal obligations even though his use of tax exemption is slight. Local pride and sentiment may support such action. A school board member or possibly even a schoolteacher may buy bonds on the local school district, even with relatively low marginal tax rates. The importance of this local market is discussed in Chapter 4.

One unhappy possibility must be mentioned. It is quite well established that federal income tax collections cover only a fraction of the volume of interest payments. The best evidence available suggests that only about 35 to 40 per cent of it is reported by taxpayers.[12] Taxpayers who do not pay taxes on their taxable

[12] Noted by Selma Goldsmith in her "Appraisal of Basic Data for Constructing Income Size Distributions" in Part VI of *Studies in Income and Wealth 13*

interest income obviously have little use for tax-exempt securities. We know very little about the income levels at which such under-reporting takes place, but evidence developed by Holland and Kahn from Audit Control Program records suggests the frequency of underreporting is greater at low income levels. But an appreciable portion of the dollar volume of underreporting is at higher income levels.

THE MARKET FOR STATE AND LOCAL GOVERNMENT OBLIGATIONS AMONG COMMERCIAL BANKS

Commercial banks follow close on the heels of individuals as the second most important group of investors in tax-exempt securities. Among institutional investors they are the most important by a wide margin. Commercial bank holdings hit their high-water mark at the end of 1951 or in early 1952, when they accounted for just over 35 per cent of all private holdings. This mark was reached after seven years of strong buying. Since that time, commercial banks have added to their holdings, but as total offerings have grown even more, the commercial bank share has declined. The first absolute decline in bank holdings of tax-exempt securities during the postwar decade came in the second half of 1955.

Commercial banks, like individuals, have been irregular buyers, dominating the market mainly in periods of easy money and withdrawing from it in tight money periods. Since commercial banks and individuals are the two most important buying groups, the timing of their participation seems to alternate. The principal features of bank ownership and participation are shown in Table 11.

The relationship of bank buying to money market conditions and the state of bank reserves is fully appreciated by the market itself. Indeed, the response of yields on state and local government obligations to Federal Reserve credit actions is sometimes more violent than that of federal government obligations. Even before 1951, which marks the postwar revival of a free and flexible Federal Reserve credit policy, the market for state and local gov-

(National Bureau, 1951). Expanded more recently by D. M. Holland and C. Harry Kahn in a paper, "Comparison of Personal and Taxable Income," which appears in the Joint Committee Print of papers submitted by panelists appearing before the Joint Committee of the Economic Report on the subject *Federal Tax Policy for Economic Growth and Stability*, 84th Congress, 1st Session, pp. 313-38.

TABLE 11

Commercial Banks' Holdings of State and Local Government Securities, 1945-1956

(dollar amounts in millions)

Year-End	Amount Held (1)	Per Cent of Total Privately Held (2)	Change in Amount Held (3)	Acquisitions as a Ratio of Change in Total Private Holdings (per cent) (4)	Holdings as a Ratio of Earning Assets (per cent) (5)	Change in Amounts Held as a Ratio of Earning Asset Changes (per cent) (6)
1945	3,970	25.4			3.2	
1946	4,395	28.0	425	634.3a	3.9	b
1947	5,276	30.9	881	62.8	4.5	39.3
1948	5,661	29.5	385	18.5	5.0	b
1949	6,548	30.9	887	43.3	5.4	15.0
1950	8,118	33.9	1,570	57.8	6.4	24.2
1951	9,198	35.5	1,080	54.3	6.9	18.2
1952	10,189	35.7	991	37.7	7.2	11.0
1953	10,821	33.5	632	16.9	7.4	15.6
1954	12,586	34.3	1,765	40.0	8.1	17.3
1955	12,698	31.7	112	3.4	7.9	2.3
1956	12,901	30.0	203	6.8	7.8	4.8

a Increase in total was negligible.
b Earning assets declined.
Source: Col. 1: Table A-3, col. 1; Col. 2: Table A-4, col. 1; Cols. 3 and 4 computed from Table A-3; Cols. 5 and 6 computed from earning assets of Commercial Banks from *Annual Report*, Federal Deposit Insurance Corporation.

ernment obligations responded with alacrity to the shape of credit policy. For example, in 1948 member bank reserve requirements were increased three different times. This action appears to have had more effect on bank purchases of tax-exempt securities than it did on their loans. Since the Federal Reserve System was still supporting the prices of Treasury securities, it could offset the reserves created by such action only by selling short-term obligations or raising reserve requirements. The third increase during that year was under temporary authority given at that time under compromise anti-inflation legislation. Bank reserves could hardly have been called tight; still, there was a halt in the expansion of deposits and currency. Under these circumstances, banks continued to increase their loans, though less rapidly than in 1947, and to sell Treasury obligations. Investment in tax exempts slowed down. This seems to characterize tax-exempt investment fairly well in general commercial bank policy during the postwar period: loans have top priority, but tax exempts come next and seem to lead all other forms of security investment in general favor. All during the decade, relative holdings of Treasury securities have been slowly dwindling. The only type of security acquired in appreciable volume, other than tax exempts, has been railroad equipment obligations. Though short maturities are available, these sometimes seem to have been bought more for reasons of customer relations than for reason of investment preference.

Commercial bank acquisition of tax exempts slackened in mid-1952, when monetary policy became a bit sterner; and continued to be slow through 1953. Again in 1955, tight money took the banks out of this market almost completely. Easy money also seems to stimulate purchases: banks were heavy buyers (relative to offerings) in early 1947, and in the second half of 1949 and all of 1950. From mid-1949 to mid-1950 these purchases could be attributed largely to easy money conditions, but in the second half of 1950 the Korean war episode sparked the conviction (wholly false, as events turned out) that there might be a shortage of tax-exempt obligations. Easy money clearly seems to have been the major stimulant of heavy bank purchases in 1954.

This concentration of bank purchases in periods of easy money would be expected to have an adverse effect on their earnings from these obligations; they buy when yields are low and prices are high. The very fact of their withdrawal from the market increases yields. Banks bid securities away from other holders in 1946 when total state and local government debt was still declining. And they paid very high prices. Their concentrated purchases in 1949-1950 coincided with declining yields; this also happened in 1954. On the other hand, banks were not in a position to take full advantage of the higher yields prevailing in 1948, 1953, and 1955. In fact, commercial banks secured higher yields in spite of what appears to have been disadvantageous timing for their principal purchases.

Such crude estimates as can be made of the rate of earnings realized by commercial banks from their holdings of state and local government securities suggest that these holdings have produced a materially better after-tax income than was received from other securities. This judgment is necessarily crude; the earnings reports of insured commercial banks on which our estimates are based do not distinguish between state and local government, and corporate securities in the "other" security category. By use of the ratio between fully taxable and tax-exempt yields in the market such a division has been estimated, as shown in Table 12. This estimate is probably a reasonable approximation of the rate of earnings from the state and local government securities held by commercial banks. The estimate cannot be far wide of the truth because these securities constitute such a large fraction of the "other" securities group in the earnings reports. Conversely, the implied yields for corporate obligations secured by this method of estimation probably should not be made to bear the weight of much interpretative analysis.

The privilege of tax exemption and availability of short maturities doubtless accounts for a large part of the interest of banks in the purchase of state and local government securities. Commercial banks are in a relatively exposed investment position; very few other financial corporations, or at least those with sizable amounts of funds to invest, are as fully exposed to tax pressures. When the income on an appreciable volume of federal securities was tax exempt, commercial banks were important buyers of them; indeed, until World War II, commercial banks paid relatively small amounts of federal income taxes. But when the federal government ceased to allow exemption from taxation for its own obligations in 1941, the only source of new issues so exempt was from state and local governments. During World War II, the volume of such new issues was negligible, but commercial banks bought state and local government securities aggressively in the secondary market. During that period, and particularly near the end of the war, life insurance companies and individuals were net sellers and commercial banks net buyers of state and local government obligations.

Commercial banks are denied by law or tradition the other investment outlets that are used by some investors to reduce the load of taxation. They cannot buy oil royalties. They cannot invest in

TABLE 12

Estimated Yield Earned on State and Local Securities by Insured Commercial Banks, 1946-1955

	State & Local (1)	"Other" Securities (2)	Interest on Securities (3)	Aa Corp. Yield to Aa S & L Yield (4) (ratio)	Estimated Yield Earned on S & L Securities (5) (per cent)
		(millions of dollars)			
1946	$ 4,301	$3,593	$176.6	2.06	1.51
1947	5,131	3,622	179.4	1.70	1.59
1948	5,511	3,421	189.6	1.44	1.82
1949	6,403	3,574	201.7	1.44	1.75
1950	7,959	4,192	225.4	1.53	1.57
1951	9,016	4,058	249.5	1.63	1.60
1952	10,006	3,867	277.0	1.52	1.74
1953	10,620	3,758	297.7	1.30	1.92
1954	12,387	3,634	324.8	1.42	1.85
1955	12,501	3,442	351.0	1.36	2.04
1956	12,717	2,829	370.0	1.34	2.24

Source: *Annual Report of the Federal Deposit Insurance Corporations*: Cols. 1 and 2, assets and liabilities of operating banks in the U.S. "obligations of states, etc." and "other bonds, etc." plus "corporate stock" respectively; Col. 3, earnings, expenses, and dividends of insured commercial banks "interest and dividends on other securities"; Col. 4, ratio of Moody's Aa corporate bond yields to Aa municipal bond yields (yearly averages); Col. 5 = Col. 3 ÷ Col. 1 + Col. 2 × Col. 4.

Stated in symbolic terms:

If S = amount of state and local government securities

r_s = rate of return from state and local government securities

O = amount of "other" securities

r_o = rate of return from "other" securities

and I = total interest income from state and local government, and "other" securities

then $r_s S + r_o O = I$

which may be transformed into $r_s = \dfrac{I}{S + \dfrac{r_o}{r_s} O}$ which is formula for computation of Col. 5.

In Table 14, col. 1 is S; col. 2 is O; col. 3 is I; col. 4 is $\dfrac{r_o}{r_s}$; and col. 5 is r_s.

dividend paying equities that promise capital appreciation taxed at the capital gains rate. They cannot invest in rental real estate properties on which depreciation may be charged. Thus the alternatives open to commercial banks are limited and most of these alternatives involve a tax liability.

Banks are also doubtless moved to invest in state and local government securities by virtue of the fact that they can underwrite and deal in them. The Banking Act of 1933 denied commercial banks that are members of the Federal Reserve System the right to underwrite and deal in corporate securities or to operate subsidiaries which engaged in this business. But state and local government obligations based on full faith and general credit were exempt from this prohibition. The great money market banks combine the operation of large investment portfolios of such securities with underwriting and dealing of the broadest sort. The two complement one another: the strategic position of an underwriter gives such banks the chance of acquiring new offerings on a most advantageous basis. And the dealer role increases the liquidity of such a bank portfolio considerably. The dealer department can work off holdings with less loss and more dispatch than is true of investors who must use the facilities of outside dealers.

Smaller banks also have an added interest in state and local government securities by virtue of the fact they can originate and deal in them. Banks, except in the great money markets, are basically local enterprises. They are tied by sentiment and by the pressure of customers to the welfare of their neighborhoods. Banks are always under pressure to support local finance, including the finance of local governmental units. A great many banks which do not consider themselves formal underwriters or dealers in state and local government obligations nevertheless do bid on and deal in the securities of nearby governmental units, albeit rather casually. In fact, the securing of the deposit balances of nearby local governmental units is not unrelated to the willingness of a bank to bid on and hold the securities of such a governmental unit. In this sense something approaching the customer relationship prevails. Even though the formalities of the open market—the public auction and bidding and the public announcement of depositary relationships—may prevail, the realities are more nearly those of negotiated arrangements. This is not to imply that such relationships are improper. Quite the contrary, they only illustrate the strong tendency in the economic history of the United States for impersonal open-market relationships to be superseded by customer relationships which are responsive to considerations other than price.

This negotiated relationship, however, clearly tends to limit the marketability of state and local government securities acquired in this way. Technically these securities are negotiable and the right of the owner to sell is unquestioned. But a banker who sold his holdings of the securities of local governmental units would be exposing himself to two kinds of criticism. In the first place, the issuing governmental unit might be offended; the sale would limit their power to sell further obligations. But beyond that, buyers would fear that a local banker had inside knowledge of local financial affairs, that he was selling to avoid expected unpleasantness. As a matter of practice, therefore, many small banks treat their holdings of nearby local state and government securities as having no greater degree of liquidity than that possessed by local loans. Not only that but in some circumstances of distress, local governmental authorities expect the local banker to furnish a market for such previously issued obligations as may turn up in the secondary market.

The great money market banks are not exempt from such influences. The fiscal authorities even of large cities and states are quite conscious of the identity of buyers for their securities. They think of buying banks as "friendly" and while they might not call those which sell their securities or fail to bid on them as "hostile" they certainly take a cool view of them. The fiscal authorities follow closely which banks organize or participate in buying groups that bid on their securities; they distinguish between those which "give them a good price" as over against bids which they interpret as ducking the market. During periods of adversity in the market, the banking underwriters very likely may feel a little more compelled to maintain a continuity of functioning than nonbanking dealers simply for this reason.

Banks, particularly those acting as underwriters and dealers in the securities of neighboring governmental units, doubtless play an important role in influencing the general financial policies of such bodies, as is generally true of customer relationships.

Since state and local government obligations are issued in serial form, the new issues market supplies some quantity of short-term obligations of the type traditionally preferred by commercial banks. This is also true of equipment trust obligations, but not of most other corporate obligations. Commercial banks, when their demand has been strong, have sometimes pushed beyond the range of maturities ordinarily acceptable to banks. The maturity distribution of bank holdings in June 1947 and in June 1956 is shown in Table 13.

TABLE 13

Maturity of State and Local Government Obligations Owned by Insured Commercial Banks, June 30, 1947 and June 30, 1956

	Amount in Millions		Per Cent	
	1947	1956	1947	1956
Maturing in one year or less	813	1,931	16.9	15.2
Maturing in 1 to 5 years	1,420	4,437	29.5	34.9
Maturing in 5 to 10 years	1,269	3,825	26.3	30.0
Maturing in 10 to 20 years	945⎱	2,539	19.6⎱	19.9
Maturing after 20 years	381⎰		7.9⎰	
Total	4,828	12,731	100.0	100.0

For reasons mentioned in Chapter 4 and explained more fully in Appendix B, banks and dealers are presumably the principal buyers of the high-coupon short-term maturities of state and local government securities. If a bank has dealer status, these securities have tax advantages since a dealer bank is not required to amortize the premium for a security held less than 30 days or having a maturity more than five years. In such a case the loss of premium may be treated as a capital loss while the coupon income is fully tax exempt. But even those banks which must amortize the premiums may still be able to improve their yield by virtue of their willingness to fuss with the mechanics of accrual accounting for income from securities. They can profit from the prejudice other investors seem to have against high coupon obligations.[13]

Direct evidence on the quality of state and local government securities purchased by banks is thin. Unquestionably the super-

[13] David Durand and Willis J. Winn, *Basic Yield of Bonds, 1926-1947: Their Measurement and Pattern*, Technical Paper 6 (National Bureau, 1947), Addendum, pp. 31-40.

visory authorities have urged high standards on banks. Probably the most comprehensive supervisory attention to this has been given by the Federal Deposit Insurance Corporation. That agency has regularly had at least one specialist in this field spending full time on the subject. The influence of this supervisory agency has been felt in the private and undocumented form of examiners' comments and in the more public form of statements and speeches.[14]

Even though official pressure for adherence to high qualitative standards is put on banks, they cannot acquire securities that are better than those being issued. Banks often have been the leading factor in the new issues market. Furthermore, they usually concentrate their purchases in the shorter maturities of the new offerings. Thus to find the volume of securities they have frequently bought, banks had to accept the general average of market quality.

THE MARKET FOR STATE AND LOCAL GOVERNMENT OBLIGATIONS AMONG FIRE AND CASUALTY INSURANCE COMPANIES

While fire and casualty insurance companies have always held a few state and local government obligations, the expansion of these holdings to major proportions and the emergence of these institutions as leading factors in the tax-exempt market did not come until near the end of the postwar decade. This development may be seen in Table 14, which shows these holdings both as a fraction of total private holdings and also as a fraction of fire and casualty company assets. Since 1948 these companies have devoted a very large fraction of their new funds to the purchase of state and local government securities.

The importance of fire and casualty insurance companies as buyers of state and local government securities is due, as might be

---

[14] As, for example, the following addresses by Raymond E. Hengren, Assistant Chief, Division of Research and Statistics, Federal Deposit Insurance Corporation. "Factors in Evaluation of Municipal Bonds," *Commercial and Financial Chronicle*, June 21, 1951, pp. 2-8 (an address before the Florida Bankers' Association). "Municipal Bonds as Bank Investments," mimeographed, pp. 21-28 (an address before the Ninth Tennessee Bankers Conference, September 7-11, 1952). "Municipal Bonds in Bank Portfolios," *Commercial and Financial Chronicle*, September 13, 1951, pp. 6-8 (an address before the School of Banking of the South Louisiana State University). *Municipal Security Analysis and Bank Investment Problems*, Municipal Finance Officers Association of the United States and Canada, August 1953 (from a paper given during the 47th Annual Conference of the Association).

TABLE 14

Fire and Casualty Insurance Company Holdings of State and Local
Government Securities, Annually, 1945-1956

(dollar amounts in millions)

Year End	Amount Held (1)	Per Cent of Total Privately Held (2)	Increase in Amount Held (3)	Acquisition as a Ratio of Change in Total Privately Held (per cent) (4)	Holdings as a Ratio of Total Assets (per cent) (5)	Proportion of Available Funds Invested in State & Local Obligations (6)
1945	$ 249	1.6			3.2	
1946	237	1.5	−12	−17.9	2.8	
1947	315	1.8	78	5.6	3.3	
1948	544	2.8	229	11.0	5.2	
1949	828	3.9	284	13.9	6.8	
1950	1,144	4.8	316	11.6	8.5	⅗
1951	1,448	5.6	304	15.3	9.8	⅔
1952	1,871	6.6	423	16.1	11.4	½
1953	2,619	8.1	748	20.0	14.7	⁷⁄₁₁
1954	3,402	9.3	783	17.8	16.7	⁸⁄₁₁
1955	4,195	10.5	793	23.8	18.8	all
1956	4,916	11.4	721	24.3	21.5	all

Source: Col. 1: Table A-3, col. 4; Col. 2: Table A-4, col. 4; Cols. 3 and 4 computed from Table A-3; Col. 5: computed from total assets of fire and casualty insurance companies in Best's *Fire and Casualty Aggregates and Averages*. Column 6: Roy Reierson and Sally Ronk, *The Investment Outlook for 1956* (Bankers Trust Company, February 1956), Table 11, page 4.

The asset figures on which Col. 5 is based are at market value. In order to estimate the proportion of new funds available for investment which was applied to the purchase of tax-exempt securities it would have been necessary to adjust for changes in market value of securities held at the beginning of the period as well as purchased during the period covered. Since we were not in a position to make such an adjustment, we used an approximation worked out by the Bankers Trust Company in its estimates of sources and uses of funds in the capital markets.

guessed, largely to their exposure to tax liabilities. To a lesser extent these holdings also represent liquidity reserves; they are combined with the holdings of other high-grade fixed dollar value obligations as general reserves against underwriting risks.

The basic investment rule prevailing among fire and casualty companies is that business liabilities should be covered by cash, receivables, and "money" bonds. "Money" bonds can be long-term as well as short-term, but they must be high grade. Business liabilities include unearned premium reserves and reserves for unsettled and unreported losses, as well as the normal liabilities. In addition, the laws of a number of states put rules on the form of investment of the capital of these insurance companies. In practice, the companies seem to fulfill their liquidity requirements in a number of ways. Some take them quite literally and hold rather short-term obligations, but others invest in relatively long-term obligations as liquidity reserves.

Fire and casualty insurance companies seem to be bound by the rule that dividends on their own stock shall be paid only out of investment income, while underwriting profits, if any, are plowed back into the business. This practice has the effect of putting rather severe income pressure on the investment managers of stock companies, which in turn produces a conflict of business interests. To raise capital, fire and casualty companies need be able to attract equity investors. The attraction of such investors depends on the ability of stock companies to produce investment income (since underwriting income, in effect, is not available for distribution to stockholders). But the production of maximum investment income may impair liquidity and therefore the ability to undertake the primary business of these concerns: the writing of insurance.

Capital gains on equities also play a role. If a company with relatively low capital funds has the skill or good fortune to achieve substantial capital gains (whether realized or not), then its basic capital position is strengthened. And to the extent the equities that produced these capital gains pay dividends at a rate above interest yield on bonds, so much the better. Under such circumstances, unrealized capital gains may be better than realized gains. In other words, fire and casualty insurance companies may become reluctant sellers of equities. But when they consider the level of equity prices high, they may overcome their reluctance, sell and reinvest in tax-exempt securities. The yields on state and local government obligations during the first half of the postwar decade discounted most of the advantage of such investment; fire and casualty insurance companies bought Treasury securities and railroad equipment obligations for liquidity protection. But in the later years of the decade, state and local government yields became relatively more favorable. At the same time equity prices rose and the capital gain potential in them became less certain.

Such a general account of why fire and casualty insurance companies might be interested in state and local government securities conceals great differences among companies. Individual companies sometimes suffer underwriting losses so severe that for several years they do not have to worry about taxes. During 1955 almost all of the net funds of fire and casualty insurance companies went into tax-exempt securities. But even in that year a significant number of individual exceptions emerged. An analysis of the investment policies of 73 of the leading companies showed the following variations:[15]

Fraction of Net Funds available for Investment Going into State and Local Government Securities during 1955	Number of Companies
"All" (and sometimes more due to sale of other securities)	17
"Most" (interpreted as over one-half)	25
"Some" (less than half)	14
"No transactions"	10
"Net sellers"	7
	73

Fire and casualty insurance companies buy mainly high quality state and local government securities. Indeed, some companies are reported to have the rule of buying nothing less than Aa bonds. It seems to be agreed that most of these companies have been important buyers of the PHA bonds. Reports of toll road bond ownership can be found, but it appears that such holdings are limited to bonds of toll roads already in proved and successful operation.

The maturity policies followed are nowhere near as uniform. It appears that some companies limit purchases to the early maturities—sometimes to as short a limit as the first five years—but in other cases purchases are made of relatively long-term bonds. Since fire and casualty companies are reputed to prefer state bonds over the bonds of local governmental subdivisions, this fact alone tends to put some limit on maturities since state bonds average to be

[15] Privately circulated memorandum by Shelby Cullom Davis, "Insurance and Investment Exposure during 1955 for Fire and Casualty Companies," March 9, 1956.

shorter in maturity than the others.[16] In general these companies are buyers of "intermediate" maturities mainly.

THE MARKET FOR STATE AND LOCAL GOVERNMENT SECURITIES AMONG LIFE INSURANCE COMPANIES AND MUTUAL SAVINGS BANKS

During most of the postwar decade neither life insurance companies nor mutual savings banks were material factors in the market for state and local government securities. This was a change from past policies: once upon a time these institutions were important buyers of state and local government obligations. Prior to World War I, when tax exemption was of no market value, mutual savings banks were the leading institutional investor in such obligations.[17] They held from one-fourth to one-fifth of the amount in private hands. Indeed, mutual savings banks holdings remained fairly large until the opening of World War II, when other investors who valued tax exemption more highly bid away these holdings. Life insurance companies became significant investors in state and local government obligations mainly after the 1920's, when demand for funds from other sources dried up. Between 1929 and 1935 life insurance companies doubled their holdings even though the gross privately held debt of state and local governments was growing only slightly. During this period other investors, principally individuals, were net sellers, apparently because of uncertainty with respect to the future of these obligations. By this action, life insurance companies showed themselves courageous as well as shrewd investors. Their reward was rather handsome profits. These holdings were increased still further until they hit a peak level in 1941.

Life insurance companies themselves were never in a position to take full advantage of income tax exemption. The exemption had some value to them but far less than to many others. In any event, life insurance companies, like mutual savings banks, began a large-scale liquidation of their portfolios during World War II. The cycle of acquisition and then liquidation ran a bit later for

[16] *Investment Policies of Fire and Casualty Insurance Companies,* by J. W. Middendorf II, privately published by Wood, Struthers & Co., cites a great many individual cases reflective of these variations in maturity policy. See pp. 23, 33, 43, 47-48, 53, 63, 72-73, and 78.

[17] Lent, *The Ownership of Tax-Exempt Securities, 1913-1953,* Appendix B, Table B-1, p. 128.

life insurance than for the mutual savings banks, but the circumstances and relative amounts were much like one another. Both of them had disposed of major fractions of these portfolios by the time the postwar period was reached.

Rebuilding did not start until several years after the postwar decade started, roughly in 1948, as shown in Table 15 for life

TABLE 15

Life Insurance Company Holdings of State and Local Government
Securities, Annually, 1945-1956

(dollar amounts in millions)

Year End	Amount Held (1)	Per Cent of Total Privately Held (2)	Change in Amount Held (3)	Acquisition as a Ratio of Change in Total Privately Held (per cent) (4)	Holdings as a Ratio of Assets (per cent) (5)	Change in Amount Held as a Ratio of Increase in Assets (6)
1945	722	4.6			1.6	
1946	614	3.9	—108	—161.2	1.3	—3.2
1947	609	3.6	—5	—0.4	1.2	—0.1
1948	872	4.6	263	12.6	1.6	7.0
1949	1,052	5.0	180	8.8	1.8	4.4
1950	1,152	4.8	100	3.7	1.8	2.3
1951	1,170	4.5	18	0.9	1.7	0.4
1952	1,153	4.0	—17	—0.6	1.6	—0.3
1953	1,298	4.0	145	3.9	1.6	2.8
1954	1,846	5.0	548	12.4	2.2	9.2
1955	2,038	5.1	192	5.8	2.2	3.2
1956	2,273	5.3	235	7.9	2.4	4.2

Source: Col. 1: Table A-3, col. 3; Col. 2: Table A-4, col. 3; Cols. 3 and 4 computed from Table A-3; Cols. 5 and 6 computed from total assets of life insurance companies in the *Life Insurance Fact Book*.

insurance companies. Both life insurance companies and mutual savings banks revived their interest in state and local government obligations because of the favorable yields which were available on some of the new revenue obligations. As described in Chapter 7, this type of financing parallels that prevailing in corporate enterprises. The credit problems, the standards of security analysis, the general economic background that dominates the choices are quite similar. The investment departments of life insurance companies and mutual savings banks which dealt with corporate financing were able to turn to these obligations without having to learn new routines and procedures.

Tax exemption is not without some appeal to both of these types of institutions. Life insurance companies have never been tax exempt *per se*, though the formulae under which they have been taxed have sometimes had that effect. But the issue of life insurance company taxation never seems to be finally settled. At present life insurance companies are subject to an investment income tax of 6½ per cent.[18] A 3½ per cent yield on a tax-exempt security provides a price advantage of about 23 basis points or ¼ of one per cent, usually enough to make toll road bonds fully competitive with corporate obligations.

Mutual savings banks, or at least some of them, have recently been given an even more compelling reason for being interested in tax exemption. In 1951 these institutions were subjected to federal income taxation at the corporate rates—with an exception. Those institutions which have capital funds equal to less than 12 per cent of deposit liabilities are, in effect, exempt from the imposition of income taxes. Only a few mutual savings banks have capital funds of 12 per cent or more, but these few included some very large mutual savings banks. The value of tax exemption became material to those banks. Others, cognizant of the fact that laws can be changed, found it prudent to acquire a few tax exempts when the opportunity to do so without material yield concession presented itself. Toll road financing during these years offered frequent opportunities of exactly this sort.

These two classes of institutions may have accounted for as much as one-quarter of the toll road bonds sold during the second half of the postwar decade.

STATE AND LOCAL GOVERNMENTS, AND THE FUNDS THEY
CONTROL AS INVESTORS IN THEIR OWN SECURITIES

State and local governments, or the special funds they control, invest in their own securities. Since these governments or their

---

[18] Small life insurance companies are taxed half this rate.

creatures are exempt from tax as such, it seems a violation of investment logic for them to own their own securities. Several reasons account for the practice. In the first place, the general conviction prevails that a governmental unit will fare better in new financing if its outstanding securities are strong on the secondary market. Buying by the issuer obviously helps.[19] Some local administrators of funds doubtless have had limited investment experience; they feel more confident in their judgments of the securities issued by their own government or nearby or well-known governmental units; they hesitate to embark on dealing in the national market for a wider range of securities. "Deep-discount" low-coupon bonds sometimes turn up on the secondary market at yields which are competitive with fully taxable issues; in such cases buying them serves the purposes of supporting local government finance without any concession in return.

Of all the factors, the overwhelming reason for this practice is probably provincialism or parochialism: good old-fashioned "keep-your-money-at-home" spirit. The laws governing investment of state and local governmental pension and retirement funds usually permit and sometimes specify investment in their own securities. These funds, incidentally, are a growing portion of all state and local government holdings, from about two-fifths of them in 1945 to over half at present. Table 16 shows the details.

OTHER INVESTORS IN STATE AND LOCAL
GOVERNMENT OBLIGATIONS

The estimates of ownership of state and local government obligations shown in Table 8 above (presented fully in Appendix A) list only three categories of investors not already discussed: nonbank dealers, taxable corporations, and fraternal societies. These three groups account for less than 3 per cent of private holdings. Since fraternal society holdings appear to be dwindling at about the rate at which such securities might be expected to mature, it is evident that they are not a market factor of much significance. But the other two have rather more importance.

Nonfinancial corporations buy some state and local government securities. It is believed that their purchases are mainly of short-

19 The point is developed at somewhat great length in Chapter 5.

TABLE 16

State and Local Government Securities Owned by the State and Local Governments Themselves, Annually, 1945-1956

(dollar amounts in millions)

| | | | | | PENSION OR RETIREMENT FUNDS | |
ar d	Amount Held (1)	Per Cent of Total Interest Bearing Debt (2)	Change in Amount Held (3)	Acquisitions as a Ratio of Change in Interest Bearing Debt (%) (4)	Amount (year end) (5)	Acquisitions as a Ratio of Change in Interest Bearing Debt (%) (6)
5	2832	14.9			1086	
6	2363	12.8	—469	neg. total	993	neg. total
7	2451	12.2	88	5.8	1084	6.0
8	2593	11.6	142	6.2	1217	5.8
9	3104	12.5	511	20.7	1407	7.7
0	3587	12.8	483	14.8	1578	5.2
1	3785	12.4	198	8.1	1659	3.3
2	4025	11.9	240	7.5	1799	4.4
3	4354	11.6	329	8.8	2073	7.3
4	4690	11.2	336	7.6	2385	7.1
5	5078	11.1	388	10.4	2728	9.2
6	5499	11.2	421	12.2		

ource: Col. 1: Table A-2, col. 2; Col. 2: Table A-2, col. 2 divided by col. 1; Col. 3: Table A-2, nge in col. 2; Col. 4: Table A-2, change in col. 2 divided by change in col. 1; Col. 5: interpola- of Bureau of the Census June data supplemented by unpublished estimates by Duane nders; Col. 6: Table A-2, change in col. 5 divided by change in col. 1.

term ones such as PHA temporary notes. Since corporate treasurers have learned about money market investment of temporarily idle funds, both the Treasury bill market and the market for high-grade short-term tax exempts have furnished such an outlet. Most of our formal knowledge of such holdings, however, comes from the reports of fully tax-exempt interest received shown in the Part 2 (Corporate) section of the *Statistics of Income*. Publication of these data is greatly delayed; at the moment 1954 is the latest year available. The capitalizing of such interest returns requires selection of an appropriate rate. If a high-grade short-term rate is used, the results show quite a lot of random variability. This evidence is of dubious reliability, however, because a similar estimate of bank holdings by capitalizing the fully tax-exempt interest they report varies considerably from the known facts. Nonfinancial corporations unquestionably buy short-term high grade obligations, but our knowledge of how much is slight; the series shown in Table 8 is presented rather tentatively. In early 1956 *Fortune Magazine* conducted a survey of the short-term investment portfolios of 276 large corporations.[20] This survey showed holdings of $240 million near the end of 1955. This would project to a total of about $1 billion if current assets were used for the blow-up ratio. The estimates shown in Appendix A have been adjusted to take account of this evidence, but they remain rather rough at best.

Nonbank dealers also present a problem. As our comments in Chapter 5 on the secondary market will indicate, dealers' inventories of securities are a factor of dominant market importance. But a large fraction of dealers inventories, such as shown in the *Blue List,* are on a "when issued" (WI) basis. Such securities are not yet issued and so not a part of the ownership record. On the other hand, it seems equally evident that dealers carry considerably larger inventories than are shown in the *Blue List.* Our evidence is as follows:

The Wharton study of over-the-counter markets developed an estimate of dealer holdings of state and municipal holdings that was more than four times the figures of shown inventory according to the *Blue List* for the same date.[21] Second, a few brokers and dealers publish financial statements. The total state and local government holdings shown by several of these were compared with *Blue List* offerings for the same dates. The balance sheet totals were almost invariably considerably more than were shown in the *Blue List.* Some brokers and dealers own tax-exempt securities even though they are relatively inactive in underwriting or dealing in them.

It appears that such holdings perform a very real investment function; firms use them as a means of employing their capital. When firms can qualify as dealers and so do not have to amortize

[20] Reported in the August 1956 issue, "Short-Term Investment Portfolios of 276 Large Corporations."

[21] Irwin Friend et al., *The Over-the-Counter Securities Markets,* Table 5-1, p. 263.

such high coupon issues as are turned over in less than 30 days, the tax advantage of such an investment is quite attractive.

The figure shown by the Wharton study cited above for nonbank dealers was used as the base figure in our ownership estimates. Changes were made by capitalizing tax-exempt interest income reported in Part 2 of the Statistics of Income blown up to cover nonincorporated brokers and dealers.

SOME CONCLUSIONS WITH RESPECT TO THE SIZE OF MARKET FOR STATE AND LOCAL GOVERNMENT OBLIGATIONS

State governments and governmental units at lower levels have unquestionably benefited in some measure from the privilege of selling securities that offer the investor exemption from federal income taxes. But this advantage has also had a clear counterpart: the market for state and local government obligations has had to be found among investors exposed to income taxation. Investors who are tax exempt *per se*—pension funds, most savings and loan associations[22] and mutual savings banks, and nonprofit foundations, for example—are not interested in such a market. Those who have limited tax liabilities—life insurance companies and lower income individuals, for example—have only a mild interest in this market. If, as some feel, the future direction of institutional investment is toward those institutions with limited tax liabilities or none at all, this forecasts a further discounting of the value of the privilege of borrowing on a tax-exempt basis.

Furthermore, state and local government securities are not the first preference of any important group of investors. Commercial banks prefer loans. Individuals, and fire and casualty companies, prefer equities—most of the time. Savings and loan associations, mutual savings banks, and life insurance companies all prefer mortgages. State and local government obligations are the second choice of many investors, the first choice of very few.

This must account for some of the jerky quality to the market for state and local government obligations and to their price instability. When banks can find all the loans they want, they do not buy tax exempts; when fire and casualty companies think equity prices are reasonable, they do not buy tax exempts. And, as a class,

---

[22] Most savings and loan associations do not have authority to invest in these obligations so the issue is largely academic.

individuals do not seem to have a true preference for tax-exempt obligations. They require a fairly clear price advantage to be enticed into the market. They will not pay out most of the value of tax exemption in buying as the commercial banks seem to do in periods of easy money. It is true that commercial banks and individuals have tended to put funds into this market at somewhat different phases of the yield cycle, a factor that tends to have a steadying influence. But unfortunately it has not been a strong enough influence to offset other unstabilizing influences.

All of this argues that the borrowing advantage of tax exemption becomes seriously depreciated except when the volume of market offerings is small, when all of the new offerings can find a resting place in the portfolios of those who actively resist tax liabilities. This is quite parallel to the point made by Shaw-Gurley: an increase in their "direct finance ratio" (direct investment by individuals to total investment) is generally accompanied by an increase in interest rates. A decrease in the direct finance ratio (an increase in the degree of institutional investment) is accompanied by a decline in interest rates.[23] When the sellers of tax-exempt obligations must find a market for a bigger proportion among investors (the equivalent of an increase in the Shaw-Gurley direct finance ratio), then rates must be pushed up. Most of the benefits of tax exemption then accrue, not to borrowers, but to investors.

[23] John G. Gurley and Edward S. Shaw, "Financial Intermediaries and the Saving-Investment Process," *Journal of Finance*, May 1956, Vol. xi, No. 2, pp. 257-76.

CHAPTER 4

The Marketing of New
State and Local Government Issues

THE demand for funds by state and local governments, discussed in Chapter 2, is dominated by the complex problem of public capital expenditures. The supply of funds, discussed in Chapter 3, is dominated by the fluctuating attractiveness of high-grade, tax-exempt but rather low-yielding securities to institutional and individual investors. The institutions for marketing state and local government obligations supply the vehicle by which the disparate requirements of these two sides of the market are equated. This market is also the place in which the timing differences that inevitably arise between these factors are ironed out. This marketing system embraces both investment and commercial banks and includes very small as well as very large financial institutions.

The function of this chapter will be to provide a narrative picture of the marketing process and to present such quantitative data —unfortunately rather scattered—as bears on and measures the operations of this market.

MARKETING PROCESS

Once a state or local governmental unit has completed the necessary legal steps that authorize it to borrow money, the marketing process follows a fairly standardized pattern. If, as is usual, the issue is to be sold by competitive bidding,[1] the intention to borrow is announced formally (informal news has already been circulated in most cases) and bids are invited. In the somewhat rarer case of a negotiated offering, a consultant or an investment banking house is engaged as a financial adviser. If an investment banking house acts as the adviser, it may also organize the underwriting syndicate. This dual role, however, is frowned on by some critics. In the more common case of a competitive sale, the second phase is that of the organization of groups for the purpose of bidding on the issue.

[1] In the year 1957, 86 per cent of the public offerings were sold through public sealed bids, 12 per cent through negotiated sales, and 2 per cent were placed directly—largely with state and local government pension funds. *IBA Statistical Bulletin*, No. 6, January 1958, p. 8.

The third stage, which almost always follows hard upon the award of the bid to the group offering the lowest borrowing cost, is the reoffering of the securities by the successful bidders to ultimate investors.

The marketing of new state and local government issues is one of the principal lines of business of the big investment banking firms, and a few firms specialize in this business. This new issues market differs from the corporate one in that commercial banks are allowed to participate in it and are an important part of the market. The shares of individual firms in underwriting syndicates are not published, and so only general impressions of relative size can be presented. From some statistics relative to syndicate management presented later in this chapter, it would appear that commercial banks underwrite somewhat more than one-half of the dollar volume of new general credit obligations. Federal Reserve member commercial banks are barred from underwriting revenue obligations, however, and so the commercial bank share of the total market is probably about two-fifths. A dozen houses or banks that are recognized leaders, capable of managing great syndicates, probably account for about half the market in dollar terms. The next dozen account for about one-sixth of the market. More than 500 firms participate to some extent in underwriting and marketing new state and local government issues. Since investment banking, as an industry, has already been adequately described in the literature of finance,[2] the function of this chapter will be to deal with the special aspects of this system that relate uniquely to the marketing of state and local government obligations.

During the postwar decade, state and local government offerings became an increasingly important part of total investment banking business. This is true if measured in terms of the dollar volume of issues handled, even more so if measured in terms of gross revenue produced. The margins on state and local government security offerings, while less than those prevailing on equity security sales, are generally considerably larger than those received from the underwriting of corporate bond sales.

The mechanics of bidding for and reoffering state and local government securities have been so well developed that investment

2 Such as *Fundamentals of Investment Banking*, Fennelly, McClure, and Clark, editors (Prentice-Hall, 1947). See particularly Section Two, Part III; Section Five; and Section Nine, Part I.

bankers can handle the issues of small as well as large governmental units quite economically. In practice, the smaller state and local governmental units seem to suffer almost no adverse effects because of their size.[3] The serial nature of the obligations, the fact that they often have complex coupon structures, and the diversity of markets complicate the marketing problem. The gross margin in state and local government underwriting needs to be larger to allow for greater marketing costs. Possibly the greater price variability which we study in greater detail in Chapter 6 is also a factor in these wider underwriting margins. Market strategy also differs; underwriting groups for an offering of state and local government issues usually are held together longer than is needed in the case of corporate marketings.

COMMERCIAL BANKS AS UNDERWRITERS OF STATE
AND LOCAL GOVERNMENT OFFERINGS

The activities of commercial banks in underwriting state and local government security offerings explain one of the major differences between this market and that for other securities such as those of corporations. Since 1933 Federal Reserve member banks have been prohibited from participating in the underwriting of securities, except the general obligations of government bodies. This fact has special significance since the commercial banking system is the biggest single institutional investor in such obligations, and the trust departments operated by the bigger member banks control the buying of substantial amounts of these securities. Thus banks are important buyers as well as sellers of these securities. The number of banks having formal dealer departments is quite large, but those who are continuously active in this new issues market appear to number not much more than fifty institutions.[4] But many more than this number maintain some degree of interest in the market. A large number of the sales of small issues are to the local banker. The reports of sales of new issues in the *Bond Buyer* disclose innumerable cases of local issues going to a nearby bank.

[3] Frank E. Morris, Research Director for the Investment Bankers Association of America, reached much the same conclusion. He seemed to feel that the "equality of advantage" went down to even lower size groups than indicated here. "Size Characteristics of Municipal Bond Issues," *IBA Statistical Bulletin*, January 1957, No. 2.

[4] In October 1955, 57 commercial banks were listed in the *Blue List* directory of advertisers. A part of this group is relatively inactive except in local issues. About 20 banks appear to maintain continuous operations in the national market.

This type of business probably should not be considered as within the category of open capital market transactions but should be treated as a kind of parochial or local finance. Many bankers feel responsible for seeing to it that their local governmental units "get at least one decent bid."[5] But, apart from community pride and other noneconomic considerations, bankers have a binding customer relationship with the local governmental units. The deposits of local governmental units often can be employed profitably. The necessary condition for getting these deposits may be to support the market for the obligations of their governmental depositors. While no geographical distribution of bank-owned state and local government obligations is publicly available, the comments of examiners and others indicate that local holdings almost always predominate.[6] The fact that many commercial banks specialize in or limit their underwriting activities to the issues of local or nearby state and local governmental units should not be thought of as indicating any substantial quantitative restriction on such activities. The largest commercial bank in the United States, located in the state of California, limits its underwriting activities to the securities of that state or of local governmental units within that state. But within this limit this bank appears to do an excellent business and holds the largest commercial bank portfolio, which also means the largest institutional portfolio of state and local government securities in the United States.[7] At the other extreme, a large New York City bank which has been one of the most active managers of underwriting accounts itself holds only a small investment portfolio of these securities.

The presence of commercial banks in the groups that underwrite state and local government obligations gives some special marketing advantages to such groups. Commercial banks, being investors as well as underwriters, do not have to fret about the financing of their dealer inventories to the same extent that nonbank dealers do. Furthermore, the leading commercial bank in a buying group may

---

[5] In scanning the lists of sales of new issues in the *Bond Buyer*, our tabulators several times noticed cases of sales of local issues at interest rates which seemed to be lower than those prevailing in the central money and capital markets, particularly in times of strain.

[6] See Hengren speeches referred to in Chapter 3, note 14.

[7] "Obligations of States and Political Subdivisions Held by the 100 Largest Banks," *Bond Buyer*, February 4, 1956.

also "bank" or finance an underwriting deal if it must be kept together beyond the date of delivery of the bonds and therefore require such financing. As a result, banks may be rather firm holders and tend to work on the side of keeping groups together when these groups are not successful in selling out their offerings quickly. In other words, the presence of one or two large commercial banks adds to the fundamental underwriting strength of a group.

The great commercial banks have close ties with many potential customers: their own country correspondents, trust departments of related banks, wealthy individuals, and other financial institutions. The general knowledge by banks of who has money for investment probably gives them a rather substantial advantage in the marketing of state and local government obligations. On the other hand, the many facets of commercial-bank customer relationships probably make them unusually cautious as to the quality of securities they merchandise. They may be effective salesmen of the highest quality obligations; their zeal in selling intermediate grades is not quite as clear.

Commercial banks which are members of the Federal Reserve System would very much like to have the present statutes, which limit them to the underwriting of state and local government general obligations, liberalized. The volume of revenue financing is large and the profit margins are higher than those on general obligations. Commercial banks would like to have access to this new sector of the market. Commercial banks can invest in these obligations and $1,849 million of such securities were in insured commercial bank portfolios on June 30, 1956.[8] The effort of commercial banks to extend their underwriting privileges is, of course, bitterly opposed by the nonbank dealers and underwriters. With one important exception, commercial banks tend to mix with the nonbank dealers in the distribution of membership of bidding groups. The one exception is in the groups that bid for the bonds of the public housing authorities. The historical reason for a sharp bank-nonbank division in this one case seems to go back to the fact that nonbank dealers initially opposed banking participation in this market. Commercial banks finally won the right to underwrite

---

[8] *Assets, Liabilities, and Capital Accounts of all Insured Banks*, June 30, 1956, Call No. 45 (Federal Deposit Insurance Corp.).

PHA obligations, but this did not salve the injured feelings. A nonbank dealer group has clung together and has won most of the offerings. They have been opposed by a so-called "bank" group which is managed by a commercial bank and has a majority of commercial bank members but which also embraces some nonbank dealers.

STRUCTURE OF SYNDICATES

In most respects the groups organized to bid on state and local government new issues are similar to those organized for the wholesale buying of corporate issues. But moderate differences in practices exist. In the first place, management fees are rather uncommon in groups organized for state and local government bidding except in the case of housing issues and negotiated deals for revenue bonds. Management fees in this latter group are quite like those prevailing in groups buying corporate securities. The groups organized for state and local government bids have more regional character than is true of corporate groups. There is often, though not always, a better market for a state and local government issue in the territory of the issuing body; local investment banking houses and local commercial banks often have an insider's advantage in selling this market. Furthermore, it is probable that managers, in forming a group to bid on a state and local government issue, emphasize sales ability over underwriting strength rather more than would be the case in bidding on a corporate obligation.

Investment banking relationships have considerable historical continuity. The same names will be associated time after time in groups bidding on a specific issuers obligations. When the market is considered to be uncertain, buying groups lose some of their continuity. Weaker firms drop out if they do not care to assume the underwriting risks; stronger firms may drop out of accounts if they do not agree on pricing policies. They may reappear later—if they do not exercise their "drop-out" privilege too frequently or arbitrarily.[9]

Many evidences of institutional pride, of syndicate politics, and

[9] The resources of this project did not permit a study of the continuity of groups but that they have such continuity is evident from a reading of the offering advertisements. A specially interesting facet of such a study, if it were ever made, would be of the rise and fall of individual houses in the rankings involved in these listings.

of strategy similar to those that can be found in the syndicates organized for corporate offerings can be observed in state and local government buying groups. Many older and better known houses will not participate in a buying group unless it be as a "major" participant: i.e., with an allotment as large as that received by any other house in the group. Some houses will not participate unless their names appear high on the list of firms in the reoffering advertisements. At least one house sometimes prefers to have its name omitted from the offering advertisements when it is not a manager of the account or cannot secure the advertising position it prefers. It is customary to have the name of the manager of a buying group appear on the left-hand side of the first line of advertisement announcing the reoffering. But the holding of this position is sometimes juggled. Suppose a New York firm and a Chicago bank start as co-managers to form a buying group to bid on a forthcoming issue of a western state. Another firm with a strong sales position on the West Coast might be willing to join the group only if it were admitted as a co-manager. In such a case, the New York City advertisement might list the New York firm in the prized left-hand first line; the Chicago bank would take this place in advertisement appearing in Chicago; the third firm might have its name in the coveted position in a San Francisco advertisement. Advertising appearing in a magazine of national coverage, such as the *Bond Buyer*, probably would come closer to measuring which firm was the real leader in the group. Other matters of position in advertising sometimes are subject to acrimonious dispute.

MANAGEMENT OF THE SYNDICATES

Both the great investment banking houses and the commercial banks that are active in the national market for new municipal issues like to assume a role of management in the formation and operation of underwriting syndicates. Part of the reason is one of profit; in some syndicates, particularly those for revenue obligations, management fees are allowed in the syndicate arrangement. Even where there are no management fees, the manager is usually in a somewhat more strategic position to dictate terms and also to effect rapid distribution of the portion of liability assumed by his firm as an underwriter. Furthermore, the manager's role is one of considerable prestige. In the negotiation for formation of a syndicate, leading firms will sometimes refuse to participate unless allowed to come in as managers or co-managers.

The recently initiated tabulations of the Investment Bankers Association of America furnished our first quantitative clues as to the relative importance of various firms in managing syndicates. Table 17 shows the first 50 firms in the order of importance in the management of new issues during the year 1957. The accounts managed by these 50 firms accounted for almost four-fifths of the total public offerings of that year. This list of firms includes 16 commercial banks and 34 investment banking firms. As can be seen from the list, the great commercial banks tend to dominate the management of general obligations accounts. Only one investment banking firm is among the first five in importance in management of general obligation accounts, and only three such firms are in the list of the ten most important ones. However, since investment banking firms control the market for revenue obligations, the total dollar volume of accounts they manage slightly exceeds that of commercial banks.

A very high degree of specialization exists in the management role. Some houses or banks specialize in public housing authority obligations; some firms specialize in toll road bonds, still others in school obligations. Some firms have special competence for dealing with water and sewer revenue obligations; still others concentrate on school building authority bonds. Regional specialization is also evident. The third most important manager in 1957 was the Bank of America, which concentrates its activities almost wholly within the state of California. Naturally regional specialization is even greater in the smaller local accounts, not included in this tabulation.

BUYING STRATEGY

Once a syndicate has been organized for the purpose of bidding on a new issue, the determination of bidding strategy takes place in several steps: the determination of the probable price (yields) at which the various maturities of the issue can be sold (the "re-offering scale"); the selection of the gross margin or spread for which the group will work; the establishment of a coupon or a coupon structure that will "produce" enough gross revenue at the reoffering scale previously determined to cover the gross margin or

TABLE 17

Principal Managing Underwriters of New Municipal Issues, 1957

(in millions of dollars)

	General Obligation	Revenue	Total
Halsey Stuart & Co., Inc.	$367	$225	$592
First National City Bank of New York	435	....	435
Bank of America, N.T. & S.A.	360	....	360
Bankers Trust Company	326	....	326
Chase Manhattan Bank	300	....	300
Blyth & Co., Inc.	76	187	263
First Boston Corporation	80	174	254
Harris Trust & Savings Bank	228	....	228
Smith, Barney & Co.	48	162	210
Lehman Bros.	112	95	207
John Nuveen & Co.	56	117	173
First National Bank of Chicago	153	....	153
Northern Trust Company of Chicago	134	....	134
Harriman, Ripley & Co., Inc.	64	66	130
B. J. Van Ingen & Co., Inc.	34	94	127
Kidder, Peabody & Co.	81	27	108
Glore, Forgan & Co.	61	39	100
Eastman Dillon, Union Securities & Co.	30	59	88
Phelps, Fenn & Co.	72	13	85
Drexel & Co.	26	52	78
First of Michigan Corporation	52	22	74
Kuhn, Loeb & Co.	57	15	73
C. J. Devine & Co.	43	26	69
Marine Trust Co. of Western New York	66	....	66
Chemical Corn Exchange Bank	56	....	56
Ira Haupt & Co.	11	40	51
F. S. Smithers & Co.	8	39	46
Continental Illinois Bank & Trust Co.	46	....	46
Equitable Securities Corporation	25	17	42
Pierce, Carrison, Wulbern, Inc.	....	35	35
Guaranty Trust Co. of New York	34	....	34
J. P. Morgan & Co., Inc.	34	....	34
Salomon Bros. & Hutzler	20	13	32
Shields & Company	17	14	31
White, Weld & Co.	10	20	30
Merrill Lynch, Pierce, Fenner & Beane	19	8	27
Ohio Company	4	22	26
Ladenburg, Thalmann & Co.	....	26	26
American Trust Co., San Francisco	21	....	21

(continued on next page)

TABLE 17 (continued)

	General Obligation	Revenue	Total
Braun, Bosworth & Co., Inc.	$21	....	$21
Security-First National Bank of Los Angeles	19	....	19
Robinson-Humphrey Company, Inc.	a	$19	19
Butcher & Sherrerd	3	16	19
Philadelphia National Bank	17	....	17
Goldman, Sachs & Co.	7	10	16
First Southwest Company	10	5	14
J. M. Dain & Company, Inc.	13	....	13
Rauscher, Pierce & Co., Inc.	4	10	14
Sterne, Agee & Leach	9	4	13
First National Bank of Portland	12	....	12

a Less than half a million.

Based on issues of $500,000 or more. In co-managed issues the amount of the issue is divided equally among the co-managers, but each co-manager is credited with one issue with respect to the number of issues.

Source: IBA Statistical Bulletin, No. 6, January 1958, p. 9.

"spread" and still permit a bid of par or better for the issue being offered.[10] The first point is primarily one of market judgment but strategic considerations enter into the second and third points.

Experienced investment bankers develop considerable skill in judging the marketability of a given issue. Judgment of a given issue is based on two distinct types of factors: the quality or market appeal of that issue in relation to the general structure of yields, and the over-all interest rate or yield structure. The larger issues announced for sale usually have been or will then be appraised by the leading investment services and have rating grades assigned to them. This rating grade determines much of the market appeal of an issue. But the judgment of investment quality is considered to be considerably more refined than can be expressed in a single rating grade. Investment bankers know that issues of some areas and of some types have greater appeal to investors than is true of other issues. Investors' preferences may be illogical—indeed they often seem illogical,[11] but these preferences determine the shape of

[10] See Appendix B. In the sale of some term bond issues and a few serial bonds, bids of less than par or of some small margin less than par are permitted, but the offering terms for most serial bond issues require a bid of par or better. In a few cases, the net price cannot be much in excess of par.

[11] Which preferences are illogical and which are not may itself be seriously

the market; they are vital data that enter into the calculation of bidding prices. It is common for those organizing buying or bidding groups to canvass the market to determine the views of leading investors with respect to individual issues, as well as the funds that such investors have earmarked for purchases of tax-exempt securities.

The degree of informal pre-bid selling is hard to judge; the testimony on this point is conflicting. Some managers of bidding groups apparently try to have most of the real selling job done before a bid is submitted. Others apparently do not put on pressure until they have "bought bonds." But if any bonds with special or unique characteristics are planned, they are certainly sold pre-bid. Pre-formal offering selling of bonds acquired in negotiated deals is much more common; in fact, it is nearly universal.

Judgment of the general state of the market apart from the investor-appeal of a given issue is largely a judgment of relative interest rates and yields. If the value of a given issue relative to that of other tax-exempt securities has been determined—and investment bankers appear to have great skill in making such value judgments —then the problem is that of picking a series of yields that will sell bonds against the general state of the money and capital markets. Investment bankers also develop considerable skill at judging this aspect of the market. But mistakes are made and for a very good reason. The judgment of quality and knowledge of investor preferences and prejudices is not subject to short-term fluctuations. Experience of the past can be brought to bear on the marketing of any given governmental units securities now. But the money

---

disputed. For example, all of the Public Housing Administration sponsored issues have the same basic credit foundation: the contractual assurance of debt service by the federal government. But the issues of some cities sell on a better basis than is true of other cities. And if the troubles potentially involved in actuating a guarantee are an onerous burden on investors these differentials may not be without some logic. Again, the fear of war damage seems to have made investors prefer the bonds of interior and particularly midwestern communities over the seaboard states and cities. Some towns seem to have an appeal to investors that cannot be explained on objective grounds of credit analysis. But it is still possible that these preferences are not without some foundation; in other words one man's logic may be another man's fallacy. For example, the bond issues of southern school districts have been severely penalized by the integration issue. In such a case it is hard to say just what is prejudice and what is canny investment logic. In any event, investor preferences are a fact investment bankers must face and a knowledge of these preferences is one of the prerequisites of a skillful buyer of municipal bonds.

and capital markets change and the pattern of change is not as predictable. This is essentially a judgment of interest rates or reoffering scales. A good reoffering scale not only should be at the right level; it should have the right slope. It should sell bonds equally well at all maturities. This is an extraordinarily difficult judgment and a certain number of mistakes is inevitable.

The reoffering scale is, as monetary economists will recognize, a kind of yield curve. It tends to follow the slope of other maturity-determined interest rate differentials. But, as we note in Chapter 6, the reofferings scales for state and local government securities often are not parallel to the other yield curves with which they would seem to be closely allied. Market strategy often seems to explain this lack of parallelism. As skilled judges of the market, the investment bankers, and particularly the great houses and banks that act as managers of the principal accounts, are very sensitive to the appeal of particular issues to various segments of the market. For example, a skilled account manager knows which issues will appeal primarily to fire and casualty insurance companies. These firms usually prefer the intermediate maturities. For such an issue the reoffering scale might be made a bit lower relatively in the intermediate maturities than at either the short or the long end of the scale. This effect might also be present, not just because a given issue was expected to appeal to fire and casualty buyers, but because this group seemed to "have money" and be in the market while other buyers were relatively less active. When the commercial banks were heavy buyers of tax-exempt securities in 1954, the lower end of the reoffering scales for state and local government obligations showed more slope than was true of the corporate maturity scale. In other words, since the market for tax-exempt securities is in some measure isolated from other sectors of the market, the slope of the reofferings scale is affected by market factors which do not operate in other sectors of the market.

Setting a coupon structure. Some of the invitations to bid specify that while the bidder may name the coupon, all maturities of the entire issue must bear this one coupon rate. When this is the case, the second part of the bidding procedure is merged with the third stage, indeed is dependent on it fully. The gross margin that the bidding group will "try for" is added to par and the lowest single coupon that will produce that amount of revenue at the agreed offering scale is attached. If the bidders are permitted to set coupons on the .05 or .10 percentage point intervals, then the margin above par can be kept low. If, however, the coupons must be named in quarters or eighths, then a rather more material margin may be required. Under these circumstances a bidding group may sometimes be faced with the choice of adopting a coupon just under the one that would have given them the margin they had initially planned on working for—and then of cutting this margin enough so as to post a par bid. This shaving of margins sometimes becomes the means by which winning bids are posted.

Usually invitations to bid permit bidders rather wide latitude in proposing coupon structures. When this is the case, the selection of a coupon system becomes a matter of considerable strategic importance.[12] The choice of coupon structure involves considerations of two sorts. As explained and demonstrated in detail in Appendix B, a coupon structure which is high in the short-term end and low in the long-term end will tend to show lower interest cost as computed by the traditional formula used in state and local government security sales. The method of computing interest cost used by municipal finance authorities has this result because the cost of a coupon paid on remote maturities has the same weight as a coupon paid next year. The mathematics of "present value" calculations, which underlie all conventional bond computations now employed in the securities markets, discounts the yield (or cost) of a remote coupon to "present value." Therefore, remote coupons have less weight than nearby ones. Under the "present value" conventions of computation no advantage would accrue to the use of "reverse slope" coupon patterns. For this reason, bidders have at least one good reason for shifting the high part of the coupon structure into the early years as much as possible. But the pattern of interest rates as a function of maturity has had a positive slope (has been "rising") for the past twenty-five years—just the opposite of

[12] Jerome Percus and Leon Quinto have demonstrated the nature of this advantage mathematically. "The Application of Linear Programming to Competitive Bond Bidding," *Econometrica*, October 1956, Vol. 24, No. 4, pp. 413-428. The severe limitation of assumptions imposed by the methods used left most of the strategic problems unexplained. The article also failed to recognize the difference between "present value" methods of interest computation and the traditional form prevailing in this bidding.

the coupon pattern preferred for cost-influencing computation. If the coupon structure and offering scale of an issue slope in opposite directions, the early maturities will sell at premiums, the later maturities at discounts.

This is not always good sales strategy. Many buyers, possibly a majority of them, prefer to purchase a bond at a price not too far from par. With the arithmetic of bond yields relatively simple, and bond yield tables widely available, it might be thought that this preference would make little difference. To some extent this is true of institutional investors. But it is not wholly true of them and hardly true at all of individuals.[13] We noted a few minor exceptions to this rule in Chapter 3 but securities which have a yield quite remote from coupon and therefore involving substantial premiums or discounts, often are hard to sell. The ability to market such "hard-to-sell" securities may be the reason why a group can afford to propose a bizarre but bid-winning coupon structure.

Dealers themselves used to prefer to hold high coupon bonds in their investment accounts since they were not until recently required to amortize premiums on securities held less than thirty days. For this reason there was an unusually active market in these bonds among dealers.

The importance of nonamortization of premiums to dealers is indicated by the considerable vigor with which they defended the practice when it came up for legislative revision. On July 9, 1957, the House Ways and Means Committee reported favorably on a Bill (H.R. 8381) to require dealers to amortize premiums on all tax-exempt bonds held by them. The IBA Municipal Securities Committee actively opposed this provision and went so far as to suggest alternatives which it claimed would close the "loophole." This committee also urged IBA members to make representations to their Congressmen that this provision would "cause an increase in financing cost in state and municipalities."[14] The report of the Committee referred to the fact that "dealers may trade premium bonds back and forth between themselves after holding the bonds slightly less than 30 days, so that they can report 'loss' on the bonds

[13] Trustees of a fund for which one person has a life interest and another is remainderman have good legal and accounting reasons for avoiding sizeable premiums or discounts.

[14] Report of IBA Municipal Securities Committee to the IBA convention in Hollywood, Florida, December 1957, as reported in the daily *Bond Buyer* of December 16, 1957.

as the premium disappears while receiving tax-exempt interest on the bonds. . . ."

High initial coupons have a long history; they have been used for at least two decades. But the low terminal coupon does not seem to have been used much before 1954 and 1955. In 1954 several issues of which the terminal maturities had coupons of 1 per cent appeared; in the fall of 1955 some bonds with the terminal maturities bearing one-fourth of 1 per cent were offered. In early 1956 this had been pushed just a bit further and at least two issues had terminal maturities bearing coupons of one-tenth of 1 per cent; one of these issues was for a forty-year maturity. The "present" value of a forty-year bond of $1,000 par with such a coupon to yield 3 per cent is slightly more than $350. In other words, a bidding group that can find buyers for oddly couponed obligations, and who are not obstructed by the lack of marketability that such peculiarities probably impart to a bond, have a special bidding advantage. Such specially couponed maturities probably have been placed before the bid is ever entered; the preselling of such special coupons therefore becomes a part of bidding strategy.

A canvass of a number of leading issues during the postwar period suggests that high initial coupons have been placed on about one-third of the new issues.[15] In most cases the high initial coupons were applied to the first five maturities, but the period was longer in some cases, shorter in others. On the basis of these two rather rough estimates, it can be guessed that about one-twentieth of outstanding state and local government debt consists of high coupon obligations, a sum now somewhat in excess of $2½ billion. The appeal of these bonds to selected buyers was discussed in Chapter 3.

The low coupons on terminal maturities, while novel, are still relatively rare and the portion of the outstanding debt represented by them is trivial. Yield concessions of from 35 to 70 basis points are needed to market abnormally low coupon bonds. Several interesting examples of split coupon structures are shown in Chart 6. The notations on each spell out the salient features there represented. The devising of special systems of coupons, however, has

---

[15] This was based on a tabulation of the 442 issues used in computing the quarterly yield series presented in Chapter 6. The proportion of issues with coupons on the early maturities which were in excess of the average coupon was slightly more than 33 per cent.

CHART 6

Selected Examples, Coupon Structure Relative to Reoffering Yield, State and Local Government Securities

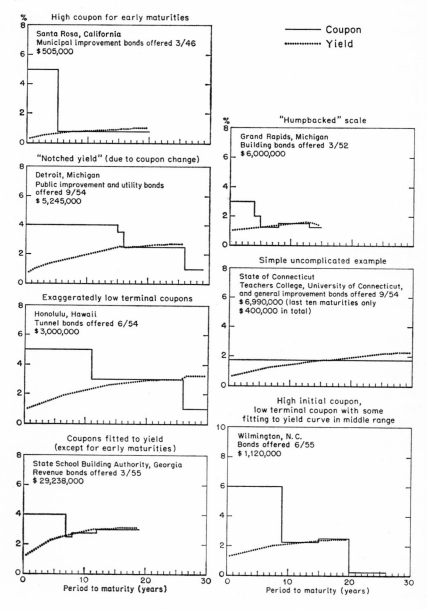

come to occupy an unusually strategic role in the selection of winning bids, far more than the subject justifies on economic grounds since coupon structures represent, not real differences in the economic character of securities, but formal differences in the somewhat archaic system of interest computation employed by state and local governments in awarding the sales of their obligations.

Gross underwriting margins. Since agreement on the kind of offering scale that is salable is general, and since all of the bidding groups have equal access to the device of special coupons, the critical difference among bids often is the profit margin planned by the various bidding groups. Data which compare the proposed coupon structures and proposed reoffering scales of losers with bid winners are not available. We can only surmise about what would be found if such data were available. But it seems to be widely felt among the managers of underwriting accounts that the important difference among groups more often than not is the size of the gross underwriting margin. This, of course, is a choice which faces all merchandisers: whether to cut margin and speed up turnover or to keep a rigid "markup" policy at the possible expense of sales. The resources of our project did not permit us to study the point statistically but the impression grew as we studied the problem that there were real differences with respect to price policy among the leading syndicate managers. Some firms are volume traders; others work to keep their margins intact.

Since the problems of group organization should not increase relative to the sizes of groups, it might be expected that bidding groups would work for higher margins on small offerings. We were able to secure data only on a few (less than one hundred) winning deals, all of them handled by national houses. Thus smaller deals handled by regional houses could not be included in this tabulation. But among those for which figures were supplied, size appears to have little effect on the margins. These data are further limited in significance since they were mainly for deals completed in the fourth quarter of 1955. The margins on the ninety-one deals for which figures were supplied are shown in Table 18.

This array discloses no evidence that big issues get preferential treatment. Quite the contrary, it suggests, if anything, that the very small issues were handled for narrower margins. But a negative relationship seems as unreasonable as a positive one. Three of the

TABLE 18

Gross Margins on Reofferings of State and Local Government Securities Competitively Bought[a]

Size of Issue	Average Margin per $1,000 Bond[b]
Under $500,000	$10.86 (6)
500,000-1,000,000	10.38 (17)
1,000,000-2,000,000	12.71 (15)
2,000,000-5,000,000	10.92 (21)
5,000,000-10,000,000	10.78 (12)
10,000,000-20,000,000	13.84 (8)
20,000,000-50,000,000	12.28 (6)
50,000,000-100,000,000	13.50 (5)
100,000,000 and over	11.28 (1)
Average of all sizes	$11.61 (91)

[a] Selected accounts opened largely during the fourth quarter, 1955.
[b] Number of cases included in each average shown in parentheses.

cases which reduced the average margin shown on deals under $1 million were winning bids submitted by a single firm. All three were for unusually high-grade even if small issues. When a deal is within the underwriting and selling capacity of a single firm, it is possible that it may be handled with quite a small margin.

It appears that profit margins are much more influenced by the quality and average maturity of offerings than by size. This is suggested by a cross tabulation appearing in Table 19.[16] This table suggests that the quality of issue is perhaps the leading factor accounting for differences in margins. Average maturity also explains a part of the differences among margins but less than quality. Size, as already emphasized above, shows no sign of being a material determinant of the margin chosen.

Gross margins are, of course, what the underwriting groups *try* to achieve. If a reoffering fails to attract buyers and price cutting becomes necessary, then margins shrink, even vanish, and sometimes become negative. This is the cost of the pure underwriting function. The extent to which such price cutting reduces margins is un-

[16] The number of cases included in this tabulation is less than that shown in Table 17 because ratings (or the lack of a rating) could be verified for only a portion of the cases for which gross margins were supplied.

TABLE 19

Gross Margins on Reofferings of State and Local Government Securities Competitively Bought,[a] by Quality and Maturity

	Average Margin per $1,000 Bond[b]		
	MOODY'S RATING		
Average maturity	Aaa & Aa	A and Lower	Unrated
Less than 10 years	$8.22 (8)	$10.65 (11)	....
10 to 15 years	9.19 (10)	12.60 (10)	$14.33 (3)
Over 15 years	9.32 (4)	15.63 (6)	14.03 (3)

[a] Selected accounts opened largely during the fourth quarter, 1955.
[b] Number of cases included in each average shown in parentheses.

known. Since markets fluctuate, it must certainly be true that in some years the frequency of such price cuts is material and must affect underwriting profits materially. But in some periods these cuts are far less common—but hardly ever absent. Even in the strongest of markets, bidding groups every now and then overstretch themselves and must use the ancient weapon of price to move their merchandise.

The data on margins which were collected covered only a brief period late in 1955; it is quite likely that in other periods margins might change in response to competitive and market conditions. For example, it appears to have been the case that the gross margins built into underwriting deals in the early years of the postwar decades were somewhat less than those put on deals in the later years. During that period offerings were scarce, sales were easy and groups were anxious buyers. Later this situation changed. During the stiffer money markets of 1956, the margins on deals widened by one to three dollars a bond; a kind of risk premium against the hazards of a market that was thought to be uncertain and even dangerous. During December 1956 the margins became particularly wide. While dealers were suffering heavy inventory losses, they were often making unusually good margins on the new deals that were well accepted. This pairing of unusual losses and gains is what brings out the highest order of strategy and courage in the investment banking community.

The margin between bids. The margins separating sealed public bids reflect both the precision of judgment involved and, to some extent, the character of bidding strategy. Many winning bids are relatively close to the second highest bids; these cases tend to be publicized. To the extent this circumstance is representative of bidding generally, it can be taken as evidence of the skill of investment bankers in judging the state of the market, assuming, of course, that collusive practices are not followed. In our inquiry we have found no evidence of such practices.

The repeated experience of the syndicates in preparing bids gives them the foundation for remarkable accuracy in bidding strategy. The process of organizing a group and preparing a bid are time-consuming and expensive enough so that few groups enter into the bidding competition unless fairly serious about wanting to buy bonds. While each group wishes to submit a winning bid, no group wants to be caught submitting one that is separated from the second bid by much of a margin. Apart from the hazards of paying too much, this margin is carefully noted by sophisticated investors and is likely to hurt the salability of an issue. Investors argue that since the bid winners paid an appreciable amount more for the issue than was offered by the second highest and other bidders, this is evidence of overpaying so that the reoffering is no bargain.[17]

The closeness of the bids, figured in terms of interest cost as it is computed in most state and local government sealed bidding sales,[18] may be deceiving; bids are calculated to minimize this cost. When bidders are permitted to name their own coupon structure, net interest cost is about the only form of comparison that can be used but it is a deceiving basis of comparison, as Appendix B shows. On sales where only a single coupon can be named, the comparison of bids is valid. When only one coupon rate can be named for an entire issue, variation among bidders would usually be covered by a range of about one-quarter of a per cent or less though this range is sometimes exceeded. The winning and second best bid

[17] This fact seems to open up the possible use of game strategy by bidding groups. In a tight and uncertain market in which only two groups are competing for an issue (and on larger issues the number of groups being formed is widely known in the "street") one group might prefer to submit a quite low bid on the general theory that at such a price they would be glad to buy the bonds. If the "winning" group pays appreciably more, the low bid of the "losing" group will embarrass the winning group in the reoffering sale. This would be the strategy of the "let-up" pitch.

[18] See Appendix B.

will often be for the same coupon with the only difference being in the amount of premium offered.[19]

The margins that separate bids can easily be minimized by looking only at the dramatic cases. About half of the time the margin between the winning bid and the second best bid is less than one dollar a bond. A close pair of bids may be separated by less than 25 cents a bond, and sometimes the margin is in pennies. But quite often the margin is not only greater than one dollar; it may be materially more. Every so often the winners' margin in a large and well-publicized sale will considerably exceed the space that separates the second from the third bids, and so on. In fact, the range of prices found in the full scale of bids is often material. While the range is usually less than ten dollars a bond, sometimes it is rather more. In the sale of big issues when the number of bidding groups is small—probably not more than two groups in the case of very big issues—the margin between the first and second bid is also the full range of prices. Such margins tend to be rather small. But an intermediate sized issue may bring out quite a few bids covering a considerable range. In the sale of very small issues, the margins between bids are often much higher. If such an issue attracts only a couple of bidders, the margin between bids may easily be from ten to twenty dollars a bond.

NATIONAL VERSUS LOCAL SYNDICATES

Larger state and local government issues are generally marketed by national syndicates, that is, syndicates managed by firms operating throughout the country and including a geographically distributed membership. Smaller issues, however, tend to be marketed either by local syndicates or occasionally by a single, sizable underwriter. There is no exact margin of size at which issues become too small to attract national interest and therefore come to attract bids only from local syndicates. One study of the underwriting of southern municipals suggest that virtually all issues of $250,000 or less were locally underwritten. Those over $1,000,000, on the other

[19] Because an arithmetically valid direct comparison is not possible we prepared only a few tentative and approximate tabulations comparing winning and other bids. The observations in the following paragraph are based on these fragments.

hand, were quite generally handled by national syndicates. The point of uncertainty was from $250,000 to $1,000,000.[20]

This study also suggested that local syndicates were more likely to handle either unrated issues or those of very high credit rating. Those of intermediate credit ratings, if of adequate size, tended to be handled by national syndicates. This study also pointed out that a national syndicate would usually include several firms located in the area of the issuing authority, presumably because of their strategic position for selling the obligations.

No evidence was uncovered as to whether the activity of local syndicates varied between areas of the country. On the West Coast leading banks often organize syndicates for securities originating in their area. These syndicates, though dominated by local houses, often should be treated as being definitely national in status. On the other hand, very high quality New England issues are often purchased by a single large firm. In other words, there is some evidence of regional diversity in the handling of the smaller and intermediate-size issues, though not a clear enough difference to furnish a foundation for further generalization.

SELLING STRATEGY OF SYNDICATES

When a syndicate is organized, it may be made an undivided account (sales efforts are pooled) or a divided account (each member is responsible for his share of sales). By reserving some bonds for syndicate account, some accounts are of a mixed nature. The issue is sometimes a cause of friction between syndicate managers and members. The sales efforts of members depend, to some extent, on the type of account of which they are a member.

The cherished hope of every syndicate manager is that when he has been successful in buying bonds, he will be able to resell them promptly at the scale agreed upon initially. Immediately after learning of winning a bid, the manager and other account members will put on a vigorous drive to sell an issue as quickly as possible; they like to have an issue "go out of the window." The mechanics of telephone selling involves strenuous and active work for the first few hours. If such a success is attained, the affairs of the syndicate

[20] "Southern versus Non-Southern Underwriting of Municipals," by Charles T. Taylor, *Southern Economic Journal*, October 1957, Vol. xxiv, No. 2.

may be completed quickly and the accounts settled and reported back to the members by the manager.

If, however, an offering does not meet with such striking success and some bonds remain unsold after the initial effort, a number of strategic decisions must be made. If it is felt that the market itself has changed between the time of entering the bid and the moment of selling, it may be argued that prices should be cut immediately to bring the issue into line with other obligations. This, however, is generally not done for some period. A syndicate would be thought guilty of remarkably bad judgment if it cuts prices quickly. By and large, syndicate managers are more likely to favor retaining initial offering prices than the smaller members who have a somewhat more nervous and uncertain attitude and may be readier to cut prices. Indeed, one of the functions of the syndicate manager of a divided liability account is to police the reoffering and to make sure that members are not covertly cutting prices in order to sell their portion of a slow issue.

The syndicate contract normally runs for 30 days but is usually subject to renewal. Accounts are frequently held together for somewhat longer periods, but at some stage after 60 days a possibility of closing out the account and distributing the unsold bonds to the members is seriously considered. Once an account has been broken up and the obligations distributed to members, each one is at liberty to follow such price or holding policies his judgment dictates or his financial position permits.

The roles of individual investment banking firms and of individual commercial banks differ greatly in a syndicate. Some firms have "good distribution" (a large or effective sales organization) but they do not have the capital to act as major underwriters. Other firms stand in the opposite position of having ample capital to take underwriting risks but of having somewhat less broad distributive outlets. Still other firms may have the kind of aggressive executives that make them natural managers; others may lack such talent and leadership. Such specialization weighs in the formation of a syndicate.

Concessions to dealers. As is customary in the reoffering of securities, the syndicates generally make "concessions" to any dealer who is a member of the National Association of Security Dealers. These concessions can be viewed as a kind of sales commission although they permit dealers to buy such securities for their own account at a price a bit below the offering price. It is also customary, although not universal, to allow slightly larger concessions to account members than to other dealers.

Because state and local government securities are usually offered in serial form, the concessions often take on a somewhat complex pattern, the usual variation being that the shorter maturities are given the lower concessions. The greater sales effort is usually thought necessary for the longer maturities, so larger concessions are given for the long maturities. But circumstances vary; in some markets the middle maturities seem to be harder to move and they are given the larger concessions. The pattern of concessions is also influenced by the quality of securities; the higher-grade securities are thought easier to sell and are given somewhat smaller concessions. A distribution of concessions based on late 1955 data is shown in Table 20. This table was based on observations for only one month; it does not reflect the fact agreed to by most observers that concessions vary according to the state of the market,

TABLE 20

Concessions Made to Members of the National Association of Security Dealers by Syndicates Reoffering State and Local Government Securities, December 1955

	SECURITIES RATED[a] (CONCESSIONS QUOTED AS FRACTION OF ONE PERCENTAGE POINT)							
	Aaa and Aa				A or Lower			
	$1/8$	$1/4$	$3/8$	$1/2$	$1/8$	$1/4$	$3/8$	$1/2$[b]
First 3 maturities	33	16	1	..	13	30	2	4
4th to 5th maturities	9	26	4	1	..	30	6	7
6th to 10th maturities	..	78	12	10	..	33	49	20
11th to 20th maturities	..	65	89	31	..	20	56	119
21st to later maturities	..	9	16	6	..	..	10	38

a Based on either Moody's or Standard Statistics ratings.
b Includes a very few cases of concessions of a $3/4$th.

Source: Reports of reofferings of leading municipal issues in the month of December 1955 as reported in the *Investment Dealers' Digest*. Since each maturity was treated as a separate issue, the totals in the table above are individual maturities, not of offerings.

small when sales are easy and larger when money and capital markets are tighter.

Since the concessions to members of syndicates for "taking down" securities are not published, we did not have access to any reliable record of these amounts. It is reported, however, that members' concessions are often larger by about one-eighth or one-fourth at each maturity except for the very short ones. If part of an issue is not reoffered, there is, of course, no concession since there is no outside sale of such a portion.

In the case of revenue obligations, which are more often in term (single maturity) rather than serial form, the concessions seem to be roughly equal to or slightly larger than those allowed on the sale of term corporate obligations. The margins on the sale of negotiated issues, particularly for turnpikes not yet constructed, have generally been at least two points (or $20 a bond) and sometimes almost twice this amount. Such an amount is materially higher than the margin for corporate underwriting. Concessions on deals of this sort have usually been somewhat larger than shown in Table 20, at least three-fourths of a point.

Concessions may be crudely estimated to account for about one-third of the gross margin on state and local government reofferings, sometimes more. This runs fairly parallel to the concession fraction prevailing in the case of public offerings of corporate bonds.

Divided and undivided accounts. The rather strong feelings of investment bankers with respect to the choice between divided and undivided liability is not related to the issue that might be indicated by these words. The financial strength of underwriters is generally such that the financially strong members of a syndicate are not usually worried about the ability of the others to perform their ultimate underwriting functions. The issue is rather one of the way in which the members discharge their liability to each other. In the case of an undivided liability with a large lot of the securities assigned for syndicate selling, the sales effort of each member is, in effect, a sales effort for the entire syndicate. A member continues to be "liable" for unsold obligations no matter what his own sale success may have been. With divided liability a member may discharge his liability by selling a proportion of obligations equivalent to his participation. In other words those syndicate members with good distributive outlets and strong sales forces much prefer divided liability. Firms with large underwriting strength in the form of capital, but with weaker distribution, prefer undivided liability.

Because of record-keeping problems, serial issues are more likely to be handled as undivided accounts, term bonds as divided accounts. In weak markets, some firms will stay in a divided account whereas they would withdraw from an undivided account because of confidence that they can be more successful in selling the bonds involved than other members of such an account.

INVENTORY POLICIES OF UNDERWRITERS

This market is quite delicately poised. While it is often in a state of equilibrium, it is usually an unstable equilibrium at best. Like a block poised on one end, it can be upset with relative ease. Profit margins relative to potential losses are small; sharp price movements produce sizable inventory losses or profits. Because of the fixed offering price in the new issues market, dealers hold to the suspicion that losses are more likely than profits and that the profits on ordinary business must be fairly good to offset the inevitable losses on some deals.

Capital margins in the securities business are thin; inventories may be rather large relative to capital. As a matter of business policy, many of the firms participating in the underwriting of state and local government issues do not have enough capital to justify the taking of what seem like very good risks. For example: suppose a given "deal" turns slow for reasons that everyone believes to be temporary. A firm with considerable capital may be justified in holding the securities involved in the deal until the expected recovery in the market takes place. But a smaller firm might, for very good strategic reasons, find it unwise to follow such a policy. Even if the chances of early recovery are excellent, the risks of the alternative are excessive. If the "deal" stays frozen, the small firm with little capital cannot enter new deals; it becomes stuck with no merchandise to sell except some securities on which it cannot cut price. Its sales force may become rusty or lost to other firms who are still active. Thus, small firms with little capital are disposed to close out and take their losses early. Large firms, particularly the leaders of groups, do not like to acquire the reputation of having managed slow deals that are broken up or on which losses are taken.

They want—if their capital permits—to hold out. Pride as much as profits often seems to account for this attitude.

The considerations that lie back of these judgments have the flavor of strategy much more than of traditional economic analysis. Many times the decision of an offering group as to whether to hold together or break up depends on the amount of free and uninvested funds available. The great institutional investors use a standard excuse if they wish to back away from a deal: they can claim to be "out of money." By this they mean that they have committed all of their investment funds; none are free. But the accounting measurement of this point seems to be ambiguous; institutional practices vary. Investors who claim to be "out of money" seem to be able to find money when the bargains get sufficiently attractive.

Any one investor can be fairly confident that if enough investors back away from the market, it will "come their way." Yields will improve and prices will go down. So the strategy of investors may be that of backing away from current offerings even though they are of the investment quality they prefer. Their funds can temporarily be invested in short-term form. The cost of holding off depends on the level of short-term interest rates. When short-term interest rates are low, investors suffer a material loss if they hold funds not fully invested at the full term their investment policy permits. Any short-term gains they may make on possible changes in the market in their favor may be lost in reduced interest income. Investment bankers, able to borrow at much less than the accruing coupons on their inventory, make a profit on their "carry," and so may be in no great hurry to sell, particularly if the visible supply of new issues forthcoming in the future periods is sparse and uncertain.

On the other hand, when short-term rates are high and close to, or even possibly above, long-term interest rates, investors can employ their money in short-term form without much loss of income, with sometimes even a little gain. At the same time, investment bankers, to the extent they use borrowed money, make no profit on carrying an inventory of unsold securities; indeed they suffer the unmeasurable losses of hobbling or inability to take on new business. If the volume of new business "visible" in the future[21]

[21] Visible supply has a number of technical definitions in the securities markets. In the municipal bond market the statistical practice of the *Bond Buyer* is to treat specifically announced competitive offerings falling within the next

should be large, the incentives for closing out of accounts is particularly high.

This delicately poised nature of the municipal bond market accounts for conditions that are sometimes described by such drastic terms as panic or near-panic. An examination of the periods described as "panics" indicates that they were those in which the structure of the market broke down; dealings became impossible and the market suffered from a kind of freezing. Drastic price declines can take place without panic if a market still exists and if buyers and sellers stand ready to do business at some price. Practical market analysts sometimes measure this by the time continuity of price quotation changes. For example, the organized stock exchanges, the New York Stock Exchange in particular, place great emphasis on the continuity of quotations. They charge the specialist with the function of "making markets," which amounts to furnishing such a time continuity of prices and transactions. Considerable discontinuities in price would not violate the economist's ideas of markets if rational interpretation of prevailing circumstances accounts for the discontinuities. But under conditions of panic a large majority of those who can, withdraw from the market either as buyers or sellers. Then those under external pressure to find a market at any price may find that no market exists; no buyers will give firm bids for any appreciable volume. Panic is really a paralysis of the market function. Withdrawal from the market accounts for such paralysis; yet this withdrawal may be prompted by quite rational behavior on the part of the principal participants.[22]

EFFECTS OF SIZE OF ISSUE ON MARKETABILITY

One of the commonest criticisms of the investment banking system as it now operates in the United States is that, while offering excellent service to the giant corporations, it fails to meet the financial needs of smaller-sized businesses. This criticism could not

---

thirty days as being a part of the visible supply. Negotiated financings are not included in the *Bond Buyer* visible supply. On the other hand, the *Investment Dealers Digest* treats any definitely announced corporate offering of debt securities as being a part of the visible supply, no matter how far off in the future.

[22] Since we do not have an economics of the individual financial firm, this point cannot be pursued very far. Common observation suggests that competition of the sort that narrows profit margins hastens the withdrawal incentives and so renders a supposedly competitive market more subject to panic than a more administered market.

be leveled at the investment banking support of smaller local governmental financing. Indeed, one of the more significant findings of this survey is that moderate sized local governmental units seem to fare quite well in the new issues market, often better than the big cities. Small state offerings often seem to fare better than those of the big states that come to the capital markets more often. Tiny local governmental units probably pay modestly higher rates than middle-sized cities of comparable credit rating, but it would be hard to support the charge that they are much penalized for their small size. Indeed, a small local governmental unit which maintains a strong credit position probably can borrow without more than a nominal discount for size.

Just how relevant this analogy is to business finance may be argued. Small business may suffer from its size as well as its credit weakness in securing access to the long-term capital markets. But if the credit standing of small business were generally as good relatively as the credit standing of small state and local government units, is it not possible that the machinery of investment banking would soon emerge to give such small business access to long-term credit on terms relatively as good as those enjoyed by smaller local government units? The point is worth reflection.

Big state and local government offerings equal the largest of corporate offerings. But at the other extreme, a large number of relatively small issues are offered on the market. The (arithmetic) average size of the long-term state and local government offerings which was reaching the pages of the *Bond Buyer* in the first half of 1956 was just a little more than $1 million. Unadvertised issues doubtless were much smaller in size. In the early years of the decade this average was only a little more than half as great. The arithmetic averages doubtless conceal considerable distributional skewness. Roughly four-fifths of new offerings are in issues of under $1 million. The median size of offering tabulated by the research department of the Investment Bankers Association for the first half of 1956 was about a quarter of a million dollars.[23]

Very small issues are typically bid for and bought by a single buyer rather than by a formally organized bidding group. As Table 21 shows, about two-thirds of the issues under half a million dollars reported in the *Bond Buyer* for the month of December 1955 were

[23] Letter from Frank Morris, Director of Research for the IBA.

TABLE 21

Winning Bidding Groups for Public Offerings of State and Local Government Securities, December 1955

No. of Firms in Group / Winning Bid	Size of Offering (in thousands of dollars)										No. of Winning Bids
	Under 200	200-500	500-1,000	1,000-2,000	2,000-5,000	5,000-10,000	10,000-20,000	20,000-50,000	50,000-100,000	100,000 & over	
1	174	61	14	4							253
2 or 3	31	48	22	5	1						107
4 to 7	1	15	26	20	7	3					72
8 to 14		1		4	15	2					22
15 to 29				2	3	1		1			7
30 to 59					1	2	4	2			9
60 to 99							1				1
100 and over								1a	1b		2
Total offerings	206	125	62	35	27	8	5	4	1	none	473

a The winning bid for a California toll bridge issue of $46 million was submitted by a group of 183 firms.
b A New York State thruway issue of $50 million was won by a group of 165 firms.

Source: Based on all usable reports in the section "Municipal Bond Sales in Detail" in the five weekly issues of the *Bond Buyer* for December 1955. Canadian issues are excluded.

awarded to single bidders. If the even smaller issues that elude reporting were included, the proportion would doubtless have been still larger. As this table also shows, the industry of investment banking seems to adapt itself to the formation of a great number of small accounts readily. The participation of commercial banks, essentially local institutions by nature, and of the smaller investment banking houses undoubtedly contributes to this result.

An interesting conclusion may be drawn from this table. The relatively small number of bonds for each member in these buying groups suggests considerable spreading of the risk. In a majority of these groups the average number of bonds per member is from 200 to 500. The underwriting of state and local government obligations is not regulated so the sizes of participation of "major" and other members of buying groups are not published. The participation of even major members, however, is bound to be relatively small when compared with the allotments in corporate bond buying accounts.

The gearing of the investment banking machinery for handling modest-sized state and local government offerings as well as the giant ones can be shown in still another way: the number of bids attracted by offerings of various sizes. If the number of bids attracted by offerings of moderate size is adequate to insure competitive vigor, it can be presumed that governmental units borrowing in such amounts do not suffer from discrimination in the capital markets. A tabulation of the number of bids attracted by offering of various sizes is shown in Table 22.[24]

As this table shows, the very small and the very large issues attract fewer bids than intermediate sized issues. This tabulation does not prove the presence of active bidding for the very small issues, nor does it prove the absence of such bidding. Very small state and

[24] One defect in this table, described in a note to it, should be emphasized so as to avoid misunderstanding. This table was based on the reports of completed sales published in the five weekly issues of the *Bond Buyer* for December 1955. While the editors make great efforts to get complete reports, the number of bidders cannot always be determined from the official reports submitted to the *Bond Buyer*. Furthermore, there is a reasonable suspicion that when an award of sale is made to the sole bidder for an issue, this fact may be obscured in the official report for reasons of pride and otherwise. The tabulation shown in Table 22 includes only those cases in which it seemed reasonably clear that all of most of the bids submitted were reported. But the chance of error and bias in this tabulation should not be minimized.

TABLE 22

Number of Bids in Relation to Size of Public Offerings of State and Local Government Securities, December 1955

No. of Bids	Size of Offering (in thousands of dollars)										Total
	Under 200	200- 500	500- 1,000	1,000- 2,000	2,000- 5,000	5,000- 10,000	10,000- 20,000	20,000- 50,000	50,000- 100,000	100,000 & over	
1	11				1						12
2	4	6	4	7	1	2	1				25
3	20	14	11	9	7	3	3		2		69
4	9	7	7	5	5	1		2			36
5	7	5	2	3	1	1					19
6	2	2	2	3	1		1				11
7		2	2		1						5
8			2		1						3
9		1									1
10		1									1
11				1							1
12				3	2						5
13											
14					1						1
Total offerings Tabulated	53	38	30	31	21	7	5	2	2	none	189

Cases in which a single other bidder was named, introduced by the phrase, "Second highest bidder was . . ." have been omitted from this tabulation. However, lists of unsuccessful bidders headed, "Among the other bidders was (were) . . ." have been included. Since many lists contained two "also-ran" bids (and additional bidders were not excluded by the heading), it is possible that, due to some custom of listing adopted to save time or space, the modal number of bids at three in so many cases is spurious. Canadian issues were also omitted.

Source: Based on all usable reports in the section "Municipal Bond Sales in Detail" in the five weekly issues of the *Bond Buyer* for December 1955.

local government units may find it difficult to attract a great deal of interest to their issues. But no such difficulty exists for intermediate sized issues. Issues of half a million dollars or more attract an ample number of bids. And, as we noted above, small issues do not seem to have a marketing cost higher than that found in largersized offerings. Though not shown by this table, it is doubtless true that the sales attracting quite a large number of bids are of moderate-sized but high-quality issues. In other words, there is a kind of "U-shaped" character to the distribution of the number of bids.[25] Very large sales will attract only a few bids because it is not practical to organize a large number of accounts. Small sales tend to attract only a few local bids. But intermediate-sized issues attract a substantial number of bids.

It seems fairly evident that this circumstance works to the advantage of moderate-sized local government units which maintain a highly regarded financial standing. They attract many bidders and probably get the advantage of low interest costs as a result. Chapter 6 develops the point that the yields on these moderate-sized issues often appear to be better than on the very large issues. Part of this superiority in the borrowing ability of these intermediate sized units is doubtless due to the fact that investors often search for such names in the process of getting area diversification. But the number of bidders must also be a substantial factor in achieving such excellent results. In the offering of very large issues the organization of only a few groups, often only two, is feasible. When only two groups are competing, they can appraise rather closely the bidding strategy of the other side; the analytical apparatus of duopoly applies. The influence of "strategic restraint" comes to bear, and pricing does not "get out of line." But when a larger number of smaller groups are bidding on a moderate-sized issue, the appraisal of strategy by opposing bidders cannot be as precise. In these cases each bidding group cannot be aware of the existence of all other bidding groups and of their composition. A "dark horse" group may easily emerge to win the bid.[26] Bids can "get out of line."

[25] Also noted by McClintock (Harriman, Ripley & Co.), in Part 1, Section 9, page 9, of the 1946 loose-leaf edition of *Fundamentals of Investment Banking* cited in note 1 of this chapter.

[26] This suggests still one more way in which game theory may have relevance to this market. When there are only two groups, the problems of strategy can be reduced to two-party, non-zero-sum game form. The circumstances in which

THE EFFECTS OF COMPETITIVE BIDDING ON THE MARKETING
OF NEW STATE AND LOCAL GOVERNMENT ISSUES

Most state and local government issues are sold by sealed public bidding. The predominance of this with respect to general obligations is shown in Table 23. This also shows that negotiated sales,

TABLE 23

Method of Offering Municipal Bond Issues, 1957
(par value in millions of dollars)

Type of Offering	General Obligation		Revenue		Total	
	(amount)	(per cent)	(amount)	(per cent)	(amount)	(per cent)
Public sealed bidding	$4,519	94.4	$1,323	65.3	$5,842	85.8
Negotiated sales	195	4.1	638	31.5	833	12.2
Private placements	71	1.5	65	3.2	136	2.0
Totals	$4,785	100.0	$2,026	100.0	$6,811	100.0

Federal government loans are excluded.
Source: IBA Statistical Bulletin, No. 6, January 8, 1958, p. 8.

though relatively more important in the case of revenue obligations, are still less frequent than competitive sales.

Competitive bidding unquestionably narrows the gross margin earned by investment bankers; there seems to be no doubt of that fact. But the procedure may be clumsy, and dating of the sale far in advance reduces the maneuverability of the borrower. A negotiated offering may be put before the market quickly when conditions appear favorable; the investment bankers' greater margin may be far more than saved in a lower interest cost to the borrower—if truly superior timing thus becomes possible. But the validity of this assumption is not proved. Perhaps the borrowers connected with investment bankers of superior judgment would benefit from superior timing, but can this be true of everyone? If a given volume of state and local government securities is to be marketed over the long run, can every borrower benefit from superior timing? If the answer to this last question is affirmative, it begins to sound as if investors suffered net lower returns from securities marketed through

larger numbers participate, however, can only be dealt with descriptively and without the more formal and rigorous apparatus.

negotiation rather than by means of competitive bidding. But this certainly does not seem to be the testimony of investors; indeed, some of them regard competitive bidding as a way of persuading investment bankers to pay too much for securities. But if this latter view is true, then it again appears that competitive bidding may have some advantages for the borrowers as over against lenders.

A more sophisticated view might be that in periods of moderate capital demand with high security prices and low yields, competitive bidding probably favors borrowers and trims the yields available to investors. But in a tight money market with high capital demand and a barely adequate flow of saving, then competitive bidding exposes the borrower to some marketing hazards. Even in such periods, the *average* cost to borrowers may be just as low with competitive bidding as with negotiation, but some borrowers then fare worse than would be true with negotiation and some fare better.

At least one contrast seems to be valid: the existence of competitive bidding does not lend itself very well to the kind of continuing secondary market that most borrowers like to see prevail for their securities. A small governmental unit comes to the market rarely and its occasional offerings are absorbed by investors without leaving much of a trace. If a few of these securities reappear in the secondary market, the turnover cost is high, but again they leave little trace in the market. But a large governmental unit that must face the market time after time, possibly with only moderate intervals between financing operations, has to worry about the supply of its securities in the secondary market. If an appreciable volume of its securities drift back into the secondary market, the prices needed to move these securities may tend to be low and to blight the chances of getting a good price on its next offering. Indeed, such a governmental unit may find it advantageous to maintain a kind of supporting operation so as to maintain a good price record for its outstanding securities.

If such a governmental unit has a negotiated and continuing relationship with a single investment banker, it is entirely possible that the trading department of this investment banker may be able to keep a healthier tone in the secondary market for the unit's securities than would be true if it was financed by means of competitive offerings. The winner of a bid will undertake to market the bonds he has "won," but he can hardly be expected to maintain a continuing interest in the market for the obligations of this issuing governmental unit.

The existence of competitive bidding does not mean that investment bankers fail to have a continuing interest in the financial affairs of public bodies. Finance officers seek the help and advice of investment bankers on market problems. The amount of time and energy the investment bankers can give finance officers is more limited than is true in the case of negotiated relationships—but investment bankers appear to take a conscientious interest in these problems.

CHAPTER 5

The Secondary Market for
State and Local Government Obligations

THE primary marketing of state and local government securities
might be thought of as their sale by the issuing governmental units
to the initial investors through the officers of the investment banking community. Secondary marketing, by residual definition, is the
sale of such securities by one investor to another investor, usually
through the intermediary services of a security dealer. Secondary
markets arise out of the fact that borrowers generally need longer
undisturbed use of funds than investors, on the average, are willing
or able to grant.

ECONOMIC FUNCTION OF SECONDARY MARKET

The principal economic function of a secondary market in securities thus is to reconcile the needs of investors with the needs of
borrowers. Borrowers need to have funds available to them for the
long periods of time that are required for most capital expenditures
projects. Repayment of debt is generally scheduled in such a way
as to fit the expected revenues of the borrowing governmental units.
While the maturities of debts may embrace a period of time less
than the life of the capital projects they finance—the standards of
conservative business finance—these maturities may be spaced out
so as to allow some margin in the coverage of debt service, figured
on the basis of cash flows.

Some investors—life insurance companies are classic examples—
can wait for ultimate repayment without worrying about access to
the funds they have invested. But this situation is far from usual.
The principal investors in state and local government securities
have, almost without exception, potential need for access to the funds
they invest before the ultimate maturity of the securities they have
purchased. Individuals, as we pointed out in Chapter 3, are the
leading buyers of such obligations. Individual life and fortune are
subject to many unpredictable hazards. An elderly investor may
find tax-exempt bonds to be an excellent outlet for his funds because of his particular tax status. But if he dies unexpectedly, or

even if his only misfortune is that of suffering reverses with his other investments, his holdings may have to be sold. When individual ownership is through the vehicle of a trust, with a life interest for one person and a remainderman's interest for another, tax-exempt obligations may be prudent for the life estate but serve no investment purpose for the remainderman. The period of the life estate cannot be forecast; it is as uncertain as life itself.

Commercial banks take an understandable interest in the marketability of the securities in their portfolios. Commercial banks' loans and other needs for funds are quite unpredictable, as recent experience has demonstrated. A commercial bank may find it quite expedient to sell off investments well in advance of maturity, if it can do this without excessive cost or losses. Fire and casualty insurance company investments represent, to some extent at least, reserves against contingencies of underwriting hazards; marketability on short notice is, therefore, an important consideration to them. Casualty companies are particularly concerned, since they appear to suffer considerable variations in their underwriting experience. Thus all the leading investors in state and local government securities have an interest in the existence of a good secondary market for their securities.

But what is a "good" secondary market? Is it a large one, i.e., one in which the volume of transactions is considerable? Is it one in which there is "reasonable equality of opportunity," i.e., one in which all kinds of securities can be handled? Is the quality of a secondary market a function of price, i.e., one in which a fairly large volume of securities can be offered without a sharp effect on price? Is it one in which the costs of marketing, the margins taken by the marketing intermediaries, are reasonable so that turnover is not prohibitively expensive? Does it have to provide good trading facilities for odd-lot as well as round-lot sales?

Investors have a direct interest in the existence of a secondary market for the state and local government securities they own; borrowers have an indirect or derivative interest. This is particularly true of borrowers who must come to the market repeatedly. After a new issue is out, the investment bankers who marketed it (and other investment bankers, for that matter), the investors who bought the issue, and the borrowers who issued it, all watch the performance of the issue on the secondary market. This interest is avid even for investors who do not plan to sell. If a newly issued security "stands up" relatively well—i.e., declines less in price than comparable issues decline or advances more than comparable issues— then each of these interests is pleased. Whenever a borrower comes to the market, the recent performance of his securities in the secondary market foreshadows more closely than any other signal the kind of bids he will get on his new offering.[1] Some issuers attempt to support the secondary market for their securities. The sinking funds maintained by some public bodies are used for this purpose; retirement and pension funds have been used as market support vehicles. The school building authorities in Pennsylvania require rental contracts equal to 120 per cent of debt service, apparently not so much to protect investors as to make possible a secondary market in these obligations.[2] The 20 per cent is apparently used for such purchases.

Simple logic would raise some doubts as to the effectiveness of such measures, quite apart from their appropriateness. If a public body supports its own securities from its capital funds, it only increases the amount of new money that must be raised later on. While this is true, some investors (and therefore investment bankers) take a kindlier view of new offerings of an issuer where known policy is to support its own obligations in the secondary market. In the end such policies may have the net effect of lowering the borrowing costs of such public bodies; some investment bankers seem to believe that they do have this effect.

ORGANIZATION OF SECONDARY MARKET IN STATE AND LOCAL GOVERNMENT SECURITIES

The secondary market in state and local government securities is an "over-the-counter" market. Because transactions in this market are shrouded in secrecy, the size and character of this market is not known except in a fragmentary way. The only systematic study of the over-the-counter market was made by a group from Wharton School at the University of Pennsylvania, financed by the Merrill Foundation, and advised by a committee of the Investment Bankers

---

[1] For example, see the comments of the Public Housing Administration on the secondary market for obligations to which it gave contracts; 8th Annual Report of the Housing and Home Finance Agency, 1954, pp. 366-67.

[2] Letter of Willard M. Wright, Jr., Manager of the Municipal Department of Kidder, Peabody & Co., Philadelphia office, to the *Bond Buyer*, March 1, 1958.

Association. This study undertook an ambitious program of data collection, most of which was centered around the months of September, October, and November 1949.[3]

The secondary market for state and local government obligations is almost wholly contained within the organizational structure of the new issues market. The bankers who underwrite a new issue are usually the same firms which maintain a continuing secondary market interest in this security. The continuity of interest is probably less than is true in the case of negotiated corporate underwritings but some connection often remains. The number of firms who maintain "positions" in state and local government securities appear to be quite large. *Blue List* advertisers number more than 600 firms of which slightly more than 50 are commercial banks.[4] While a large proportion of these firms are local in their operations, the minimum advertising contract in this vehicle is sufficiently costly to suggest that few firms are likely to maintain *Blue List* listing purely for prestige reasons.

The Wharton study estimated that transactions took place in at least 4,000 different state and local government issues during the three-month interval from September through November 1949.[5] The number seems high; it is possible that in some cases different serial maturities of the same issuers were counted separately. If so, the number of *issuers* whose obligations were traded at least once in the three-month period would be considerably less. As a basis of comparison it might be recalled that anywhere from 20,000 to 25,000 state and local governmental units probably have debt securities outstanding.[6] At the time of the Wharton study the *Blue List* was showing 900 issues daily.[7] Near the end of 1955, the number of issues which show in the *Blue List* had risen to over 2,000.

A large fraction of the secondary market in state and local government securities is a dealer-to-dealer market. This, of course, is quite characteristic of all over-the-counter markets. A dealer who cannot supply a customer with the type of security desired from

---

[3] Friend et al., *Over-the-Counter Securities Markets, op.cit.*

[4] *Blue List* directory of advertisers, October 1955.

[5] Friend et al., *Over-the-Counter Securities Market, op.cit.*, Table 2-6, p. 57, and discussion, pp. 58-62.

[6] Chapter 1. National Quotation Bureau had a record of 8,700 issues in 1949. See Friend et al., *op.cit.*, Table 2-3, p. 53.

[7] Friend et al., *op.cit.*, p. 59. In the tabulation made by Hoffman, each serial was counted as one issue.

his own inventory ("position") will acquire it from another dealer. One function of the *Blue List* is to permit dealers to service their customers from the whole range of offerings made by all other dealers. Since the Wharton tabulations of dealer-to-dealer transactions combines both new issues and secondary market transactions, the basis of comparison is not too precise, but they show that 40 per cent of these combined transactions were of such a nature.[8]

THE ROLE OF DEALERS IN THE SECONDARY MARKET FOR STATE AND LOCAL GOVERNMENT OBLIGATIONS

In terms of institutional organization, the secondary market largely overlaps the market for new issues. As we noted before, most underwriting houses have a continuing interest in the securities they sell; one of the most tangible forms of such interest is to "make a market" in these securities. The process of "making a market" is that of offering to be either a buyer or a seller; to bracket transaction prices with a bid price and an ask price. But to "make a market," a dealer must take a "position," that is, be willing to be long or short of a security. Short positions are dangerous in this market; finding the specific issue and maturity of a given issuer to cover is hard except for a few issues which are widely traded. As a result, dealers tend to have net long positions which they "offer" (or hold unoffered for investment) and if they have no inventory of a security for which they get an inquiry, having been sellers, they generally know how to locate such securities.

Underwriters are not automatically dealers, but a majority of them maintain trading departments. A few firms specialize in "making market," with trading being more important to them than underwriting.

However, trading is not the sole reason why dealers maintain "position." The reasons for maintaining a dealer "position" include the following cases. A new issue, when offered, may stay in investment banking ownership after the initial offering syndicate or account has been broken up for either of two very good reasons. If the security offering is a great success, dealers may buy for their own account and hold off the market for a little while expecting to reoffer later in the secondary market at a better price. At the other extreme, if an offering has not gone well, the syndicate ac-

[8] Friend et al., *op.cit.*, Table 4-20, p. 183.

count may be dissolved and the securities divided up among the participants. These will be offered in the secondary market sooner or later. Quite apart from new offerings, dealers like to maintain an inventory of merchandise. They are often buyers from investors in order to supply themselves with an inventory. The securities in the portfolios of investment bankers are not all for sale; some are retained for investment purposes. Most investment banking firms find it desirable to keep firm capital invested in some fashion, whether the firm be a partnership or a corporation. For the reasons developed in the preceding chapter, the more desirable alternatives for most investors are either equities or tax-exempt securities. In other words, U.S. government securities, corporate bonds, and other debt forms, the interest on which is taxable income, are not particularly desirable forms of investment for firm capital. Equities can sometimes promise capital gains. Income from tax-exempt securities is just that: tax exempt. Furthermore, for the technical reasons developed in the following chapter, the short-term high-coupon tax-exempt obligations often have special appeal to dealers in state and local government obligations if they can be moved along before thirty days have past.

For these and other reasons, the volume of dealings among dealers is considerable. In general this volume of inter-dealer transaction appears to be more than just a speculative churning about; it seems to serve real market and economic functions. The services of the secondary market to ultimate investors are improved by virtue of a free and active market among dealers. Investors can get access to a much wider range of buyers and a much wider range of security offerings through the interdealer transactions.

Dealer operations of the routine sort in United States government securities apparently produce less profit than position speculation. A dealer who maintained the minimum inventory with which he could do business might make his rent and overhead, but his profits would be slim. We have little evidence about the results of dealer speculation in state and local government securities, but such as we have does not suggest the existence of a parallel.

In some periods dealers make large inventory profits; in other periods they incur large inventory losses. Since inventories seem to lag behind prices more often than leading them, it would not be unreasonable to conclude that dealers, in the postwar decade, have had at least as many losses as profits on inventory holdings. Since turnover margin, which we treat later in this chapter, gets mixed up with capital gains and losses, the point might be hard to support even if earnings records were available to us—which they are not. It must be recognized that dealers have more incentives than merely successful inventory speculation for the maintenance of positions.

SIZE OF SECONDARY MARKET IN STATE
AND LOCAL GOVERNMENT OBLIGATIONS

The size of a secondary market is usually thought of as the gross volume of transactions, of the "amount of business done." Our evidence on size has been borrowed almost wholly from other sources, mainly the Wharton study. This study gives us data for one three-month period; our knowledge of changes in the level of activity is fragmentary. But it is quite clear that the secondary market for state and local government obligations is far less important than the new issue segment. It is less in gross volume; it is less, almost certainly, in terms of gross revenue produced for dealers; it is less important as an economic function. But, while smaller than the new issues market by any such tests, it is still of considerable importance.

The estimates made in the Wharton study of activity agree quite closely with such other evidence as can be brought to bear. The Wharton estimate was that $1,056 millions of resales of state and local government securities occurred during the three-month interval covered.[9] During the same period the respondents reported $1,152 millions of new issue sales of state and local government security offerings. The volume of new issues, both long-term and short-term, reported by the *Bond Buyer* for the comparable interval amounted to $1,100 millions. With the new issue sales from the two sources so close, the figures for secondary market sales may well be a fair representation of size at that time. Two elements of these figures deserve special attention. The activity figures compiled by the Wharton survey suggest that the degree of activity (rate of turnover?) in the secondary markets for state and local government securities, while considerably less than for marketable U.S. Treasury securities, is quite a bit higher than for corporate bonds. This is shown in Table 24.

9 Friend et al., *op.cit.* Table 3-2, p. 116.

TABLE 24

Amount of Bonds[a] Resold in Over-the-Counter Market Compared with Amount Outstanding

	Resold[b] (quarter year Sept.-Nov. 1949)	Outstanding[c] (Dec. 31, 1949)	Annual Rate Resale to Outstanding (per cent)
	(millions of dollars)		
U.S. Treasury marketable securities	24,444	152,500	64
State and local government securities	1,056	20,875	20
Corporate bonds	782	56,534	6

a Including short-term debt securities.
b Wharton over-the-counter survey cited above in note 8.
c *Survey of Current Business*, May 1956, "Debt Changes in 1955," pp. 6-14.

This comparison suggests that state and local government securities are only about one-third as active as those of the U.S. Treasury. This comparison, however, is far from valid since the federal marketable debt in 1949 was roughly one-half in maturities of less than three years; the comparable proportion of under-three-year state and local government obligations probably was less than one-fifth. Short-term securities are presumed to be rather active in the secondary markets; they are used by their holders more for liquidity purposes. But even with allowance for the differential rates of secondary market activity for the short-term and the long-term securities, the rate of activity for longer-term federal government marketable securities probably is greater than that for state and local government obligations, but not by a very large margin.

Corporate bond turnover appears to be even slower than that of state and local government securities. This comparison, however, is subject to a number of qualifications. A large fraction of corporate long-term bonds was originally marketed by direct placement and with investors such as life insurance companies who are notoriously infrequent sellers in the secondary markets. If the secondary market turnover of corporate bonds could be compared with those publicly offered, the turnover ratio obviously could be as much as a half higher. But even after application of such a correction, the secondary market turnover of state and local government obligations appears to be considerably above that of corporate bonds but below that of Treasury securities.

The Wharton tabulations also suggested that the secondary market in state and local government securities was somewhat more concentrated among nonregistered brokers and dealers, including banks, than was true of new issues. This is shown in Table 25.

TABLE 25

New Issue Sale and Resales by Registered
and Nonregistered Brokers and Dealers,
September to November 1949

	New Issues	*Resales*
	(millions of dollars)	
Registered brokers and dealers	797	548
Nonregistered brokers and dealers		
(including commercial banks)	355	508
Total	1,152	1,056

Source: Friend et al., *op.cit.*, Tables 3-3 and 3-4 (percentages in 3-3 applied to 3-4).

A series approximating secondary market offerings was derived from *Blue List* totals. The *Blue List* is to the municipal bond market roughly what the *National Quotation Service* is to the over-the-counter market for corporate stocks and bonds. The series was derived by subtracting the amounts left unsold in major accounts (as reported weekly by the *Bond Buyer*) from the total offerings shown by the *Blue List* for the same date. The logic of this computation is that the total of issues offered in the *Blue List* less the amounts of new issues unsold in major new issues should equal secondary market offering (except for new issues not in major accounts; probably a small amount). The results are shown in Chart 7.

While interesting as an exhibit, this series is only a rough approximation of the time pattern of secondary market sales of state and local government securities. In the first place, the number of small new issue offerings which are not counted as "major" accounts but which are advertised in the *Blue List* undoubtedly is of modest importance. And since such offerings presumably were more frequent in the later part of the decade, this fact probably added an upward cant to the series. Second, even a cursory examination of just a few issues of the *Blue List* indicates clearly that many of the listings of securities, even if no longer in the "new issue"

CHART 7

State and Local Government Securities Reoffered in the Secondary Market

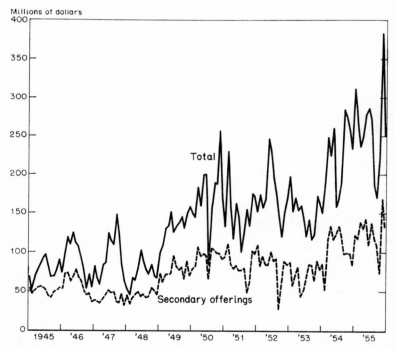

Source: Total offerings shown in *Blue List* corrected for new offerings.

category, are of recently offered securities. In the majority of cases such recently new issues are offered by dealers who were members of the reoffering syndicate; sometimes, but not too often, they are shown by dealers who were not original underwriters. While the bonds of an unsuccessful syndicate are generally shown only by the members of the reoffering group, the bonds of a successful offering may be shown by other dealers.

It seems quite evident that dealers "free-ride" on one another's successful and popular offerings and try to improve on the concessions granted outside dealers by holding these bonds for a slightly higher price after the syndicate books have been closed. To some extent, this may be done by the members of buying groups themselves. Furthermore, it appears that all new issues, whether or not considered successful initial offerings, tend to churn around in the market a bit before they find their way into the portfolios of ultimate investors.

If these data are a fair representation of secondary market offerings, some interesting conclusions follow. In the first place, the secondary market for state and local government securities appears to have been relatively much more active in the early postwar period than later on. The data show also that secondary market offerings have represented a sharply dwindling proportion of the total offerings in the market of state and local government securities during the postwar decade.

This is quite natural. In the early postwar period there was something very much like a shortage of tax-exempt securities. As Chapter 6 shows, during 1946 the value of tax exemption was given a premium even greater than the marginal tax rate applying to corporate income. Under such circumstances holders who could not take much advantage of tax exemption, such as the life insurance companies and mutual savings banks, had a strong price incentive to sell what they owned in the secondary market. This they did, as the ownership estimates indicate.[10] Since then there have been far fewer circumstances in which differential tax situations offered so strong an incentive for a redistribution of ownership.

Since 1953, and particularly in 1954 and 1955, the secondary market in state and local government securities has received a boost from the practice of "tax-swapping." This practice is followed mainly by banks, but in certain circumstances other investors can advantageously swap.[11] A tax swap is an almost simultaneous purchase-sale in which an investor sells securities in order to establish

[10] See Appendix A and Chapter 3.

[11] Commercial banks are permitted to deduct security losses from current income after offset against capital gains.

either a capital gain or loss and simultaneously buys similar securities. Tax-exempt securities do not furnish quite as satisfactory a vehicle for tax swapping as is true of taxable obligations since the advantage may be used only when the market has declined during a given tax year. But in churning markets, tax exempts furnish a good tax-swap vehicle, hence the interest of commercial banks in these bonds even if they are not dealers and cannot use the full coupon as a tax deduction.[12] Tax swapping probably tends to swell the volume of secondary bonds shown on the *Blue List* as indicated in Chart 7: dealers may "offer" bonds which are still owned by bank customers but are not a true part of dealer positions. Because tax swapping in municipal obligations takes time and often involves large amounts, such showings are a necessary marketing device.

CHARACTER OF ISSUES IN THE SECONDARY MARKET

Our knowledge of type of issue in the secondary market is limited; it comes from only one source, a scanning of the *Blue List*. This is a fair representation of securities offered in the national market but it probably misses most of the more local issues. In the national market some types of issues seem to appear more frequently and in greater volume than other types. Toll road bonds, for example, appear frequently on the *Blue List* and a number of dealers advertise the "making" of a market in these obligations. Evidence as to volume is negligible, but dealers report that the more speculative of these issues enjoy rather sizable if volatile markets. Toll road issues, for obvious reasons, are marketed before construction of the projects which they finance. The revenue-producing prospects of these projects are all surveyed extensively by engineering and special market survey firms which concentrate on projects of this type. These advance estimates have suffered the inevitable fate of forecast: they have often been quite wrong. The prices of all public authority revenue obligations depend to some extent on the degree to which their service requirements—interest and principal—are covered. News of these projects affects the prices of the bonds which financed them. Even during construction and before there has been a test of revenue production, news of the rate of construction, of how costs are matching advance estimates and of the adherence

---

[12] And then only if turned over each thirty days or less.

to the timetable of construction, all affect the prices of such securities.

It appears that investors in these obligations include many who take a quite speculative view of the results. Bad news may loosen the affections of some investors and increase the market supplies of the underlying securities. But low prices also appear to bring out some speculative interest. In other words, the volume of transactions in each issue of revenue obligations in the secondary market seems to be subject to special factors. Overall, the rate of turnover of revenue obligations appears to exceed that of publicly offered corporate obligations; at least the frequency of their appearance on offering sheets would so indicate.

The obligations of housing authorities issued under contract with the Public Housing Administration (which are in effect guaranteed by the federal government) seem to turn up on the *Blue List* quite frequently. As is true of all new issues, the frequency of listing jumps considerably when new offerings of these obligations appear on the market. But even between financing dates, the volume of housing authority bonds with PHA contracts on the *Blue List* is generally a bit larger relative to volume outstanding than is true of state and local government obligations generally.

A scanning of the *Blue List* also shows that well-known names and issuers tend to dominate; state issues and those of the large cities are shown in sizable volume. This indicates, as we had already surmised, that the issues of small governmental units appear only infrequently in the national security markets. Dealers all testify that there is a tendency for issues to gravitate toward the home market in secondary dealings. At time of original sale, the obligations of a small governmental unit, if it be judged to have high credit quality, can be sold on the national market. But if such securities appear on the secondary market, knowing dealers look for bids on such issues at or near the place of issue. It seems quite certain that a significant part of the secondary market for state and local government obligations is purely local in nature. The typical advertisement of regional houses is "wire offerings" or "offerings wanted." Everyone understands that these offerings would be of securities of governmental units close to their location. While the Wharton survey tried to cover all nonregistered brokers and dealers,[13] they surveyed only the banks with formally recognized dealer departments. Just as small banks without formal dealer departments often buy the issues of small local government units, they undoubtedly furnish a kind of informal secondary market for such issues.

BUYERS AND SELLERS IN THE SECONDARY MARKET

On most points our knowledge of the secondary market is fragmentary; on one it is almost completely blank: the identity of the investors who sell in the secondary market and those who buy in it. There is some presumption that institutional investors buy a large fraction of their holdings from the new issues markets. The gross purchases of fire and casualty insurance companies, which are shown in detail in officially deposited reports, at least those of the 1953-1955 period which we examined, appear to be almost wholly from the new issues market. And very few sales were shown. But aside from such fragments we know little about participation in this market. It is not impossible that the secondary market is supported mainly by individuals and smaller institutional investors, but we have no facts with which to buttress such a presumption.

PRICES IN THE SECONDARY MARKET FOR STATE AND LOCAL GOVERNMENT OBLIGATIONS

Buyers and sellers are interested in the level of secondary market prices relative to that of the new issues market and the general level of security yields. Sellers are also concerned about the discount from prevailing yields they must accept as a kind of marketing or selling cost. Our knowledge on the second point, while far from complete, is considerable. But a judgment of the first point should be based on a detailed examination of transaction prices, something that was beyond the scope of this project.

It is widely believed (though research has not yet confirmed the point) that prices of corporate bonds, and probably for corporate equities (at least corporate preferreds), are somewhat higher in the secondary market than in the new issues market. In other words, the investor who buys from the new issues market presumably can share in the full economic underwriting profit of converting a new

---

[13] Though with a rather small response; see tables cited in note 8, above, and comments on coverage and response, Chapter 3.

issue into a "seasoned" one. A similar judgment appears to be true of the relative prices of large revenue bond issues in term form. In the case of most successful underwritings, the bonds soon appear in the secondary market at a premium over the offering prices. This, of course, is not true of unsuccessful offerings. But since successes outnumber the failures, there is a presumption that a buyer of new issues should get better bargains than if he waited to buy in the secondary market.[14]

To some extent the same phenomenon can be observed in the sale of general obligation serial bonds of the larger issuers. Soon after the successful sale of a large state and city issue, some of the bonds may start appearing in the *Blue List* marked up a bit from the original offering price (yield marked down). But this market observation does not quite settle the basic question about relative yields and prices in the secondary as over against the primary or new issues market. If an investor buys prudently from the new issues market and if the relative credit quality of the issue he has bought is unchanged, can he expect to be able to resell his holdings later at about the same relative yield, less the prevailing turnover cost, or can he expect an improvement due to seasoning, or a further discount due to obscurity or other factors?

We are unable to answer that question satisfactorily, but the testimony of a number of market observers suggests the following: the holder of a small or obscure issue must expect to face a rather substantial marketing cost and probably some relative discount from the new issue price he paid. Buyers with modest investment needs who are discerning of quality can often get superior yields in buying such issues from the secondary market. But if a given issue appears in ample supply in the secondary market it probably means that the yields on such an issue are a bit higher than for comparable quality in other issues. In such a case, the governmental unit whose issues appear in large volume on the secondary market may find that its own new issue costs are somewhat higher relative to its basic investment quality than is true of the issues of a governmental unit for whose issues there is some scarcity value. To be specific, most of the dealers interviewed were of the opinion that

---

[14] This is without recognition of the fact that a large investor could not cover his requirements in the secondary market without driving up prices far beyond the initial quotations. Our hypothetical "buyer" should be thought of as a small investor.

New York City bonds sold at yields higher by 15 to 25 basis points (from ⅛ to ¼ of 1 per cent) than the bonds of other cities of comparable quality which were not in such regular supply in the secondary market. It was also agreed that the bonds of governmental issuers having some scarcity value tended to command something like a premium on the secondary market. In other words, there is no clear evidence that yields on the secondary market are clearly above or below those for comparable credit quality on the new issues market. The differential is one that should be treated as a marketing cost rather than a generalized price differential.

One price aspect of the secondary market seemed to be clear; no appreciable volume of offerings could be marketed by the usual mechanics of secondary market offerings. If a large block of state and local government securities comes into the secondary market, it is common to negotiate the formation of a buying syndicate, very likely to publicize the issue with something like an official offering circular or statement, and to use the marketing mechanics that prevail for new issues. Furthermore it is interesting that private holders marketing such large blocks often seem to negotiate such secondary sales even if the securities were originally marketed by competitive bidding.[15]

Judgments about prices in the secondary market must be qualified by still one more consideration: we do not know the extent to which publicly announced prices such as in the *Blue List* or on offering lists are the prices at which transactions take place. *Blue List* prices are suspect; the same issue may be quoted at several different prices over a fairly wide range—what is more, these differentials may persist for several days. Presumably buyers will seek out the lowest price, but the margin within which bargaining can take place apparently is fairly wide.

Ambiguity about prices is complicated by one of the trading customs prevailing in this market. Most state and local government securities, or at least those in serial form, are quoted in terms of yield rather than price. But in new issue offerings the concessions

[15] The secondary sales of state and local government revenue bonds included in the *Issuer Summaries* published by the Counsel for Defendants in the antitrust case against certain investment bankers shows that in the period of mid-1933 through 1949, 15 secondary offerings involving $81,664,000 were sold by negotiation whereas only 3 secondary offerings involving an amount of $10,263,000 were sold by public sealed bids.

allowed dealers are quoted in common fractions: eighths, quarters, etc. Thus on a new issue offering, one dealer may buy a given serial of a given security from another on the basis of a quoted yield less the concession: i.e., the ten-year maturity of a given issue may be sold on a "2.50 yield basis, less ⅜." This practice has spread to the secondary market for state and local government obligations. The *Blue List* quotes almost all serial issues in yield terms, a few in dollar terms, but never in a combination form.[16] But the dealer-to-dealer price is usually such a combination. Assume a given security is offered on the *Blue List* on a 2.65 yield basis. The trader for a firm interested in buying this security will call the offering firm and bid "2.65 less a point." Bargaining usually follows, and the final transaction may take place at some such price as "2.65 less ⅝ths." This form of quotation, however, does not seem to apply to transactions with nondealer customers.

THE MARKETABILITY OF STATE
AND LOCAL GOVERNMENT OBLIGATIONS

The literature of investment management is replete with judgments about the relative "marketability" of various types of securities. The folklore of the capital markets makes much of this concept. But the concept of "marketability" has never been reduced to terms that give it explicit content, to something about which an operational research project could be planned.

The popular ideas of marketability seem to apply primarily to the secondary market. Certain judgments seem to be a part of the common folklore: i.e., that the securities of the United States Treasury are highly marketable; that real estate properties are often not very marketable; and that equipment trust obligations, while of high quality, have limited marketability. The character of the comments makes it reasonably clear that several ideas are implicit in the common meaning of marketability. In the first place, extreme price volatility seems to be contrary to the commonly accepted meaning of marketable; price stability seems to be regarded as a necessary prerequisite to marketability. For example, many corporate equities, although they can be sold readily in large quantities, are subject to rather wide price swings. They are not con-

---

[16] This is not true of the National Quotation Service lists; in them the combination form of quotation, though not common, is sometimes encountered.

sidered marketable by many investors when selling would cause realization of losses.

Then there is a quantity aspect to marketability. Some securities can be sold easily in limited quantities, but large quantities seem to drive prices down; in other cases large offerings do not seem to depress prices quite as much. Economists might be tempted to identify this behavior as a reflection of the elasticity of demand: an inelastic demand marks the first case and elastic demand the second one. But the concept of elasticity does not seem to offer much help in accounting for the differences among observed cases. The matter is more one of the rationality of market behavior. To a considerable extent, securities of a type such as state and local government obligations are homogeneous in character. They all have the common characteristic of offering tax exemption. While quality and other differences among securities are material, none of them seem so considerable that they could not be ironed out by differential pricing. Thus, large offerings of an issue of tax-exempt securities might tend to depress the entire market for tax-exempt obligations but why should it depress the quotation for this one particular issue unduly?[17] To the extent that tax-exempt securities are a homogeneous commodity, the price effects of increased supply should affect the whole market but not just the one issue. But tax exempts are not homogeneous. The appearance of an unusual volume of a given issue on the market depresses the quotations for that issue. This concentrated pressure on one area may also be a general market factor but one so diffuse that its influence cannot be traced.

In this sense, it appears that small holdings of state and local government securities are reasonably marketable.[18] But the market is not geared to accept individual issues in large volume without recourse to special procedures which are rather costly. Most investor's portfolios are rather widely diversified and, except for term revenue bonds, few investors have large holdings of individual issues and individual maturities. In the amounts individual issues

[17] Judges of market quality will be quick to point out that enlarged issue of securities by an issuer reduces the quality of this issuer's obligations and therefore should increase his costs relatively. This would be true on the new issues market, but it is not true of the secondary market. The sudden appearance of a large volume of securities of a given issuer on the secondary market does not change the amount *outstanding*.

[18] This is not true of odd lots. (An odd lot is less than five bonds or a block of bonds that is not a multiple of five.) Odd lots are salable but at a high cost.

are held, most holdings are reasonably "marketable." Indeed, it appears that the investment practice of diversification is not only useful for the purpose of spreading credit risks but it also tends to make portfolios more marketable.

MARKETING COSTS FOR STATE AND LOCAL GOVERNMENT
SECURITIES IN SECONDARY MARKET

The other element in marketability is that of relative marketing cost. The cost of "getting in and out" or the cost of turning over a portfolio position certainly has a real bearing on the judgment of the investor and the speculator. Even though the cost of marketing new equities issues is high, the cost of buying and selling equities on established exchanges or in the bigger over-the-counter markets is moderate; listed or actively traded equities are considered "marketable" even though subject to considerable price volatility. If we apply this standard to state and local government obligations, they can still be judged reasonably marketable. The margin taken in the secondary marketing process is not far different from the margin applying to new issue sales, and the margins for state and local government bonds do not appear to be much different from those prevailing in secondary market sales of corporate bonds.

But there is one important difference: the cost of marketing a tax-exempt obligation absorbs relatively more income. This higher cost may deter the ordinary investor from buying these obligations if he anticipates that shifting his investment position prior to maturity may be expensive. Our evidence on this point is as follows: the Wharton study developed quite a bit of data on the margins taken in over-the-counter trading in state and local government obligations.[19] Unfortunately the estimates prepared in this inquiry combined the margins on over-the-counter transactions in recently offered issues with those of a true secondary market nature. This inquiry found that the average cost of marketing a state and local government obligation was about 1.0 per cent. This represents the margin between the initial seller and the nondealer investor in which case the security might have gone through the hands of two dealers. This 1.0 per cent margin for tax exempts compares

[19] Most of this evidence may be found in Chapter 6 of Friend et al., *op.cit.* The specific data cited in this paragraph were taken from Tables 6-17 (p. 344), 6-18 (p. 346), 6-19 (p. 346), 6-21 (p. 351), and 6-26 (p. 358).

with a margin of 0.8 of one per cent for corporate bonds, of 2.0 per cent for preferred stocks, and of 4.6 per cent for common stocks on the over-the-counter market. The average margin for the individual dealer was 0.7 of one per cent; this margin was 0.8 of one per cent for transactions handled as a principal and 0.2 per cent for transactions handled on an agency basis. Transactions with customer banks involved a margin of only 0.3 of one per cent; those with other financial institutions 1.5 per cent; while, surprisingly enough, those with individuals amounted to only 0.6 of one per cent. The explanation of the high rate for other financial institutions probably grows out of the fact that these sales were mainly of newly issued term revenue bonds on which the marketing margin is quite wide.

The testimony of dealers suggests that margins for round lots in the secondary market are in fact somewhat higher than the combined margins shown by the Wharton tabulations. The margins mentioned in interviews were about as follows:

P.H.A. contract guaranteed notes	4-month maturity, 10 to 15 basis points
P.H.A. contract guaranteed notes	one-year maturity, 5 to 15 basis points
High-grade tax warrants	6-month maturity, 10 to 20 basis points
Housing Authority bonds (PHA contract)	long-term, ½ to 1 point (per cent)
New York City bonds	long-term, ½ to 1 point (per cent)
Small high grade issues	long-term, ¾ to 1½ points (per cent)
Small intermediate grade issues	long-term, 1 to 3 points (per cent)
Toll road bonds—good quality	long-term, ½ to 1½ points (per cent)
Toll road bonds—intermediate quality	long-term, 1½ to 4 points (per cent)

While these margins certainly do not bind investors into their existing holdings, they are a deterrent of some importance to portfolio fluidity. Furthermore, our evidence—the Wharton study and the interview of money market dealers—probably failed to reveal the margins that exist in the marketing of truly local issues, those that do not come into the national markets or of odd lots.[20] Secondly, the income from tax-exempt securities being somewhat below that prevailing on alternative forms of investment, the cost of changing investment position is not immaterial. This can be shown in the following tabulation which is based on the median points

[20] The cost of marketing an odd lot may amount to two or three full points.

of the margins shown on the previous page and using the average yields prevailing for such obligations in mid-1956.

	Income Foregone in Marketing: Equal to:
P.H.A. contract guaranteed notes 4-month maturity	10 days interest income
P.H.A. contract guaranteed notes one-year maturity	18 days interest income
High-grade tax warrants 6-month maturity	15 days interest income
Housing Authority bonds (PHA contract) long-term	4 months interest income
New York City bonds long-term	4 months interest income
Small high-grade issues long-term	6 months interest income
Small intermediate grade issues long-term	8 months interest income
Toll road bonds—good quality long-term	3 months interest income
Toll road bonds—intermediate quality long-term	6 months interest income

The cost of marketing small local issues might, if we had the facts, amount to as much as one year's interest income. In other words, investors cannot afford to shift investment positions without strong and compelling reasons. These margins suggest that speculation in state and local government securities, except for dealers for whom marketing costs are largely a matter of overhead, is awkward and costly.

CHAPTER 6

Tax-Exempt Interest as a Cost to Borrowing Governments and as a Yield to Investors

SUMMARY

The full story of postwar interest rate developments has yet to be written. This chapter cannot cover the entire subject; it can only concentrate on interest rate developments that were unique to the field of state and local government borrowing.

The most important fact to be considered is that yields on tax-exempt securities increased much more than almost any other comparable interest rate since World War II. During the almost unbroken boom of the postwar decade interest rates increased considerably. The largest relative increase for any major long-term yield, however, was that experienced in state and local government borrowing. The basic long-term yield on high-grade issues of this type increased from one per cent in the spring of 1946 to almost 3½ per cent in the late summer of 1957. Short-term tax-exempt yields went up relatively even more, as was true of all short-term interest rates. Because the underwriting margins also increased, the cost of borrowing by state and local governments increased even more than yields. Such an increase in interest costs meant that the total amortization cost of a 20-year serial debt with equal maturities increased by almost a fourth; for a 30-year debt the total amortization cost increased by more than a third.

One commonly offered explanation of the exceptionally large increase in tax-exempt yields is that restrictive monetary policies influenced them in an unusual degree. Monetary policy doubtless had a powerful and pervasive effect on interest rates generally. The case for a differential impact, however, is far less clear.

The narrowing differential between tax-exempt and fully taxable interest rates cannot be explained by tax expectations; quite the contrary, the expectations as to tax rate changes should have produced quite different differentials from the ones that, in fact, prevailed.

The most convincing explanation, and the one most in accord with both logic and fact, is that in order to market the increased volume of state and local government securities, new investors had to be brought into the market and that these new investors had a lower marginal use for tax exemption. This point has already been developed in Chapter 3. In other words, to find markets for the considerably increased volume of offerings, the privilege of tax exemption had to be bargained away for less and less to investors for whom tax exemption had a relatively low marginal value.

Another significant observation with respect to tax-exempt interest yields during the postwar decade was that they fluctuated through a somewhat wider range than had been true of other long-term interest rates. One possible line of explanation explored in this chapter is the somewhat more volatile character of new issue yields compared with those which prevail in the secondary market. Since most of the customary measures of open-market interest rates depend on secondary market sources, there is a danger that these commonly cited figures conceal the true course of events. Though there is some merit in the point, our investigations suggested that new issue versus secondary market experience would not account for the wider fluctuations in state and local government yields except to a relatively small extent. The more convincing reason appears to be that commercial banks have been an extraordinarily important part of this market. For reasons of general banking policy, commercial banks have been quite volatile investors. Indirectly, of course, this may reflect the influence of monetary policy.

The third major characteristic of the postwar market for state and local government securities has been that the interest rate differential between lower credit quality and higher credit quality borrowers persisted more than the comparable differential in the corporate field. This is an extraordinarily puzzling fact. Various hypotheses that might explain it were tested, but none of them yielded satisfactory results; the question is worthy of further investigation. The principal significance of this finding, however, is that the financial problems of state and local government in the future may be even more acute than some forecasters have suggested since an increased volume of borrowing inevitably means some reduction in the quality of the securities issued. On this basis it may be expected that there will be increasing problems in financing state and local government capital improvements.

The fourth major characteristic of postwar state and local government tax-exempt yields is that the yield curves or the relationship between yield and maturity for these securities were not parallel to those found in other sectors of the capital markets. The differences were sometimes so sharp that they cast doubt on the popular hypotheses that the maturity-yield relationship of interest rates reflects risk of loss on long-term obligations. Experience has shown that the serial offering scales of tax-exempt obligations often depart from the other yield curves appreciably. How much of this is due to the inflexible supply of unpopular maturities cannot be estimated. Experience with term bonds such as of toll roads is still too brief to forecast the pattern they will develop. It presumably will be similar to that of term corporate securities. The only hypothesis that seems to explain this interesting fact is that the market for state and local government securities is a highly segmented market. Demand in one segment of the market can vary considerably from the demand that prevails in other portions of the money markets or the capital markets.

The net effect of all four of these factors, but particularly of the first and third, has been to create a vast shift in the way in which the benefits of tax exemption are divided between borrowing governments and investors. The economic (if not the political) equivalent of tax exemption is that of a subsidy. Near the beginning of the postwar period it would appear that a very large part of the tax revenue foregone by the federal government was recaptured by state and local governments in lower borrowing costs. In fact the quantity of borrowing was small and so what in actuality took place was that investors in tax exempts from earlier periods were given the chance to realize capital gains. State and local governments did not get much advantage from this brief episode. But as the decade went along, this condition changed and investors were able to demand a larger and larger portion of the benefits of tax exemption and state and local governments were able to retain less of them. The subsidy lost much of its effectiveness. In the final part of this chapter, some admittedly rough estimates of the way in which this differential has been divided between borrowers and investors are presented.

RELATIVELY GREAT INCREASE IN TAX-EXEMPT YIELDS
DURING POSTWAR DECADE

The much greater increase in yields on tax-exempt state and local government securities is evident in any comparison of interest rate changes. In the spring of 1946, a top-rated state and local governmental unit could have sold its twenty-year obligations at an interest cost of less than 1 per cent. In the late summer of 1957 a similar borrower would have had to pay almost 3½ per cent for twenty-year money. The unusual degree of this increase in interest costs is disclosed by a comparison with other yield changes. During the same interval, the yield on fully taxable U.S. government twenty-year obligations went from about 2¼ per cent to almost 3¾ per cent, an increase of 1½ percentage points. The interest cost for newly marketed high-grade corporate bonds rose from about 2⅝ per cent to more than 4⅝ per cent, an increase of two percentage points. Increases in yields on high-grade corporate bonds in the secondary market were less, about the same as for U.S. Treasury long-term bonds. If yields on state and local government securities had increased only in the same proportion as those on U.S. Treasury or high-grade corporate bonds they would have risen only to about 2 per cent. In other words the major part of the tax-exempt yield increase must be explained by factors applying uniquely to that market.

The contrast between tax-exempt state and local government security yields and those on corporate bonds was (and is) greatest for the highest grade obligations. The differences were considerably less for intermediate-grade securities. This is shown in Chart 8. In this chart, the Aaa tax-exempt yield is shown as a ratio of the Aaa corporate yield; the Baa tax-exempt yield is also shown as a ratio of the Baa corporate yield. For comparative purposes, the corporate tax rate (for large corporations) is also shown. This chart demonstrates that the erosion of the borrowing advantage of tax exemption during the postwar decade has not been a steady matter; the differential has moved erratically.

Using 1946 as the starting point for our tax-exempt yield comparison undoubtedly results in some bias. The volume of new issues was very small and market supplies in the secondary markets were also limited. The 1946 yields were priced in a very thin market.

The extremely low yields on state and local government obligations in that year were partly due to a fear that there might be a shortage of tax-exempt investment outlets now that tax exemption was not available on newly offered federal obligations. In retrospect the fear seems odd, but editorial comment at that time confirms its

CHART 8

Municipal Bond Yields as a Percentage of Comparable Corporate Bond Yields

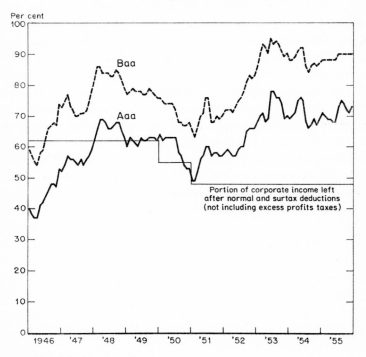

Source: Moody's Investors Service.

reality. With full allowance for the market effects of this fear, one cannot help wondering why tax exemption should have been given such a high value at that particular juncture. Applicable income tax rates had just been lowered and in that short idyllic interlude before the threat of war once more revived, the expectation must have been for even further tax reductions.

As other studies have shown, saving through financial intermediaries appears to have gained relative to direct individual investment.[1] Many of the principal institutional investors are themselves either exempt from federal income taxation, pay only low marginal rates of taxes, or are unable to pass along the value of tax exemption to their equity investors as was elaborated in Chapter 3. Life insurance companies are now subject to a $6\frac{1}{2}$ per cent gross investment income tax rate. Public and private pension funds, both among the most rapidly growing investment institutions, can, and usually do, qualify for complete tax exemption. Mutual investment companies can qualify for tax exemption but cannot pass the benefits of tax exemption on their investments along to their stockholders. Among institutional investors, the only two important groups subject to the full corporate tax rate are commercial banks; and fire, marine, and casualty insurance companies. Both of these types of institutions have frequently been important investors in tax-exempt securities; on some occasions they have put a large fraction of their accruing money in this market. But tax-exempt securities are hardly the most desirable form of investment for either type of institution. Customer loans continue to be the favorite outlet of commercial banks. With the special 85 per cent dividend credit on corporate equities, fire, marine, and casualty insurance companies pay taxes of only 7.8 per cent on dividend income (52 per cent times 15 per cent). This makes equity investment very attractive—except when equity prices get very high.

Individual investors with high incomes can choose tax-exempt obligations with considerable logic. But this is a defensive form of investment; it preserves only the dollar integrity of principal and shelters income from taxation. The widespread forecast of secular inflation has led many investment counselors to emphasize more the preservation of real value than of dollar amounts. Capital gains have been more emphasized as an investment objective; they have some tax and many strategic advantages. Other shelters from taxation can be found in such investment media as oil royalties and rental real estate.

The timing of the shrinkage in yield differentials suggests that monetary policy is only a partial explanation at most. Much of the

---

[1] Raymond Goldsmith, *Financial Intermediaries in the American Economy* (Princeton University Press for National Bureau, 1958), Chapters VII and IX, particularly Table 91, p. 304.

shrinkage had occurred before 1951, when monetary policy was reactivated. Furthermore, it is hard to find any persuasive reason why monetary tension should have had an unusually severe effect on the tax-exempt market, except that commerical banks are unusually important investors in this market. Commercial banks are probably more directly affected by monetary policy than other financial institutions. It is true, of course, that state and local governments rely less on current surplus for capital expenditures and are less facile in the temporary use of short-term credits, both features of which help business corporations minimize the impact of monetary policy.

One would expect the differential between tax-exempt and fully taxable yields to respond not only to accomplished changes in tax rates but also to expectations as to future tax rates. This is particularly true of long-term tax-exempt obligations which discount tax rate expectations rather far into the future. Unfortunately the facts do not give much support to the hypothesis that this was a significant market factor. In the beginning of the postwar period, tax cut expectations were high but have since been dimmed by the course of international political developments. On the basis of these expectations the differential should have started narrow and become wider—the opposite of actual events.

Tax rate expectations clearly have been a market factor from time to time. In the fall of 1950 the prices of tax-exempt securities were bid up when other prices were going down. This was true likewise in earlier periods. After World War I the level of income tax rates was reduced sharply; the value of tax exemption was correspondingly discounted. During the New Deal period in the 1930's most investors, bitterly opposed as they were to the prevailing political temper of the times, found it hard to believe that steeply progressive rates of taxation were an enduring element in the political system. Much the same could have been said during the early phases of World War II. But the size of the federal debt and many other factors changed the views of many investors. By the time the postwar period was underway, most investors had come, no matter how reluctantly, to believe that relatively high tax rates were likely in the foreseeable future. When high-grade tax-exempt yields for twenty years dipped under one per cent in 1946, buyers of tax exempts were, in effect, discounting this privilege over the next twenty years at a marginal rate in excess of 60 per cent. This is shown with Aaa and Baa municipal yields as a relative of similar corporate yields in Chart 8. Since this was considerably in excess of the 38 per cent rate on corporations at the time, the valuation of the market is hard to understand.[2] When Congress was considering a revision of tax rates in 1948, the prices of tax exempts were weak for a while but this was reversed in the mild recession of 1949.

The other side of the story is that the yield discount (price premium) of Aaa municipal bonds in 1953 came to be as low as 22 per cent. The value of tax exemption was only about two-fifths of the corporate tax rate and was equal to the marginal tax on income of individuals with only about $10,000 of income per annum. In neither case can it be said that expectations of tax rate changes justified such a change. In fact if a boom period reduces the expectation of tax reductions and enhances the prospects of individuals' advancing to higher tax brackets, as would seem reasonable, this factor should moderate the price reduction for tax-exempt securities. But, as shown above, the actual course of price developments has been quite the contrary.

Tax rates clearly have some relationship to yield differentials, as would be expected. One investment counsel service determines a "normal" relationship between Treasury yields and tax-exempt yields by a multiple regression using Treasury bond yields, existing tax rates for higher income individuals and for corporations as independent variables. Correlation coefficients of about .9 prevail between the presumptive normal yields and the actually observed yields.[3]

Even though this indicates a considerable relationship of yield differentials to tax rates, this analyst also observed that expectations appeared to lead actual tax rate changes by an appreciable margin. Time-lagged correlations were not computed, but this relationship seemed evident in the charts of this counseling service. This correlation was computed only for Aaa or Aa securities. These securities have preserved the greatest amount of differential, as indicated in

[2] Particularly so in light of the fact that individuals appear to have been selling tax exempts or at least failing to maintain their investment position in them while commercial banks were the only buyers during first half of 1946.

[3] J. Eugene Banks of Brown Brothers Harriman and Company, institutional investment counseling service.

another section of this chapter. Among securities of lower credit quality such high correlations might not be found.

Failure of the market for the privilege of tax exemption to expand probably explains most but not all of the differential yield movements. In the first place, the significance of the under-1-per cent yield on twenty-year state and local government obligations at the beginning of the decade may be questioned. The volume of new issues was negligible; almost the only bonds available were those in the secondary market. The *Blue List* of that period showed offerings only slightly in excess of 100 million. The proportion of issues of top quality was not unusually high. In other words, the yields quoted at that period must have been based on a relatively thin market.

Another factor that might account for a high-grade yield change would be a change in the proportion of state and local governmental units with high credit standing that are borrowing. At the beginning of the decade, the governmental units with high credit standing were borrowing very little; most of those coming to the market had an intermediate credit standing.[4] It could have been said that the supply of high-grade issues was short relative to the supply of issues of other qualities. But the widespread need for large state and local governmental capital expenditures brought more conservatively financed and richer communities into the market. Public Housing Authority issues, which are of the highest quality, became an increasingly important factor in the market. There was no shortage of high-grade issues at the end of 1956!

While the supply of high-grade issues increased relatively, this factor cannot explain the over-all yield increases. Yields of intermediate-grade state and local government securities increased by just about as much as those of high-grade issues. The general quality of state and local government credit probably has not changed materially. Large borrowing may have reduced it a bit but at most from something like a "superb" to a "very good" rating.

The large increase in state and local governmental yields compared with the relatively and absolutely much smaller one which has been shown by U.S. Treasury obligations must be considered against the background fact that the marketable debt of the federal government increased relatively little over the decade, while that

[4] See Table 7.

of state and local government had risen to more than three times its earlier level. The U.S. Treasury had to raise some new money, but its major problem was that of refunding the outstanding debt. While the total debt grew moderately in the postwar period, the marketable portion of the net debt changed very little.

But this relatively greater increase in debt is not the whole story. While the new money demands of state and local government were large, so were those of corporations. If the demand for new money explained the differential advance in state and local governmental yields, then the increase in corporate yields should have more nearly paralleled that of state and local governments than that of treasury obligations. This was not true: corporate yields, if measured by the cost of new money, went up only a bit more than yields on U.S. Treasury obligations: a matter of ⅜ of a percentage point at most. Corporate yield experience was much closer to that of Treasury financing than to that of state and local government borrowings. Tax exemption clearly isolated the market for state and local government securities from other capital markets.

WIDE PRICE FLUCTUATION OF STATE
AND LOCAL GOVERNMENT SECURITIES

The yields of long-term state and local government securities fluctuate through a wider range than any other important long-term interest rate. Any chart showing the history of bond yields demonstrates the fact adequately.[5] The large-scale buying of tax exempts in late 1950 produced a drastic price effect. The prices of tax exempts dropped more when the U.S. government security market was unpegged in early 1951 than did the prices of Treasury bonds themselves. The further drop in prices to mid-1953 was also greater for tax exempts than it was for taxable bonds. The recovery of prices after mid-1953 to mid-1954 was also greater for tax exempts than for taxable obligations. Again in late 1956, tax-exempt prices went down more than other bond prices.

The wider amplitude of price fluctuations is also shown in Chart 9. This chart is based on a series of prices derived from yields. To furnish comparability, the prices were derived for state and local government and corporate securities having a rating of Aa. Both

[5] As, for example, the bond yield chart in the *Federal Reserve Historical Chart Book.*

CHART 9

Relative Price Movement of Corporate and Municipal Bonds

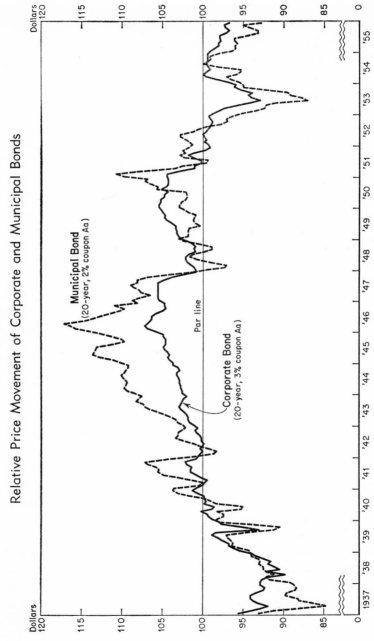

Price comparison based on prices derived from Moody's Aa municipal and corporate bond yields; a coupon of 2% being assumed for the municipal bond and a coupon of 3% being assumed for corporate bond; both bonds assumed to have 20-year maturity.

series were taken from Moody's Investors Service, as were the ratings. In both cases, the prices were those representing a constant twenty-year maturity bond. To facilitate comparison, the corporate bond was given a 3 per cent coupon which brought its average near par; a 2 per cent coupon for the municipal did likewise. In other words, the prices do not represent a single bond (which would shorten in maturity as time passed) but an assumed average of a portfolio with a constant maturity of twenty years. This was felt to approximate more closely the price experience of investors than any other form of representation. The much wider range of price fluctuation for state and local government securities is easily evident to the eye. The average variation of price for the municipal series was more than twice that of the corporate series for the entire 1937-1955 period. In the period since March 1951 (the Federal Reserve-Treasury "accord") both fluctuated a bit more than before and the difference in range is not quite as large, with the municipal average range a little less than twice that of corporate bonds.

The wider range of yield fluctuation for state and local government obligations than for corporate or U.S. Treasury bond yields appears to be due to a combination of circumstances. In addition to the general economic influences that apply to all capital markets equally, the valuation of state and local government securities involves pricing the privilege of tax exemption. This makes it a narrower market.

A further circumstance influencing state and local government security yields is that this market is more subject to inventory adjustments. The supply of corporate obligations in the secondary market is seldom very large; the supply of new and unsold corporate issues is more often zero than any other amount. The supply of Treasury obligations in the market is concentrated in the shorter maturities; supplies of the longer maturities are seldom truly large. Sometimes one or two dealers will be holding a speculative position in long bonds, but inventory is more sporadic than regular. When market signs are adverse, these inventories are cleared out quickly.

But the market for state and local government securities apparently cannot operate satisfactorily without an inventory of significant size; sometimes it seems to need quite a large amount. Even though dealers may see the signs of marked adversity, they find it hard to reduce inventories quickly. Since many state and local

government finance authorities in offering their securities for competitive bidding do not respond quickly to adverse market developments, inventory may pile up from new-issue marketing much more
than is true of the corporate field, where the units are larger,
financing plans can be changed more quickly, and the proportion
of negotiated deals is larger. The influence of unsold inventory
on this market is material. Several periods of this influence stand out
quite evidently. In the fall of 1947 when the Federal Reserve started
supporting Treasury bond prices, and on Christmas Eve when this
support was dropped to par, both the corporate and the tax-exempt
market responded by weakening. But whereas the initial response
of the corporate market accounted for most of its change, the tax-
exempt market continued to be weak well into 1948 until inventory
had been worked back to more normal proportions. Much the
same was true in 1951 when the Federal Reserve dropped par
support altogether. In the spring of 1953 when the entire capital
market was relatively tight, tax-exempt securities followed the
general pattern of weakness. Although the recovery of Treasury
and corporate bond prices started in early June after Federal Reserve easing was evident, it did not show up as promptly in the
tax-exempt market; some inventory had to be worked off before
the influence of credit ease was fully evident.

The unusual coupon practices that prevail in this field (see
Appendix B) and the wider range of outstanding coupons may
account for some, though probably only a small part, of the greater
price volatility of state and local government securities. When
Durand and Winn were studying bond yields in the early postwar
period, they encountered the fact that, other things being equal,
high-coupon tax-exempt obligations sold at a higher yield than
those with coupons near the levels of market yields.[6] Investors
apparently did not like to pay the large premiums involved in
high-coupon obligations; trust administrators had to amortize them
to preserve equity between life tenants and remaindermen but
amortization sometimes involves legal problems. In smaller portfolios reinvestment of principal is awkward. Since the Durand-Winn
survey was made, yields have gone up a great deal. Some high-
coupon long-term bonds are still outstanding, but the effect of
coupon on yield is far less clear than it was earlier. Durand and

---

[6] Technical Paper 6 (National Bureau, 1947), pp. 31-40.

Winn solved the problem of quality uniformity by use of New York City bonds and corporate stock.[7] The subsequent retirement of a large number of the high-coupon issues meant that similar comparisons must be based on fewer observations. But a number of other coupon effects were noted and confirmed by traders. In periods of relatively easy money in 1949 and 1954, high-coupon short-term issues sold at lower yields than comparable maturities with lower coupons. Banks sometimes prefer high-coupon issues for reasons outlined in Chapter 3 and paid a slight premium for them. But in 1955, when bank credit was tight, high-coupon short-term issues sold at higher yields than comparable issues with lower coupons. High-coupon long-term issues generally sell at slightly higher yields if their coupon throws their price materially above par. This premium is large in a low-rate period such as when Durand and Winn were making their observations but it has been far smaller recently.

Another coupon-induced effect has emerged in recent periods: when yields have gone up so that low-coupon issues sell below par, their yield is also slightly above comparable high-coupon maturities of comparable quality. This effect is confined to municipals, rather the reverse being true of corporate obligations. The reason for this phenomenon seems to be as follows: if the low-coupon issue was originally sold at par, the holder can claim tax exemption only for the amount of the coupon; the approach of such an under-par security to par by the working of amortization mathematics is treated as a taxable capital gain. So the full yield of such a low coupon obligation is not tax exempt, only the coupon. For example, in January 1957, $1 million of 1¾ per cent general revenue bonds of the Triborough Bridge and Tunnel Authority maturing in 1960 were offered in the secondary market priced to yield 3.25 per cent. On the same day City of San Antonio Electric and Gas Systems Revenue Improvement bonds—an issue of comparable (or at least no higher) quality—were offered with the 1960 maturity (coupon 4 per cent) priced to yield 2.80 per cent. Seattle school district bonds, also of comparable but no higher quality, were offered on the same day priced to yield 2.80 per cent on the 1960 maturity (coupon 6 per cent).[8]

---

[7] They also paired bonds of one corporate issuer.
[8] *The New York Times,* January 21, 1957, financial advertisements.

Only the 1¾ per cent coupon on the Triborough bonds was tax exempt; the other 1½ per cent of the offered yield was subject to capital gains taxation. Allowing for taxation of this at the prevailing 25 per cent level for long-term capital gains, the net tax-exempt yield of the Triborough bonds was slightly more than 2.85 per cent, quite in line with the offering yields of comparable new issues.

When it was originally sold at a discount, the holder of a low coupon bond can claim the original yield as being tax exempt. Thus low-coupon[9] terminal maturities may offer full tax exemption. But even in these cases, low coupons are not popular in the market and require from 35 to 70 basis points higher yields.

From these observations, the following statement might be generalized: the effects of a high coupon on a short-maturity issue depend on the state of the money markets. Both a high coupon on a long-term issue and a low coupon on all issues (particularly if sold at a low yield by the issuer) tend to sell at higher yields than comparable maturities with coupons near to market yields. Investors, with the exceptions noted above, prefer municipal securities that sell near par.[10]

The hypothesis that is the most persuasive one in accounting for the considerable volatility of tax-exempt security prices is that commercial banks have been such important but unstable investors in them. As the evidence in Chapter 3 showed, commercial banks have absorbed as much as two-thirds of the new issues offered on the market in some semiannual periods; in others they absorbed none of the net increase. No other class of investors has alternately entered or retreated from the market with such great variability.

The reason commercial banks are such volatile investors in these securities is that they do not give them a top priority among the investment alternatives open to them. Commercial banks are dominantly customer-lending institutions. The next priority is for liquidity, and even short-term tax-exempt securities are not particularly liquid. The purchase of tax-exempt securities thus has a relatively low priority in the application of funds. For this reason

---

[9] See Chapter 3 and Appendix B for an account of why such coupons are offered.

[10] Investors buying callable corporate securities in the secondary market prefer low-coupon securities selling under par since these will not be "lost" to a call as readily. Thus, in a price decline, this factor sustains the prices of low-coupon corporate issues whereas low-coupon municipals sell off just that much more.

commercial banks may have been far less dependable buyers of tax exempts than the institutional investors that have accounted for the principal purchases of corporate bonds, such as life insurance companies and pension funds and other trust accounts. To the extent that this hypothesis is valid it raises an interesting question for the future: will the growth in money supply requirements, which guides the release of reserves by the central bank, be at such a pace as to expand or constrict the relative proportions of securities taken by commercial banks?

THE INFLUENCE OF CREDIT QUALITY ON YIELD

One of the most significant differentials among state and local government security yields is that induced by differences in the qualities of individual securities. The yield differentials between grades of corporate securities shrank considerably during the postwar decade. But the differentials between grades of state and local government securities continued to be large. These differentials are shown in Chart 10 in absolute amounts (of yield) and in relative amounts (yield differential as a ratio to highest grade yield) in Chart 11.

Neither basis of comparison is wholly satisfactory. An investor might consider the risk premium he would require to be a proportion of the basic high-grade yield available to him. For example, in a given circumstance an investor might assume a given risk gladly if he could improve his yield from 2 per cent to 3 per cent. He might, however, hesitate to assume the same risk in order to improve his yield from 5 per cent to 6 per cent. But if the differential is looked at as a fund that might be accumulated in reserve form, then an absolute amount is more nearly consistent with the actuarial nature of risk than a relative amount. The market does not seem to hold clearly to just one of these views; both are shown for reference purposes.

The measure of quality we used has been that of the ratings assigned by Moody's Investors Service. This source furnishes unusually comparable data because they not only prepare the ratings of individual securities but also compile yields by the same quality ratings. Such experience as has accumulated with rating systems suggests that they are reasonably accurate judges of quality. While

CHART 10

Municipal Bond Yield Differentials by Quality of Issue, in Basis Points*

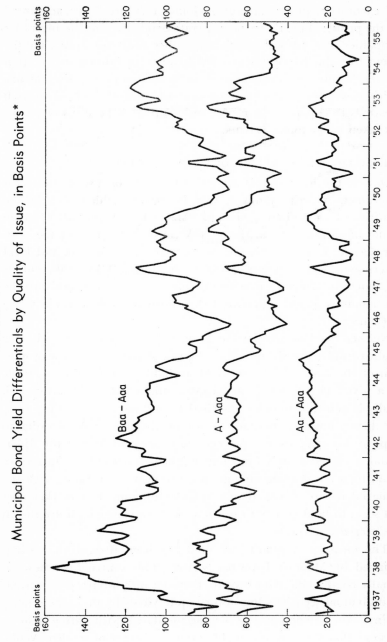

* A basis point is one-hundredth of one per cent of a yield quotation.
Source: Moody's municipal bond yields for Aaa, Aa, A, and Baa issues.

CHART 11

Municipal Bond Yield Differentials by Quality of Issue, in Relative Terms

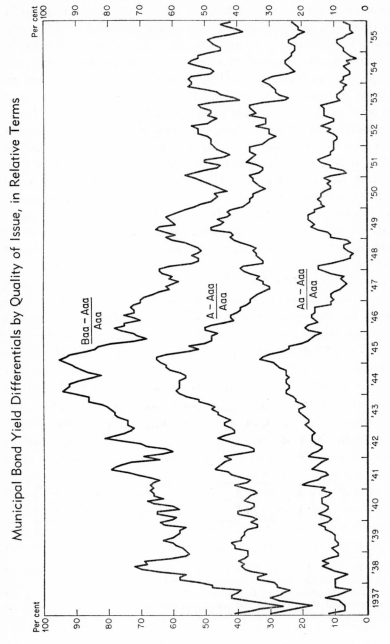

Source: Moody's municipal bond yields for four top rating groups.

this record has been tested only for corporate bonds,[11] we have no reason for expecting the accuracy of municipal bond ratings to be less than that of corporates. The fundamental quality differences among the various rating groups probably are moderate. Practically all municipal credits that are rated fall within the top four rating groups. The rating agencies class securities in all four top groups as being of "investment quality." In other words, they judge state and local government credits to be generally good; some are better than others, but most of them are rated good. No rating agency gives even a Baa rating to a credit if it has dubious characteristics; rather, it is a good credit but with less margin of protection than the very top qualities. The Hickman survey of corporate bond quality cited above found that the differences in investment experience among quality ratings, while positively correlated, were smaller relatively than the yield differentials. In other words, the corporate bond market exacted a considerable surcharge for the risk element in corporate credit.

The quality yield differentials found in municipal bonds are so large as to raise questions as to the rationality of investment behavior. For example, the margin between the Aaa yields and Baa yields has averaged close to one percentage point during the postwar decade. Without some quantitative measure of risk this figure cannot mean much in itself. We can be confident, however, that the worst investment experience of a reasonably diversified portfolio of tax exempts in the Great Depression would have been far more than covered by a 1 per cent risk premium. The highest default estimate anyone made was 15 per cent (most were much smaller) and no one believes that ultimate losses to investors were more than 1 per cent of the debt outstanding. As shown below, a diversified portfolio of Baa state and local government securities should be able to accumulate a risk reserve that would allow for a Great Depression every few years and still show a handsome margin over the Aaa yields. Even the margin between the two highest grades

[11] W. Braddock Hickman, *Corporate Bond Quality and Investor Experience* (Princeton University Press for National Bureau, 1958), Chapter 3, particularly pp. 174-210. Hickman found the agency ratings were better for large than for small issues and these ratings did not anticipate the unfavorable experience of some industries such as railroads. But, with allowance for these qualifications, agency rating of corporate bonds was a fairly good forecaster of relative default experience.

has run from 10 to 20 basis points.[12] A margin of 10 basis points would accumulate an appreciable reserve over a long period of time.

The significance of yield differentials as risk premiums is probably best measured by calculating the reserve fund that could be accumulated with such differentials. As a starting point we might assume that periods of distress in municipal finance come rather rarely; they are considerably more than twenty years apart. Aside from such periods of widespread difficulty, the record of municipal credit has been remarkably good. Thus if a twenty-year period be used, and if the yields and yield differentials of the year 1955 be used, the following results are shown:

    a. The Baa yield margin over the Aaa yield would accumulate a fund of about $260 over a 20-year period per $1,000 bond.

    b. The A yield margin over the Aaa yield would accumulate a fund of about $125 over a 20-year period per $1,000 bond.

    c. The Aa yield margin over the Aaa yield would accumulate a fund of about $35 over a 20-year period per $1,000 bond.

This overestimation of risk coverage is not as surprising as it first seems. The PHA obligations furnish an interesting example. The bonds of various local housing authorities covered by a contract with the Public Housing Administration guaranteeing service of these bonds amounts to a tax-exempt credit guaranteed by the federal government. But in the sales of these securities, differential yields are put on the securities of differing authorities but of the same maturity.[13] Some "names" sell better than others. The investment bankers making the offerings concede the irrationality of such differentials, but they know from experience that investors prefer the securities of some localities and they allow for these preferences in their bids. As many as three or four reoffering scales may be used indicating three or four types of judgment made by the market.

Every so often a small high-quality issue, sold virtually simultaneously with a batch of new PHA contract housing authority bonds, will fetch a better price (offer a lower yield) than is obtained from the housing bonds. Why will investors buy such issues with a

---

[12] A "basis point" is one-hundredth of one percentage point in the expression of yield; i.e., a change of yield from 3.16 to 3.12 is referred to as a drop of four basis points.

[13] See Chapter 4, note 11, for a possible rationality in these differences.

thinner return than that prevailing on a tax-exempt issue backed by the credit of the federal government? Sometimes local tax exemption accounts for such differentials but this advantage accrues only to local citizens and these bonds are being offered on the national market.[14]

While these differentials indicate something less than perfect rationality in the market, they are usually small differentials. In the end, the most important unanswered question is why the market demands such a substantial yield differential for intermediate-grade securities, a differential that exceeds any risk calculation that might be made. The reasons that seem to have the greatest cogency are institutional and traditional. The two principal institutional buyers are commercial banks, and fire and casualty insurance companies. Both of them prize liquidity and both should be considered conservative investors. The liquidity of a high-quality credit instrument is admittedly greater than that of one of intermediate quality. While we have no solid evidence to support the point, opinions of dealers seem to be that the marketing cost of selling a lower-grade security often is considerable. If an investor has to sell an intermediate-grade security before maturity, its higher income may fail to cover the added costs of liquidating the holding.

To the extent that institutional investors want to preserve liquidity for periods of economic adversity, the reasons for avoiding intermediate-grade securities are multiplied. As the two differential charts show (Charts 10 and 11), a recession of the 1937-1938 magnitude increases the yield differentials materially and doubtless would impair the liquidity of the intermediate grades.

Still another view of commercial banks as investors is that they are more anxious to maximize their loan income than their investment income. Loans not only bear a higher rate of return; they are important to customer relationships and are often determinate of a bank's ability to attract deposits—the life blood of the business. The returns from tax-exempt holdings are important, but they cannot claim top priority. And so banks do not attempt to maximize their returns from this segment of their assets; they rather lean

[14] As mentioned in Chapter 3, state and local government securities are only tax-exempt as respects federal income taxes and usually the income tax of the state of issue. States tax one another's issues freely.

on its quality and liquidity. Banks also take a special interest in local government and the home state.

On top of this, some weight must be given to the incentives working on professional investment officers in commercial banks. An aggressive policy of investment involving some concession to usual quality standards might increase the rate of return on the portfolio. But if this policy should involve no more than one or two conspicuous defaults, the officer rightly fears that he might lose in salary, prestige, and possibly even in job more than he would gain from a better rate of earnings. Even if he could demonstrate to his board of directors that, as an actuarial calculation, the bank was ahead by virtue of a higher rate of return on portfolio, directors do not like losses. They would find it hard to support this philosophy before bank examiners. Bank examiners seem to take a dim view of what might be called the actuarial view of investment risk. They criticize calculated risk-taking even though earnings may suggest the advantage of such a policy. The customs of the financial community do not tolerate much risk assumption.

The investment policies of fire and casualty companies are quite similar. They also look to tax-exempt holdings for liquidity and for that reason prefer high-quality securities. Indeed, it is reported that the boards of directors of some companies have adopted policies of not buying less than Aa rated bonds.

The investment policies of individuals vary widely. Dealers report that some individuals shop for high returns and will assume risk. But individuals will not take risks for trivial yield differentials. They will buy a toll road bond with an income approaching 4 per cent rather than a high-grade 2½ per cent obligation, but probably not for a small differential. Individuals who buy tax exempts generally are not of a speculative temperament; in fact, it appears from the Harvard study interviews[15] that investors in tax-exempt securities tend to be those who would be classed as "conservative" or capital conserving investors. They are not calculating risk-takers; they are cautious.

To the extent that individual investment in state and local government securities is controlled by trust investment policies, one can be sure that caution and conservatism prevail, that calcu-

---

[15] J. Keith Butters, Lawrence E. Thompson, and Lynn L. Bollinger, *Investment for Individuals* (Harvard Business School, 1953).

lated risk-taking is rare. A trust department that aggressively improved the returns for most beneficiaries would get few thanks for the yield improvement; but if they have just one or two publicized losses, the word might spread and they could lose trust business. This is a high order of rationality on the part of trust investment officers as a safeguard against the irrationality of trust beneficiaries.

In other words, the natural market for tax-exempt securities is among investors who prize safety and who are not aggressive yield improvers at the cost of some risk-taking. This comparison can be made even more explicit: life insurance companies and some self-administered pension funds have shown themselves yield-conscious; they are not exactly risk-takers but they are not cautious to the point of avoiding some balancing of risk with yield improvement. But these institutions, though of growing importance in the capital markets, are of moderate importance as buyers of rated tax-exempt securities. The buyers of tax exempts thus tend to pay a higher price (or accept a wider yield differential) for investment safety than is true elsewhere. This fact in turn affects the market for state and local government obligations in this way: as long as the volume of offerings is moderate, investors will pay a good price for tax protection. But when the volume of offerings increases, as it has in the past few years, the inevitable averaging down of quality and the need to broaden the groups of buyers tends to have a sharp effect on yields. The greater fluctuation in yield and price of tax exempts is not unreasonable in the light of such demand inelasticity.

TERM STRUCTURE OF YIELDS ON STATE
AND LOCAL GOVERNMENT OBLIGATIONS

Maturity-yield differentials and the patterns into which they fall are a market factor of considerable importance and have become one of the most frequently employed empirical foundations for interest rate theorizing. When maturity is the sole difference between otherwise homogeneous securities, differences of yield for various maturities seem to offer clues for answering basic questions as to why interest is paid or for what service investors demand the payment of interest. Heretofore analytical attention has been given mostly to differentials in the high-grade fully taxable markets. Maturity-yield differentials for tax-exempt obligations as represented by offering scales introduce a new factor: the discount of tax rate expectations.

Maturity-yield differentials appear to have been implicit in the market structures of interest rates for as long as we have reasonably dependable figures. But detailed measurement of the differentials and plotting of so-called yield curves did not come until the 1930's. In the middle of this decade Macaulay tested the hypothesis that the long-term short-term interest rate relationship was a kind of implied forecast: an upsweeping yield curve forecast rising interest rates and a downsweeping curve forecast falling interest rates.[16] Though he believed that such forecasting was implied, he found it to be unsuccessful. He found no evidence that the long-term interest rates of a period had been anticipated by the preceding long-term short-term interest rate relationship.

Another hypothesis advanced as an explanation of maturity-yield differentials was that of liquidity preference: investors, fearing the risks implicit in the price fluctuations of long-term bonds, would accept lower returns on shorter maturities as a form of loss prevention as well as liquidity assurance. This hypothesis implied that an upsweeping yield curve was the normal expectation; that any other form of curve was a temporary abnormality. But the historians of interest rates showed that downsweeping yield curves appear to have been just about as frequent as upsweeping ones.

A third hypothesis was simply imperfection in the market structure. The smoothness of the yield curves suggested that there was some arbitraging of nearby maturities but that the market was segmented to such a degree that remoter extremes of maturity for otherwise homogeneous obligations could sell at quite different yields.

Macaulay's pioneer work on the relationship of long-term and short-term interest rates was followed by the National Bureau's corporate bond survey. Because the subject of this inquiry was limited to corporate bonds, early work on the term structure of interest rates (done by Hickman[17] and Durand[18]) was similarly

[16] *Movements of Interest Rates, Bond Yields and Stock Prices in the United States since 1856* (National Bureau, 1938).

[17] W. Braddock Hickman, *The Term Structure of Interest Rates, an Exploratory Analysis* (National Bureau unpublished manuscript dated November 16, 1942).

[18] David Durand, *Basic Yields of Corporate Bonds, 1900-1942*, Technical Paper 3 (National Bureau 1942).

focused. A second study by Durand and Winn,[19] published in 1947, covered other kinds of bonds including some serial municipal issues. It is possible that even earlier work was done on this subject by the technical staff of the Treasury Department, but their work records unfortunately are cloaked in official secrecy.[20]

Very little work has been done on the empirical character of maturity-yield relationships for tax-exempt securities except for that of Durand and Winn cited above. The reason could hardly be lack of data since the yields assigned to various maturities of serial offerings by underwriters in the form of "offering scales" furnish a readily available source of data. But there are problems of comparability of these scales to those derived from analysis of other segments of the capital markets.

The securities of the U.S. Treasury and most corporate securities are offered on the market in single maturity or "term" form; measurement of the relationship between yield and the period to maturity is therefore based largely on secondary market observations. Serial corporate offerings are found only in the form of railroad equipment trust obligations. The measurement of the corporate yield-maturity relationship, the "term structure," is therefore more difficult than is true of state and local government securities. For this reason it was only feasible within the resources of this project to compute an annual term-maturity pattern for each of the postwar years. The computation was made for the first quarter of each year and the observations were limited to the month of February so far as possible. These are shown in Table 26. Term maturity structures derived in this way are reasonably comparable to the Durand-Winn corporate and municipal bond yields.[21] The sole difference is that new issue yields were used rather than those from the secondary market. This can be viewed as more of an advantage than a disadvantage: the quality of issues in the secondary market is diverse and scattered; in some periods it is almost impossible to get enough observations for the drawing of

[19] David Durand and Willis J. Winn, *Basic Yields of Bonds, 1926-1947: Their Measurement and Pattern*, Technical Paper 6 (National Bureau, 1947).

[20] The first yield curve published by the Treasury appeared in the *Treasury Bulletin* for February 1939, but this analytical device had been used internally for some time previous to this publication date.

[21] Cited above; the basic corporate yields have since been kept up to date in the National Industrial Conference Board Economic Almanac.

TABLE 26

Maturity-Yield Relationship for Aaa State and Local Government Obligations

(per cent)

Years to Maturity	1945a	1946a	1947a	1948a	1949	1950	1951	1952	1953	1954	1955	1956
1	.40	.25	.65	.80	.65	.70	.90	1.00	1.15	.80	.80	1.50
2	.45	.30	.70	.90	.80	.80	.95	1.05	1.25	.90	.95	1.60
3	.50	.35	.75	1.00	.90	.85	1.00	1.10	1.35	1.00	1.05	1.70
4	.55	.40	.80	1.10	1.00	.90	1.03	1.13	1.40	1.10	1.15	1.77
5	.58	.45	.85	1.20	1.10	.95	1.05	1.15	1.45	1.15	1.23	1.80
6	.62	.50	.90	1.27	1.18	1.00	1.07	1.18	1.50	1.20	1.30	1.85
7	.66	.53	.95	1.33	1.25	1.05	1.10	1.22	1.55	1.25	1.38	1.87
8	.70	.57	.98	1.38	1.30	1.10	1.13	1.26	1.60	1.30	1.45	1.90
9	.73	.60	1.02	1.42	1.35	1.15	1.15	1.30	1.65	1.35	1.50	1.92
10	.76	.63	1.05	1.47	1.40	1.20	1.18	1.35	1.70	1.40	1.55	1.95
12	.82	.68	1.12	1.55	1.50	1.30	1.20	1.43	1.77	1.50	1.65	2.00
15	.90	.80	1.20	1.70	1.65	1.45	1.28	1.50	1.95	1.65	1.80	2.05
20	.98	.90	1.30	1.80	1.85	1.55	1.35	1.55	2.20	1.90	2.00	2.15
25	1.05	.96	1.38	1.85	1.90	...	1.45a	1.75	2.40a	2.15a	2.20	2.25
30	...	1.00	1.40	1.90	...	...	1.55a	1.80	...	2.30a	2.35	2.30
35	...	...	...	...	...	...	1.60a	2.00	...	2.35a	2.40	2.40
40	...	...	...	...	...	...	1.60a	2.05	...	...	2.45	2.40

a Rough approximation.

Source: Yields based on observation of yield curves drawn from offering scales of Aaa obligations brought to the market in the month of February for each year. If no Aaa offerings came in that month, observations were based on offerings of the preceding or following month or on Aa offerings with slight adjustment.

yield curves. New issues were relatively infrequent when the Durand-Winn municipal yield curves were being derived and the secondary market was relatively active.[22] Their choice of data was appropriate to that period. But conditions have since changed and emphasis is currently on the new issues market. Three of the years in this series overlap the period computed by Durand-Winn. The results are so similar that the new-issues basis seems to be fully justified.

The municipal yield curves are generally not parallel to those for Treasury obligations and corporate bonds in the following cases: (a) the upward slope of yields within and after the intermediate maturities is greater for municipal obligations than for Treasury or corporate bonds; (b) the dip at the very short-term end of the scale for Treasury obligations is not found in either the corporate or the municipal yield curves in anything like the same degree.

Both observations are consistent with recognized market characteristics. The two principal institutional buyers of municipal obligations—commercial banks and the fire and casualty insurance companies—both prefer the intermediate maturities. Indeed commercial banks prefer the quite short maturities but, as shown in Chapter 3, they are unable to meet their investment requirements within this range. The number of truly long-term investors is relatively less than in the corporate bond market. Life insurance companies and pension funds which dominate this latter market buy the longest maturities, but neither one is an important factor in the market for serial municipal obligations. Individuals buy long-term obligations but at a price. Thus the flatter slope to the intermediate range of the municipal yield curve squares with market logic. The very short-term end of the Treasury security market is the liquidity market—the one for bills, certificates, and the like. It is used for in-and-out investment. This special function of the Treasury security market often reduces short-term yields rather sharply. In this respect, short-term municipal obligations are rather more like corporate obligations than Treasury obligations.

Since railroad equipment obligations are issued in serial form it might be expected that the municipal and rail equipment offering scales would tend to be parallel. This is true only part of the time. Equipment trust offering scales parallel the Treasury yield curve

[22] See Chapter 5.

rather closely and usually show a little more bow in the intermediate range than is true of municipal bonds. In a period such as the fall of 1955, the parallel virtually disappeared. Equipment trust obligations then offered had little slope in their yield curve. In a number of cases, all the individual maturities were sold "flat," i.e., at the same yield. Commercial banks tapered off their buying, and equipment trust obligations had to be sold to pension funds. But pension funds require as high a yield for a short obligation as for a long-term one. During this same period, the slope to the offering scales for municipal obligations was usually fully as great or greater than that of Treasury obligations.

In 1956 further disparities in yield structures developed. When the money markets became tight, the yield-maturity pattern for U.S. Treasury obligations beyond the first few years became "humpbacked." Intermediate-term yields were above both short-term and long-term yields. But while the slope of the tax-exempt curve declined somewhat during this period, it never flattened out altogether. Explanation of this dissimilar experience appears to be the segmentation of the market. The tax-exempt market is dominated by a different group of buyers from the other capital markets. These buyers have different maturity preferences, hence variations in slopes of yield curves. Without buyers having adequate resources and sufficiently catholic tastes in maturities to arbitrage these markets, such differentials could persist indefinitely. Commercial banks are the only investors having these characteristics; when they are active, interest rate relationships show a more rational pattern. But when commercial banks withdraw from one of the capital markets, as they did in the latter part of 1955 and early 1956, yield arbitrage becomes more erratic.

As would be expected, the term structures of intermediate grades of securities do not parallel those of the top qualities. Generalized term structures for Baa bonds for a selected number of years were prepared for comparison with the Aaa term structures and are shown in Chart 12. As would be expected, the differentials for very short maturities are modest and tend to widen out for the longer maturities, with one exception. That exception is the year 1946 when the two term structures were virtually parallel from the one- to thirty-year maturity. The investment logic that accounted for this relationship is far from clear. The differential continues to widen up to about the fifteen-year maturity in most cases and thereafter tends to be a constant. The year 1948 is an exception. In that year the differential continued to spread out to the longest measureable maturity. But 1948 appears to be the one year which conforms to investment logic. Risk presumably is partly a function of time; the more remote the

CHART 12

Basic Yield Curves for Aaa and Baa Municipal Bonds, Selected Years

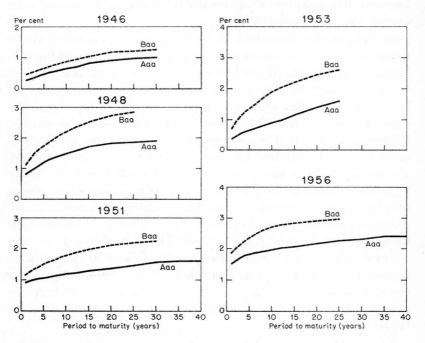

maturity, the greater the range of unforeseen contingencies. The logic of rating investment quality is largely that of margins of protection. No security is given one of the top four ratings unless it offers an "investment" quality likelihood of being paid according to contract. The margin of protection for the highest two grades is so large that it is hard to conceive of hazards that would upset the repayment probability. But this margin is not quite as generous in the intermediate grades. Time may erode this margin even further. And it would be logical that the more remote the time interval, the greater the possibility, per unit of time, that such erosion could take place.

The humpbacked nature to the yield curve for Treasury obligations in 1956 was basically due to the fact that commercial banks dominate the intermediate-term market. In that year commercial banks were both net sellers of intermediate-term obligations and also active traders of such securities in tax swaps.[23] Furthermore, it can be deduced that the very long-term yields on U.S. Treasury obligations were below those prevailing on intermediate-term obligations because relatively few long-term securities were outstanding or were being traded in the market. The few which were offered could be absorbed by investors who preferred U.S. Treasury obligations for special legal reasons—small state and local government pension funds, for example.

The offering scale of state and local government obligations, however, continued to have quite a bit of slope, possibly because the marginal expectation of investors in tax-exempt obligations is for higher interest rates. The very longest term obligations can be sold only if they offer investors somewhat more than can be earned in the intermediate market. The long maturities have to be baited with more yield than the shorter maturities of the same issues with which they are compared by investors.

Still another fact adds further evidence in support of this hypothesis. The offering scales of intermediate-grade tax-exempt obligations have had even more slope than those of the highest grades. Investors apparently felt that credit risk was not a proportionate but an increasing function of time. In other words, the maturity-yield relationship in the market for state and local government securities

---

[23] The foundation of the process of tax switching lies in a provision of the Internal Revenue code permitting commercial banks to charge all capital losses in excess of capital gains against current income. If a security, which is quoted considerably below book value, is sold and replaced with a security of similar maturity and yield, the current tax rate applies only to the coupon of the replacement issue: the accrual of discount is treated as a capital gain. Thus the greater the loss now taken, and the greater the proportion of subsequent income that can be taken on a capital gains basis, the more tax liabilities are reduced. The principal operating requirement is that commercial banks time their capital gains and losses in such a way that each tends to be concentrated in separate tax years. This is necessary so that losses do not have to be offset against gains but can be charged against current income. The deep discounts and high yields which characterize the prevailing humpbacked yield curve reflect the fact that few investors other than commercial banks are active traders in this part of the market.

apparently did not parallel the relationship prevailing in the market for Treasury obligations because investors in tax-exempt obligations compounded the joint influence of two risk appraisals: the risk of further increases in yields (and in capital losses on outstanding bonds) and also of a more rational time-function credit risk for lower-grade tax-exempt obligations.

One negative conclusion can be drawn from the comparison of maturity-yield differentials in the tax-exempt market with those prevailing on fully taxable obligations: investors do not imply complex tax-rate forecasts in their differential yield appraisal. At almost every juncture, the observed differentials made no sense if tested by prevailing expectations as to tax rates. This is a most odd conclusion. Investors certainly do have tax-rate expectations. During most of the postwar decade they apparently were prepared to pay as much for tax exemption in a remote period as in a nearby one: a pessimistic forecast of future tax rates! The most probable explanation is that many investors prefer a defensive posture; they will forego some yield to provide against the unknown and probably hostile future.

DIVIDING THE TAX-EXEMPTION SUBSIDY

A rational investor presumably invests in tax-exempt securities only at yields which are at least equal to, or greater than, the after-tax yield on fully taxable securities of comparable quality. This means that the yield differential between tax-exempt and fully taxable securities should not be a greater fraction of comparable fully taxable yields than the tax rate applying to this investor's marginal income. In practice, prudent investors probably do not go this far. Tax rates are known only for the present and immediate future; an investor may also be rather uncertain about his income expectations. Thus a prudent investor presumably would buy tax-exempt securities only if they offered some comfortable margin of protection against unexpected changes in tax rates and in income.

To the extent that this describes investment behavior correctly, the revenue lost by the federal government as a result of state and local governmental units selling tax-exempt securities will be only partly reflected in lowered borrowing costs to these governmental units. The tax revenue lost by the federal government is, in effect, split up between investors and state and local government borrowers. Tax exemption can be viewed as a subsidy of somewhat less than complete effectiveness; a direct subsidy from the federal to state and local government presumably would not have to be shared with investors.

The sharing of this revenue loss (or subsidy if one wishes to stress the equity considerations) can be viewed as a test of the balance of market power. If state and local governmental borrowers retain most of the revenue lost to the federal government in the form of lower borrowing costs the market could be said to reflect a strong demand or limited supplies of securities or both. If investors get most of the benefit, the market reflects a weaker demand, an ample supply of tax-exempt securities, or both.

A comparison of the yields on tax-exempt and full taxable obligations such as shown in Chart 8 suggests that there was a considerable shift in this division of gain during the postwar decade.

Estimation of this margin is statistically difficult. The measurement of revenue lost to the federal government as the result of tax exemption presents many technical obstacles; the estimation of reduced borrowing costs is almost as difficult. The revenue lost by the federal government depends on the marginal tax rates and alternative investment opportunities of those who buy and own tax-exempt securities. Present owners have bought the securities they now hold at varying times in the past: some acquired them directly from the underwriters when they were first publicly offered; others were bought in the secondary market. One of the functions of the secondary market presumably is to transfer tax-exempt securities from those who can make less complete use of the privilege of tax exemption to those who can make maximum use of the privilege. The chore of estimating the revenue losses for all outstanding securities thus presents a formidable problem. Estimation of the reduced borrowing cost on all outstanding securities would involve going far back into the history of such offerings, comparing market yields for fully taxable and tax-exempt obligations. Even though relatively simple in concept, the volume of historical research required to complete such an estimate would be impossibly burdensome.

A rough approximation of this relationship was made by limiting the comparison to new financing. One year's borrowing cost reduction for all securities issued during a year was compared with one year's loss of revenue to the federal government based on the tax rates applying to those who initially purchased these securities. Even this simplified form of comparison involves some conceptual and statistical difficulties. Changes in the holdings of tax-exempt securities provided by the ownership estimates are net; they are the result of gross purchases offset by sales or retirements by call or maturity. No method could be found by which net changes in the ownership estimates could be transmuted into a gross purchases series.

To approximate the revenue foregone, the estimated average tax rates for the two principal classes of buyers were applied to the yields on comparable fully taxable securities. The selection of what is "comparable" for various classes of investors is itself a matter of judgment. Some alternative investment outlets were introduced into these estimates: i.e., individuals might switch from tax-exempt securities to equities rather than to a fully taxable fixed-dollar form of security.

Estimation of the reduction of borrowing costs follows a similar pattern; the amount borrowed is multiplied by the differential in yield between the obligations actually issued and yields on comparable fully taxable obligations assumed in this case to be corporate bonds. Because acquisitions were net, the estimated borrowing cost reduction had to be adjusted by the ratio of net to gross acquisitions to make them comparable with the reduction-of-revenue estimates described above.

Such estimates for the years 1947-1955 are shown in Tables 27, 28, and 29. Table 27 presents the estimate of revenue lost by the U.S. Treasury. The owner-buyers of tax exempt obligations are divided into two groups for purposes of this estimate: corporations and individuals. A single marginal tax rate is used for individuals; our knowledge of holdings by income levels does not permit a more refined division of this group. The assumed investment alternatives were corporate bonds and stocks. In one estimate the investment alternative was assumed to be one having the same yield as Moody's corporate bond series. On the second estimate the investment alternative was assumed to be one having the same yield as Moody's corporate stock series. A third estimate assumed the proportions to be half of one and half of the other. Assumed differences as to in-

TABLE 27

Alternative Estimates[a] of Revenue Loss to Federal Government by Tax Exemption on State and Local Government Securities, 1947-1955

	Net Investment in Tax-Exempt Securities (millions of dollars)	Corporate Bond Yield[b]	Common Stock Yield[b]	Average Tax Rate	TAX LIABILITY	
					Bond Investment[c]	Equity Investment[d]
		(p e r c e n t)			*(millions of dollars)*	
Investment by Taxable Corporations[e]						
1947	959	2.86		38	10.7	
1948	614	3.08		38	7.2	
1949	1,171	2.96		38	13.2	
1950	1,886	2.86		45	24.3	
1951	1,384	3.08		52	22.2	
1952	1,414	3.19		52	23.5	
1953	1,380	3.43		52	24.6	
1954	2,548	3.16		52	41.9	
1955	905	3.25		52	15.3	
Investment by Individuals						
1947	498	2.86	5.13	60	8.5	15.3
1948	1,058	3.08	5.78	60	19.6	36.7
1949	650	2.96	6.63	60	11.5	25.9
1950	550	2.86	6.27	60	9.4	20.7
1951	430	3.08	6.12	60	7.9	15.8
1952	1,143	3.19	5.50	60	21.9	37.7
1953	1,814	3.43	5.49	60	37.3	59.8
1954	794	3.16	4.78	60	15.1	22.8
1955	1,748	3.25	4.06	60	34.1	42.6

Revenue Lost by Federal Government (millions of dollars)

	Bond Investment by Individuals Assumed[f]	Equity Investment by Individuals Assumed[g]	Half Bond/Half Equity Investments by Individuals Assumed[h]
1947	19.2	26.0	22.6
1948	26.8	43.9	35.3
1949	24.7	39.1	31.9
1950	33.7	45.0	39.3
1951	30.1	38.0	34.0
1952	45.4	61.2	53.3
1953	61.9	84.4	73.1
1954	57.0	64.7	60.8
1955	49.4	57.9	53.6

(notes on next page)

a Estimate for first-year revenue loss based on net purchases of principal investors.

b Assumed to be fully taxable investment.

c Net investment in tax-exempt securities times corporate bond yield times average tax rate.

d Net investment in tax-exempt securities times common stock yield times average tax rate.

e Consist of commercial bank and casualty insurance companies.

f Net investment in tax-exempt securities times corporate bond yield, times average tax rate for taxable corporations, plus comparable figure for individuals.

g Net investment in tax-exempt securities by individuals, times common stock yield, times average tax rate, plus comparable figure for taxable corporations based on corporate bond investment.

h Mean of f and g.

Source: Net amount in tax-exempt securities: Table A-3. Corporate bond yield: Moody's corporate bond annual average yield series. Average tax rate for taxable corporations is from tax rate tables in *Statistics of Income*. Average tax rate for individuals is an estimate made by C. Harry Kahn of the National Bureau staff. Kahn computed an average of the marginal tax rates for the various income levels reporting corporate dividends and tax-exempt interest in 1940, weighted by the amount of income so reported. In that year both items were adequately reported and tabulated in the *Statistics of Income* (Part I). He then computed a similar weighted average marginal tax rates for corporate dividends in 1947, 1952, and 1954. Tax-exempt interest was not reported in those years. By adding the absolute rate differential that prevailed in 1940, an estimated average of weighted marginal rates for holders of tax-exempt securities was reached. The estimates for the three years were 58.7, 62.9, and 59.8 per cent, respectively. A flat 60 per cent rate was used since the estimates gave no indication of secular movement either up or down. All other columns are computed.

---

vestment alternatives affected the final results less than might have been expected.

The reduction in borrowing cost for state and local governments (Table 28) was assumed to be the differential between tax-exempt and corporate bond yields of a comparable quality. State and local government offerings were arrayed by quality of issue. The yield differentials for each quality of issue and between tax-exempt municipals and the comparable corporate bonds, based on Moody's annual average yield series, was assumed to measure the reduction of borrowing cost. Unrated tax-exempt issues were assigned values a bit below those applying to Baa issues, the lowest rating grade for which a borrowing cost differential was computed.

The reduction in borrowing cost is compared with the revenue loss in Table 29. In 1947 from three-fifths to three-fourths of the revenue lost by the federal government was recovered by state and local governments in reduced borrowing cost. Up until 1952 this proportion varied from levels down to as low as two-fifths. But in 1953 it fell to a level between 20 and 30 per cent. It rose slightly in 1954 and 1955.

Computation of the estimated division was not made either for 1956 or for 1957. It seemed reasonably evident, however, that investors reaped most of the benefits of tax exemption. The amount state and local governments saved on borrowing costs was only a fraction of the revenue lost by the federal government; investors retained the bulk of this margin. While the differential seems to be sensitive to money markets and business conditions, even in a period such as 1954 state and local government did not recapture a great deal of the advantage of tax exemption. In the second half of the postwar decade more of the advantage of tax exemption went to investors than was retained by state and local governments. No development now in sight threatens (or promises) to change this relationship.

The general methods of estimating both the revenue foregone and the increase in cost of borrowing have precedent in earlier estimates made by the Treasury Department.[24] In 1939 they estimated on essentially this same basis that the amount of revenue lost by virtue of tax exemption on states and local government obligations was about double the amount that borrowing costs would increase if tax exemption were removed.

Conditions were, of course, considerably different at that time. Exemption from income taxation could also be secured by investment in various federal government securities. Rates of corporate taxation were much lower and the income stage at which progression was steepest for individuals was considerably higher. After allowing for these differences, however, the results are fully consistent with the estimates shown in Table 29.

The estimates presented here may minimize the differential between yields in periods of tense money markets because they are based on secondary market quotations. The gap between new issue yields of tax exempts and of taxable obligations may have been more fully maintained than those which prevailed in the secondary markets. New issue yield series for corporate and state and local government obligations have not been projected over the entire postwar decade in a statistically satisfactory way.[25] It is probably

[24] Hearings before the Committee on Ways and Means, House of Representatives, of the Seventy-sixth Congress, first session: *Proposed Legislation Relating to Tax-Exempt Securities*, June 28 to July 11, 1939, Exhibits 12 and 13, pp. 34-47.

[25] In the appendix of this chapter an 18-month new issue yield series for state and local government securities prepared by the Investment Bankers Association is examined.

TABLE 28

Reduction of State and Local Government Borrowing Costs as a Result of Federal Tax Exemption; Estimate for First-year Cost Reduction on Obligations Issued, 1947-1955

(dollar amounts in millions)

Class of Security	1947	1948	1949	1950	1951	1952	1953	1954	1955
Aaa									
1. Amount sold	262.1	642.8	200.7	322.1	630.9	631.5	926.3	798.0	831.1
Reduction in[a]									
2. Interest rate	1.16%	1.02%	1.01%	1.12%	1.25%	1.16%	.89%	.86%	.88%
3. Interest cost	3.0	6.6	2.0	3.6	7.9	7.3	8.2	6.9	7.3
Aa									
4. Amount sold	800.0	489.5	642.7	1,048.2	734.3	570.3	1,210.6	959.4	1,110.9
Reduction in[a]									
5. Interest rate	1.10%	.90%	.90%	.99%	1.13%	1.04%	.77%	.86%	.86%
6. Interest cost	8.8	4.0	5.8	10.4	8.3	5.9	9.3	8.3	9.6
A									
7. Amount sold	322.6	591.7	816.3	830.2	667.9	1,140.5	1,216.4	1,354.1	1,310.8
Reduction in[a]									
8. Interest rate	.87%	.62%	.65%	.79%	.96%	.83%	.46%	.58%	.59%
9. Interest cost	2.8	3.7	5.3	6.6	6.4	9.5	5.6	7.9	7.7

Baa									
10. Amount sold	185.6	198.7	427.3	305.0	270.4	284.4	418.1	392.0	457.5
Reduction in[a]									
11. Interest rate	.74%	.52%	.72%	.94%	1.04%	.82%	.33%	.42%	.39%
12. Interest cost	1.4	1.0	3.1	2.9	2.8	2.3	1.4	1.6	1.8
Unrated issues[b]									
13. Amount sold	783.5	1,117.0	908.5	1,188.1	974.7	1,774.7	1,786.5	3,465.1	2,266.1
Reduction in[a]									
14. Interest rate[c]	.60%	.40%	.60%	.75%	.90%	.70%	.25%	.30%	.30%
15. Interest cost	4.7	4.5	5.5	8.9	8.8	12.4	4.5	10.4	6.8
All issues									
16. Total sold	2,354	2,990	2,995	3,694	3,278	4,401	5,558	6,969	5,977
17. Interest cost reduction	20.7	19.7	21.6	32.3	34.2	37.5	29.0	35.0	33.2
18. Net purchases by taxed investors	1,457	1,672	1,821	2,436	1,814	2,557	3,194	3,342	2,653
19. Per Cent of total[d]	61.9%	55.9%	60.8%	63.5%	55.3%	58.1%	57.5%	48.0%	44.3%
20. Interest cost reduction on such purchases	12.8	11.0	13.1	20.5	18.9	21.8	16.7	16.8	14.7

[a] Reduction due to tax exemption.
[b] Includes a small amount of issues rated but less than Baa.
[c] Rough estimate based on Line 11.
[d] Since the estimates in Table 27 are for revenue lost on net purchases of principal investors, the cost-of-borrowing estimate for all securities issued is reduced in this step to an amount equivalent to the net purchases of the principal investors.

Source: Lines 1, 4, 7, 10, from percentages in Table 7 source times line 16. Line 18 from Table 27. Lines 2, 5, 8, and 11 are the differences between Moody's corporate bond annual average yields and Moody's series of annual average yields on state and local government general obligations for securities of same rating group. All other lines computed or derived as indicated.

TABLE 29

Percentage of Federal Tax Loss Retained by State and Local Governments as Reduced Borrowing Cost

| Year | INVESTMENT ASSUMPTIONS | | |
	Corporations: Corporate Bonds Individuals: Corporate Bonds (1)	*Corporations: Corporate Bonds Individuals: Equities* (2)	*Corporations: Corporate Bonds Individuals: Half Corporate Bonds and Half Equities* (3)
1947	67	49	58
1948	41	25	32
1949	53	34	43
1950	61	46	53
1951	63	50	56
1952	48	36	42
1953	27	20	23
1954	29	26	28
1955	30	25	27
Simple average	47	34	40
Weighted average	42	32	36

Source: Col. 1: Line 20, Table 28 ÷ Line 11, Table 27. Col. 2: Line 20, Table 28 ÷ Line 12, Table 27. Col. 3: Line 20, Table 28 ÷ Line 13, Table 27.

true that if such new issue yields were available the tax-exempt corporate differential probably would be larger in periods of tense money markets. Nevertheless, since the only clear differences between new issue yields and those in the secondary markets have come in periods of tight money markets, it is only in those periods that the criticism is relevant. For example, in 1954 it was quite clear that new issue yields were not greatly different from secondary market yields. In other words, the cyclical variability of the division is less than indicated by our estimates. Nevertheless, with full allowance for this factor, it seems clear that in the period since 1950 investors captured much more of the benefit of tax exemption than was retained by state and local governments.

Two other facts also seem indisputable. The savings in borrowing cost were least for the lower-grade securities and it was for these that the revenue lost by the federal government was the greatest. In other words, those units of state and local government that would seem to have been most deserving of aid in reducing borrowing cost or subsidy received the least benefit. The second fact is that this differential became greater in years of heavy borrowing. If allowance could be made for the fact that securities are probably shifted in the secondary market from those who make lesser use of tax exemption to those who maximize its use, the disparity between revenue lost to the federal government and reduction of borrowing cost would probably be even more striking than suggested by these estimates.

Appendix Note to Chapter 6

Measurement of Yields in State and Local Government Market

Measurement of yield in the market for state and local government securities presents an unusual number of technical problems. In the first place, the market is composed of thousands of individual issues, each of which has special characteristics. Secondly, we have too few prices of verified transactions. The offering scales on new issues are published but these prices represent actual prices only for successful offerings. On others concessions are common. We have no record of prices in the secondary market for serial issues except the asking prices of the *Blue List*.

These problems are encountered in other bond markets and

would not be particularly difficult except for still another problem, that of discontinuity. The continuity needed for index number construction is hard to manage. Two solutions are possible and both are employed: a time series can be built up on the basis of hypothetical quotations supplied by experienced traders, or the new issue yields of successful offerings can be used as a measure of the market. Three of the trade yield series—Standard Statistics, Dow-Jones,[26] and the Bond Buyer two series—solve the problem in the first way. In each case a basic list of bonds is prepared. Each week dealers are called and asked to supply quotations for each of these bonds. In some cases several quotations are received; in others one quotation for each bond is secured. In two of the three series, the dealers are asked to supply a quotation for a twenty-year bond of the given city or issuing body. No such bond need exist; it can be purely hypothetical. One of the series tries to use actual bonds that average near twenty years in maturity and makes substitutions from time to time.

Thus these series have some elements of unreality. It is known, for example, that in some periods actual transactions are shaded more from *Blue List* offering prices than is true in other periods. This may easily be true of these series; they are subject to the uncertainties of the market. In quoting to a statistical service, dealers are under no compulsion to "shade" price as if they were trying to make a deal. One other feature of some significance is the fact that two of the three series use relatively high coupon bonds. It is not clear that in their hypothetical bids the dealers make allowance for this factor.

The second alternative is followed by Moody's Investors' Advisory Service. Using their own rating grades, they array the offering scales by grade. Using the scales of offerings that are successful (or of revised offering scales when such are available) the yield value for the twenty-year maturity of each quality rating is determined. The yields of the four top grades are then averaged to produce the combined index.

The week-to-week and month-to-month variations in the several indexes move with considerable similarity. But more surprising, they seem to retain about the same relationship over long periods

[26] Dow-Jones formerly computed a revenue bond index but discontinued publication in February 1957.

of time. The one limit—and this is something that seems to apply to all of them—is that they lag a bit behind events. This reflects some lag in the informational process: the levels at which transactions take place take the form of revisions and price shading, but dealers, although fully conscious of the process, hesitate to reflect the change in quotations that are to be used for index computation until the change is widely known. This lag probably applied more on the down side of the market than on the up side.

None of the yield series now compiled generalize the maturity-yield relationship. Although provision of new primary material on interest rates was not a part of our project, we attempted to fill two gaps: to provide a quarterly series of yields, by quality, for several maturities: 1-year, 5-year, 10-year, 15-year, and 20-year. The latter was included primarily so as to provide a connecting link with the existing yield series. The second contribution, mentioned in the body of Chapter 6, was to determine generalized maturity-yield relationships for high-grade obligations annually. This was timed for February of each year and thus was aimed at extending the Durand-Winn basic yield series.[27] Maturity-yields were also generalized for Baa offerings in selected years to test the effect of quality on this relationship.

The testing of the various yield series led to one somewhat unexpected conclusion: general obligation state and local government securities in ordinary serial form apparently do not have the yield improvement or "seasoning" gain which is usually characteristic of corporate obligations. Revenue bonds in term form do pass through such a stage but a general obligation may never sell on a better basis relatively than when it is first issued. Thus the difference between new issue yields and yields in the secondary market, which plagues the measurement of corporate bond yields, has no evident counterpart in this market.

This does not mean that no such differences exist. It only means that from such evidence as exists, mainly from a short time series prepared by the Investment Bankers Association of America, the differences do not have a clear pattern; so far they seem to have a somewhat random quality.

A comparison of the new issue reoffering yields estimated by the Investment Bankers Association statistical service with yields

[27] Cited fully in the opening to Chapter 6.

in the secondary market such as shown by Moody's statistical service offers some interesting comparisons. In the first place, the new issue yields for a given quality of security are almost always materially lower than yields for the same grade in the secondary market. It is not clear that strict quality comparability prevails. From the side of cyclical analysis, an even more interesting point is that new issue yields are clearly more volatile than secondary market yields. New issue yields rise more quickly and by a greater amount in tight money periods and fall rather more quickly and by greater amounts when monetary ease returns. These differences are reflected in Table 30. As this table shows, the prompter and more considerable response is evident in all grades of securities. It is quite clear, however, that the most volatile response is found in the highest-grade obligations. This might be interpreted to mean that yields on lower-grade obligations are less influenced by monetary factors and are more influenced by quality of security.

The relationship of new issue yields to those prevailing in the secondary market apparently are not the same for tax-exempt securities as they are for long-term corporate bonds which are fully taxable. Since time series for tax-exempt new issue yields cover such a short period of time and since corporate series are not much longer the point cannot be affirmed with complete confidence. It appears, however, that on a new issue yield basis there would be less of a differential between corporate securities and tax-exempt securities than indicated by Chart 8. Even with allowance for this point, tax-exempt yields appear to fluctuate more than corporate bond yields even when measured on a new issue basis.

New issue yields for securities of varying quality do not always move in the same direction, as is evident in Table 30. Indeed, the variations by quality of security are so considerable as to suggest that some of the fluctuations in the market for tax-exempt securities might be due to fluctuations in the relative proportions of securities of various quality offered on the market. If the quality mix of this market is relatively volatile it may mean that new issue yields for given qualities of securities have a somewhat random character.

TABLE 30

New Issue Reoffering Yields, 1957 to June 1958

(median yields on 20-year maturities of general obligation bonds)

Month	Aaa		Aa		A		Baa	
	IBA New Issue	Secondary Market	IBA New Issue	Secondary Market	IBA New Issue	Secondary Market	IBA New Issue	Secondary Market
January	2.73	2.99	2.83	3.24	3.40	3.64	3.95	4.16
February	2.60	2.79	2.85	3.05	3.30	3.37	3.65	3.96
March	2.80	2.88	3.00	3.15	3.40	3.42	3.85	3.97
April	2.80	2.88	3.00	3.15	3.40	3.43	3.83	3.95
May	3.05	3.00	3.20	3.26	3.60	3.54	3.95	4.10
June	3.15	3.19	3.55	3.41	3.85	3.69	4.25	4.32
July	3.15	3.17	3.30	3.41	3.80	3.73	4.18	4.29
August	3.30	3.37	3.60	3.64	4.03	3.90	4.33	4.43
September	3.15	3.43	3.50	3.68	3.95	3.96	4.30	4.49
October	3.10	3.31	3.30	3.50	3.70	3.78	4.20	4.38
November	3.00	3.24	3.23	3.42	3.60	3.68	3.95	4.35
December	2.70	2.92	2.78	3.05	3.25	3.33	3.70	4.00
Monthly av.	2.96	3.10	3.18	3.33	3.61	3.62	4.01	4.20
1958								
January	2.45	2.75	2.70	2.94	3.10	3.18	3.60	3.81
February	2.63	2.72	2.88	2.96	3.25	3.13	3.65	3.79
March	2.70	2.79	2.90	3.04	3.40	3.22	3.65	3.88
April	2.70	2.70	2.75	3.00	3.18	3.17	3.60	3.78
May	2.65	2.69	2.80	2.95	3.10	3.12	3.50	3.71
June	2.73	2.74	2.90	3.01	3.25	3.20	3.45	3.78

Source: *IBA Bulletin*, No. 6, Jan. 1958, p. 3.

CHAPTER 7

The Market for Tax-Exempt Revenue Obligations

ONE of the principal features of postwar state and local government finance has been an increasing resort to so-called "revenue" financing. A governmental project that is revenue-producing may be separated from other governmental activities and made to support its own financing. Revenue may come from sale of a public service or it may be based on a lease with a public agency such as a school district. The full faith and general credit of sponsoring governmental agencies is not pledged in support of such debt. The line of demarcation that sets a revenue obligation apart is often not clear. Some revenue projects are based on leases under which the lessee government agency covenants that it will collect taxes sufficient to service the lease contract. Some revenue bonds are even directly supported by ear-marked taxes even though not "full faith and general credit" obligations. The IBA estimated that tax or lease contracts supported about one-fifth of the revenue bonds sold in 1957.[1] The forms of revenue projects are almost as numerous as ingenious lawyers and investment bankers can devise. Because of the diversity in form, the Governments Division of the Bureau of the Census has bracketed the many forms of these obligations under the general title of "nonguaranteed" debt.

During the postwar period the amount of revenue or nonguaranteed debt has grown from about one-tenth to over one-quarter of the outstanding long-term debt of state and local government, as shown in Table 31. More than one-third of the net increase in tax-exempt debt since 1948 was in the form of revenue obligations. The proportion of net increase was greater than that of offerings because of the long average maturity of these obligations.[2] Explicit knowledge of the amount outstanding cannot be pushed back of 1948, the first year for which the Bureau of the Census collected a separate figure for this type of debt. However, until 1949 the Census compiled figures of so-called "enterprise" debt: the obligations of government-owned enterprises. For the two years

[1] *IBA Statistical Bulletin*, Oct. 1957, No. 5, p. 2.
[2] Over 40 per cent of those sold in 1956-1957 had a maturity in excess of thirty years. *Ibid.*, p. 1 and 2.

TABLE 31

Nonguaranteed State and Local Government Long-term Debt

| Year | LONG-TERM DEBT | | Nonguaranteed as a Proportion of Total (per cent) |
| | Nonguaranteed | Total | |
	(millions of dollars)		
1948	1,920	17,614	10.9
1949	2,474	20,141	12.3
1950	3,264	23,141	14.1
1951	4,197	25,549	16.4
1952	5,314	28,720	18.5
1953	6,524	32,004	20.2
1954	8,645	36,898	23.4
1955	11,733	42,272	27.8
Increase, 1948-1955	9,813	24,658	39.7

Source: Bureau of the Census, Governments Division publications: "Government Debt" series (G-GF) for 1948 to 1951. "Summary of Government Finances" series for 1952-1955 data; Table 17 in 1955 summary. Figures for 1949, 1950, and 1952 were revised upward in the subsequent census tables presumably because of identification of additional cases. If this accounts for the revisions, the data for the early years may be low by as much as 10 to 15 per cent. Because of incomplete revision of the earlier data, the 1948-1955 increase shown above may be somewhat overstated.

These data do not square with those shown in Appendix A and used elsewhere in the text because they are based on the census fiscal year figures.

of overlap in which both figures were compiled, 1948 and 1949, the amount of enterprise debt was about three times the amount of nonguaranteed debt. But the growth appears to have been parallel. This slim evidence suggests that nonguaranteed or revenue debt had earlier been an even smaller portion of the total.[3] The portion of revenue obligations in new public offering has also been increasing though not with the unbroken regularity shown by the outstanding debt; this is shown in Table 32. This table, being based on tabulations prepared by the trade publication, the *Bond Buyer*, may not classify securities in exactly the same way as that followed by the Census in its tabulation of "nonguaranteed" debt.

[3] Revenue obligations are mentioned as ". . . increased in importance and popularity," by Harry L. Severson in *Municipals* (National Association of State Bank Supervisors, 1941), p. 34.

But we have no reason to suspect a fundamental difference; indeed the ratio of revenue to total obligations in the new offerings series apparently should produce just about the ratio of nonguaranteed and total debt shown by the Census.

TABLE 32

Revenue Obligations as a Proportion of New State and Local Government Security Offerings

| Year | Revenue | Total | Revenue as a Ratio of Total |
	(millions of dollars)		(per cent)
1946	206	1,204	17.1
1947	386	2,354	16.4
1948	550	2,990	18.4
1949	683	2,995	22.8
1950	600	3,694	16.2
1951	730	3,278	22.3
1952	1,463	4,401	33.3
1953	1,567	5,558	28.2
1954	3,214	6,969	46.2
1955	1,710	5,904	29.0
Total: 1946-55	11,109	39,347	28.3

Source: The *Bond Buyer*, sales summaries.

Two other bits of evidence concerning the growth of revenue financing may be cited. The *Issuer Summary* compiled from evidence presented at the anti-trust trial of the investment bankers shows that the defendant investment bankers handled 1.7 billions of new issue "municipal" revenue bond sales from July 1933 through 1945.[4] Although the use of revenue financing came to have material significance only in the 1930's, isolated intervals of its use may be found much earlier.[5]

[4] Vol. 2, end section.
[5] In 1871, Lawrence, Kansas, issued bonds with which to build a dormitory for the newly established University of Kansas. Although initially general obligations of the city, they were later made a kind of revenue obligation by a special act of the state legislature. A. M. Hillhouse, *Municipal Bonds: A Century of Experience* (Prentice-Hall, 1936), p. 96.

FACTORS ACCOUNTING FOR RECOURSE
TO REVENUE FINANCING

The circumstances underlying the growing importance of revenue financing can be roughly divided into two general groups. One reason was developed in Chapter 2: the fact that many state and local governmental units have approached debt limits that circumscribed their activities. The devices invented by lawyers for relief of this situation have often taken the form of a new governmental entity which had a kind or degree of borrowing power denied the basic governmental unit.[6] But since it was generally not possible to give these new creatures of government taxing powers without breaching the basic prohibitions of the law, these new bodies had to be given a source of revenue with which to service their debts. Thus the school building authorities or corporations[7] are created to provide the buildings; their revenues come from leases with the underlying school districts which have many of the same characteristics as a tax dedication.

But the most important circumstance lying back of revenue financing generally has usually been the inauguration of new business-type activities to which state and local governments have been willing to extend the privilege of tax exemption but not of their basic full faith and general credit. Some of this is a quite old story. During the period when development of public power facilities was considerably more important than it has been recently, such enterprises were usually subsidized by access to the privilege of making their securities tax-exempt. But this was felt by some to be an adequate subsidy and the second step of granting the subsidy of shelter under the public credit was denied them.[8] This sort of circumstance accounts for a great proportion of the cases of revenue obligations: water and sewer systems, irrigation and drainage districts, bridges, tunnels, toll roads, off-street parking facilities, ports, airports, college dormitories, and sometimes even factories and

[6] The Commonwealth of Pennsylvania has over one thousand authorities, most of which have borrowed.

[7] Such as in Pennsylvania, Kentucky, or Indiana.

[8] Public housing has been given both subsidies: tax exemption of its financing and a guarantee by the federal government. This is achieved by making the individual public housing authorities local governmental units (not federal) so their borrowing enjoys tax exemption, but the federal government then enters into a contract with each one up to their allotted quota of construction, for underwriting of debt service.

hotels sponsored by local government to attract outside business. The philosophy is that since individual citizens do not benefit equally from all these various types of activities, the credit of "all the people" should not be used to support them. But the line is not sharply drawn. Toll road systems of two large states—New York and New Jersey—are financed by a combination of revenue and guaranteed obligations. A further possible flaw in the logic is that many investors in these obligations seem to assume that the sponsoring governmental agencies that created these creatures would not let their obligations go into default. Although this assurance is carefully and explicitly denied in each revenue financing, the hope apparently is a market factor of not inconsiderable importance.

The Investment Bankers Association has condemned the use of tax exemption (by cities mainly) to build industrial buildings and hotels which are used as bait to attract new businesses. But the importance of these instances is small; a far more important type of activity has been the use of tax exemption to finance the construction of electric power generation facilities for the service essentially of private enterprises.

Most of these cases are found in the western part of the United States where the public-private power issue is still a hot one. Special power districts or even irrigation districts have sometimes borrowed on a tax-exempt basis for the construction of a power plant, usually a hydroelectric one.[9] The significant point in most of these cases is that the revenue bond financing was supported and made palatable to investors by being founded on a long-term contract with a financially responsible private utility firm for the sale of power at rates sufficient to service the bonds. This is not to say that the private utility benefited indirectly from tax exemption. Presumably the rates at which it resells the power to the public reflects its costs.

Sometimes tax exemption is used to support the revenue financing of public operation of utilities that have experienced serious financial problems under private operation: street railway systems are

[9] In at least one case an irrigation district built a steam-generating plant with the candid intention of "rounding out" its power-generating facilities. In most cases the hydroelectric installations have some semblance of connection with the basic irrigation plans of the sponsoring districts, though in some cases it is hard to find much engineering justification for the projects on such grounds.

a leading example. Isolated cases can also be found of ferryboat systems or other struggling public utilities that have been taken over after failing to survive under private and fully taxed operations.

FORM OF REVENUE OBLIGATIONS

The popular identification of revenue obligations with toll road bonds has led to the assumption that most revenue obligations were in term (single maturity) rather than serial form. An IBA analysis of the revenue obligations sold in the year ended June 30, 1957 showed that only about one-quarter were in term form; the great bulk were in serial form.[10] Water and sewer bonds are almost always in serial form, as is true of most school building corporation and college dormitory bonds. On the other hand, most toll road, many port, airport, bridge, some public utility, and "industrial" bonds are in term form. Some toll road authorities have financed with a combination of serial and term bonds.

In some cases, by the wondrous magic of legal invention, it has been possible to issue tax-exempt "industrial" bonds which were convertible into common stock or to which common stock warrants were attached.

When term bonds are used, they are almost always callable. Call for refunding purposes is often made costly and sometimes prohibitive. But call by lot of bonds to be retired by earnings is generally permitted. And in most of the projects, the margin of coverage is such that—if realized—the outstanding issues would all be retired before ultimate maturity.[11] Call provisions are being attached to serial bonds with increasing frequency.

NATURE OF THE MARKET

The market for revenue obligations is partly but not altogether set apart from the market for full faith and credit obligations. Buyers tend to treat them as more nearly like corporate obligations, and the yields on them are often quite comparable to yields available on corporate bonds. Informed security analysts study the supporting economic expectations back of a revenue obligation very

[10] *IBA Statistical Bulletin*, October 1957, No. 5, p. 4.
[11] Some such projects then pass into the realm of free public facilities: toll roads become free roads, toll bridges become free bridges, etc. Or school buildings revert from ownership by the authority or corporation to the ownership of the leasing school district.

much in the same way that corporate obligations are scrutinized. The ratio of funds available for debt service to the minimum requirements is computed, the margins for under-realization of expectations given respectful attention. If the coverage is adequate and the basic revenue source has some degree of assurance and stability, then the obligation merits a high rating; if not, it is given a more modest standing.

High-quality revenue obligations are often bought by investors in tax-exempt obligations along with full faith and credit obligations. Since Federal Reserve member commercial banks cannot underwrite these issues, they are less enthusiastic investors in them; the remote maturities of most term issues are also inappropriate to their needs. (Nevertheless they owned $1,849 million of them in mid-1956, or about one-sixth of the total amount outstanding.) A few of these bonds also turn up in the portfolios of fire and casualty companies.

Some of the larger and more publicized revenue projects have been new ventures. The investment rating agencies, as a matter of policy, will not assign ratings to an untested venture, so the obligations of such projects are sold "unrated." This has given the impression that revenue bonds are not of top credit quality. This impression is wrong. A very large proportion of revenue projects financed are of continuing and proved projects and so have relatively good credit standing. In the IBA survey of revenue bonds financing for the year ending June 1957, they found that almost 30 per cent of the obligations had a credit rating of Aa and another 30 per cent were rated A.[12] "Unrated" obligations were about one-third of the total, and obligations having a rating of Baa were less than 8 per cent of the total. None of a lower rating were marketed.

INVESTORS IN REVENUE OBLIGATIONS

In spite of the relatively good credit rating of revenue obligations, the market for them appears to be somewhat more limited than that for full-faith and general credit obligations. The investors who buy these obligations apparently view them much as they would the obligations of corporate ventures and apply some of the

[12] *IBA Statistical Bulletin*, October 1957, No. 5, p. 4.

standards of investment analysis to them that are commonly applied to corporate obligations.

Individuals apparently buy most of the more speculative revenue bonds. A tax-exempt security with fairly generous returns appeals to investors who wish to enjoy tax protection combined with some opportunity for capital appreciation. Both life insurance companies and mutual savings banks have also concentrated their buying of tax-exempt obligations among revenue bonds. Life insurance companies particularly are concerned about their current earning rate. Since their marginal federal income tax liability is only 6½ per cent (see Chapter 3) they are not disposed to pay a large price for tax exemption. But the future is uncertain and tax laws are frequently changed; the value of tax exemption could be greater and life insurance company investment managers doubtless have had this in the backs of their minds. If their forecasting of these revenue projects turns out to be astute, they can then decide whether to realize the capital gains that will follow or to continue to use and enjoy the privilege of tax exemption at a fairly good rate of return, compared with cost. Mutual savings banks are in a similar position except that some are already exposed to federal income taxation and others are within its shadow.

COSTS AND YIELDS FOR TAX-EXEMPT REVENUE FINANCING

The costs of financing a project the revenue from which supports the credit cannot be generalized. The matter is one for security analysis, as we have already explained, and the basis of judgment depends on the individual case. There is a life cycle for most revenue projects not unlike that which prevails in business finance. When an enterprise is started, credit analysis is really a matter of forecasting. No matter how bright the prospects, investors quite reasonably expect a better rate of return as the price for risking their money on an unproved project. But, of course, all projects are not equally unproved. Water and sewer plants for residential communities that are already in existence and growing represent little gamble—the basic demand for these services is hardly touched by fluctuations in general business conditions. The operating problems of such public services have been encountered and solved many times before; few technological risks remain to be faced. A toll road or a toll bridge is something else. One much publicized toll bridge was built over a section of the Missouri River, which at that time was a dry branch. This was done with the expectation that army engineers would later rechannel the Missouri back into the stream bed that ran under this bridge. But Congressional appropriations were cut in the postwar economy drive and the river was not restored to its original channel. The investment banking firm which had marketed the bonds made strenuous efforts to secure the appropriation needed to put the river back in the channel which would have made the bridge useful. In 1953 such appropriations were made and the river was restored to its original bed. In 1956 tolling was finally started on the bridge.

INTEREST COST OF REVENUE FINANCING

It is not uncommon to find the coupon required to sell an unrated revenue bond about 2 percentage points above high-grade tax-exempt yields. A great deal of the financing of new toll roads has been at about this differential. After an enterprise has been in operation for some period, and has demonstrated adequate capacity to earn, then its obligations may appreciate to a lower yield basis. The record is not unmarred; several projects have only barely earned their debt service requirements and a few have failed to do even this much. An authority which has established the record of planning and executing successful revenue-producing projects can usually get money on its new ventures advantageously. The Port of New York Authority, which operates not only port facilities but three tunnels, a bridge, and four airports, furnishes a good example. Port of New York Authority financing is generally at relatively favorable rates for revenue obligations.

But revenue financing nevertheless involves the payment of a materially higher price for money than is true of full faith and credit financing. In the spring of 1956 the Port of New York Authority borrowed at a net cost to itself of 3.04 per cent. In the same week, two private utilities with the same credit rating as the "Port" also borrowed; their cost averaged 3.6 per cent. At the same time, high-grade full-faith and credit tax-exempt obligations of about the same maturity were being marketed at a cost of about 2.5 per cent. In other words, investors were accepting a return that was 30 per cent lower for the privilege of exemption from federal income taxes for the good general obligations. For the obligation of a public authority with demonstrated earning capacity and some diversification of revenue sources, investors were willing to concede only a 15 per cent lower return for the privilege of tax exemption. A few weeks later, when the general market had improved another comparison could be drawn. The General State Authority of the Commonwealth of Pennsylvania sold a moderate-sized block of revenue bonds ($20,000,000) at about the same time some full-faith and credit obligations of California for bonus payments were sold. The cost differential was about 30 basis points for equivalent maturities. It is invidious to compare the quality of credit of these two great states, but both deserve a high rating. It seems clear that most of the differential was due to the revenue status of the Pennsylvania borrowing.

Margins or differentials required for revenue financing can be tested in one more way: an examination of the borrowing costs of the school building authorities or corporations in Pennsylvania and Kentucky and Indiana. Exact measurement is impossible; comparison of the credit of school districts across wide areas is dangerous. But a general judgment, supported by the opinions of market observers, is about as follows: when these revenue devices for circumventing the debt limits were employed, investors required margins of from 1½ per cent to 2½ per cent over the going rate on general obligations. In the early postwar days these obligations required returns of 3½ to 4 per cent to find a market when general obligations were selling from 1½ to 2 per cent. In 1954 and 1955, with judicial testing of these obligations and some investment experience, they settled down to a differential of from about ¾ of 1 per cent to 1½ per cent over general obligations.

It is thus quite evident that the costs of tax-exempt revenue borrowing lie somewhat between full faith and credit costs and the yields of fully taxable obligations, but rather nearer the latter. One further point seems fairly evident: when revenue financing has been substituted for full-faith and credit financing—such as in school building—this has not wholly sheltered the market for general obligations. Investors cannot put their money both places; if they buy tax exemption in one form, they have withdrawn their demand for other types of tax-exempt instruments.

Although it is not feasible to compare borrowings costs of different debtors, particularly over periods of time, the secondary market for outstanding revenue bonds can be measured. This had been done by the *Wall Street Journal.* Until February 1957 they computed an index based on ten outstanding revenue bonds, the yields being the market reports of dealers but not based on actual transactions. The series is shown in Chart 13, together with the Moody's

CHART 13

Offering Yields on Toll Road Bonds Compared with Yields on Outstanding Revenue Bonds

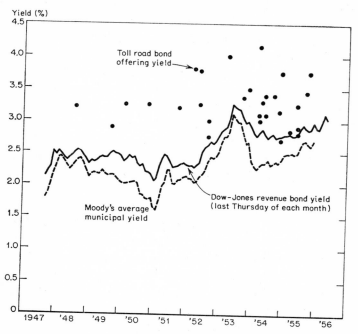

index. The ten bonds included in the Dow-Jones index, with two exceptions, would be counted as unusually high-grade revenue obligations. This series, therefore, cannot be used to measure new money costs. As indicated earlier, toll road bonds require the seasoning which can come only from actual operations. This is shown by the plotting of the new issue yield of most of the major toll road issues marketed during this period. Toll road bond interest rates show no clear pattern of conformity to the general market for outstanding obligations, though individual offerings clearly are so influenced.

APPENDIX A

Statistics of State and Local Government Debt, 1945-1956

TABLE A-1

Gross State and Local Government Debt, End-of-Year, 1945-1956

(millions of dollars)

Year end	Gross Debt (1)	Noninterest Bearing Debt (2)	Interest Bearing Debt (3)	Short-term Debt (4)	Long-term Debt (5)
1945	19,242	296	18,946	353	18,593
1946	18,819	296	18,523	454	18,069
1947	20,354	322	20,032	551	19,481
1948	22,699	371	22,328	625	21,703
1949	25,234	432	24,802	781	24,021
1950	28,528	459	28,069	932	27,137
1951	30,998	480	30,518	919	29,599
1952	34,235	524	33,711	1,194	32,517
1953	38,026	570	37,456	1,645	35,811
1954	42,475	602	41,873	1,847	40,026
1955	46,193	600	45,593	1,579	44,014
1956	49,641	600	49,041	1,527	47,514

Source:

Column:

1   Privately held interest bearing state and local governments securities outstanding was calculated by applying the Securities and Exchange Commission worksheet series "Total Net Change" (SEC-w19, line 5) to the June 30, 1955 census figure in the *Annual Report of the Secretary of the Treasury*, 1956, page 499, table 49, column 10, Part v. "Noninterest-bearing securities," from Table A-1, col. 2, and "state and local government securities held by governments," Table A-2, col. 4, were then added to this series.

2   Straight line interpolation of Treasury Department June figures, *Annual Report of the Secretary of the Treasury*, 1955, page 512, Table 49.

3   Col. 1 minus Col. 2.

4   A seven-month moving total of short-term offerings in the *Bond Buyer's* "A Decade of Municipal Finance." Technique suggested by Friend and Natrella.

5   Col. 3 minus Col. 4.

TABLE A-2

Publicly and Privately Held State and Local Government Securities, End-of-Year, 1945-1956

(millions of dollars)

Year end	Total Interest Bearing Securities (1)	PUBLICLY HELD BY			Total Private Held (5)
		State and Local Governments (2)	Federal Government (3)	Total Governments (4)	
1945	18,946	2,832	505	3,337	15,609
1946	18,523	2,363	484	2,847	15,676
1947	20,032	2,451	503	2,954	17,078
1948	22,328	2,593	573	3,166	19,162
1949	24,802	3,104	488	3,592	21,210
1950	28,069	3,587	555	4,142	23,927
1951	30,518	3,785	816	4,601	25,917
1952	33,711	4,025	1,138	5,163	28,548
1953	37,456	4,354	806	5,160	32,296
1954	41,873	4,690	480	5,170	36,703
1955	45,593	5,078	480	5,558	40,035
1956	49,041	5,499	530	6,029	43,012

Source:
Column:

1	Table A-1, col. 3.
2	*Federal Reserve Flow-of-Funds worksheets* (FRB-w22, col. 1).
3	*Federal Reserve Flow-of-Funds worksheets* (FRB-w22, col. 2).
4	**Sum** of Col. 2 and Col. 3.
5	Col. 1 minus Col. 4.

Privately Held State and Local Government Securities, End-of-Year, 1945-1956

(millions of dollars)

	Commercial Banks (1)	Mutual Savings Banks (2)	Life Insurance Companies (3)	Fire and Casualty Insurance Companies (4)	Fraternal Societies (5)	Nonbank Security Dealers (6)	Miscellaneous Financial Institutions (7)	Nonfinancial Corporations (Except Dealers) (8)	Agencies of Foreign Banks (9)	Residual, Mainly Individuals (10)	Total Privately Held (11)
					SECURITIES HELD BY						
1945	3,970	93	722	249	342	300e	21	319	34	9,559	15,609
1946	4,395	63	614	237	348	340	19	321	23	9,316	15,676
1947	5,276	65	609	315	343	243	21	357	35	9,814	17,078
1948	5,661	71	872	544	347	267	22	409	97	10,872	19,162
1949	6,548	86	1,052	828	342	252	23	460	97	11,522	21,210
1950	8,118	88	1,152	1,144	326	370	43	528	86	12,072	23,927
1951	9,198	147	1,170	1,448	325	384	48	580	115	12,502	25,917
1952	10,189	325	1,153	1,871	328	228	51	645	113	13,645	28,548
1953	10,821	407	1,298	2,619	317	430	57	736	152	15,459	32,296
1954	12,586	600	1,846	3,402	327	500e	76	955	158	16,253	36,703
1955	12,698	637	2,038	4,195	348	600e	108	1,205	205	18,001	40,035
1956	12,901	669	2,273	4,916	348e	500e	123	1,280	250e	19,752	43,012

Source:
Column:

1   Federal Reserve all-bank statistics reported either in *Federal Reserve Bulletin* table "Loans and Investments of Commercial Banks by Classes", or in the G-7 release.

2   *Annual Reports* of the Federal Deposit Insurance Corporation.

3   *Life Insurance Fact Book*, annual table, "State, Provincial and Local Bonds Owned by U.S. Life Insurance Companies."

4   1945-51 from Federal Reserve flow-of-funds worksheets. 1952-56 from *Best's Aggregates and Averages* adjusted for undercoverage of mutuals and to exclude Traveler's Insurance Company.

5   *Postwar Capital Markets* statistical summaries.

6   Rough estimate using benchmark estimate from Wharton's study of over-the-counter markets projected by changes shown in the *Blue List.*

7   Federal Reserve all-bank statistics combined with *Postwar Capital Markets* tabulation of investment company holdings.

8   Securities and Exchange Commission savings worksheets.

9   *Postwar Capital Markets* worksheets.

10   Computed: cols. 11 minus sums of cols. 1-9.

11   Table A-2, col. 5.

TABLE A-4

Percentage Distribution of Privately Held State and Local Government Securities,
End-of-Year, 1945-1956

Year End	Commercial Banks (1)	Mutual Savings Banks (2)	Life Insurance Companies (3)	Fire and Casualty Insurance Companies (4)	Fraternal Societies (5)	Non-bank Security Dealers (6)	Miscellaneous Financial Institutions (7)	Nonfinancial Corporations (Except Dealers) (8)	Agencies of Foreign Banks (9)	Residual, Mainly Individuals (10)	Total Privately Held (11)
				PER CENT OF SECURITIES HELD BY							
1945	25.4	00.6	04.6	01.6	02.2	01.9	00.1	02.0	00.2	61.3	100.0
1946	28.0	00.4	03.9	01.5	02.2	02.2	00.1	02.0	00.2	59.4	100.0
1947	30.9	00.4	03.6	01.8	02.0	01.4	00.1	02.1	00.2	57.5	100.0
1948	29.5	00.4	04.6	02.8	01.8	01.4	00.1	02.1	00.5	56.7	100.0
1949	30.9	00.4	05.0	03.9	01.6	01.2	00.1	02.2	00.5	54.3	100.0
1950	33.9	00.4	04.8	04.8	01.4	01.5	00.2	02.2	00.4	50.5	100.0
1951	35.5	00.6	04.5	05.6	01.3	01.5	00.2	02.2	00.4	48.2	100.0
1952	35.7	01.1	04.0	06.6	01.1	00.8	00.2	02.3	00.4	47.8	100.0
1953	33.5	01.3	04.0	08.1	01.0	01.3	00.2	02.3	00.5	47.9	100.0
1954	34.3	01.6	05.0	09.3	00.9	01.4	00.2	02.6	00.4	44.3	100.0
1955	31.7	01.6	05.1	10.5	00.9	01.5	00.3	03.0	00.5	45.0	100.0
1956	30.0	01.6	05.3	11.4	00.8	01.2	00.3	03.0	00.6	45.8	100.0

Results of Conventional (Nonaccrual) Method of Computing Interest Cost Which Prevails in Competitive Bidding for State and Local Government Issues

INTEREST cost computations are all based in some measure on rules or conventions. No one method can be considered categorically "right" and all other methods wrong. But in practice it is widely agreed that the "present value" method of computing the value of bonds as it is used in preparing bond tables presents a close approximation to what is normally thought of as interest cost or interest expense.[1] It is true, of course, that even this method has some elements of approximation, the greatest one being introduced by the existence of a term structure of interest rates. For example, when a bond with its attached coupons is discounted to its present value, the calculated yield assumes the same rate for discounting each maturity. But this assumption does some violence to the facts of the market; sloping yield curves often prevail. However, for most purposes this flaw is not important so long as both parties to a transaction in securities understand this fact.

The computation of interest cost made in picking winning bids for virtually all state and local government bond issues in the United States, however, is not based on a "present value" type of computation; it is based on an older formula. This formula will be demonstrated in detail later in this appendix, but it amounts to a simple ratio of coupons to principal weighted by the period the principal is outstanding.

Because such a large proportion of state and local government securities are in serial form, the persistence of this older form of computation is understandable. Other rules would make for more complex calculations. But its existence is largely an anachronism which often tends to focus attention on the wrong factors. Later in this appendix we shall argue this point at greater length. At this juncture it would be better to illustrate this method of com-

---

[1] The "present value" form of calculation is also sometimes referred to as the "accrual" or "annuity" method of computing bond values.

putation and then to study some of its variations in practice. A hypothetical illustration has been devised and then elaborated to help in the exposition of this problem (see Table B-1).

TABLE B-1

Hypothetical Illustration of Conventional (Nonaccrual) Method of Computing Interest Cost Prevailing in State and Local Government Borrowing

Part 1. Assume $10,000 borrowed in 1956 to mature in equal annual instalments of $1,000 over the next ten years and assume coupons shown in Column 5

Maturity	Years to Maturity (Assumed)	Principal Maturing Each Year	Principal Outstanding for One Year (Col. 2 × col. 3)	Coupon (Assumed)	Interest Cost (Col. 4 × col.
1957	1	$1,000	$1,000	4	40
1958	2	1,000	2,000	4	80
1959	3	1,000	3,000	4	120
1960	4	1,000	4,000	2¼	90
1961	5	1,000	5,000	2¼	112.50
1962	6	1,000	6,000	2½	150
1963	7	1,000	7,000	2½	175
1964	8	1,000	8,000	2½	200
1965	9	1,000	9,000	2½	225
1966	10	1,000	10,000	2½	250
Total			$55,000		1,442.5

Interest cost computation: $1,442.50 ÷ $55,000 = 2.6227 per cent.

Part 1 of the illustration sets up the basic circumstances that might prevail in a very simple and uncomplicated state or local government financing. To ease the computations, small amounts have been used and all figures are rounded to the extent possible. The only departure from utter simplicity is that involved in the coupon structure assumed. In this case, we have used three different coupon rates. As was developed in Chapter 4 above, such a coupon system would not be far from those which often prevail: high for the first few maturities, i.e., 4 per cent; dropping back to 2¼ per cent in the middle and then up a bit again to 2½ per cent in the later maturities. The so-called interest cost is simply the number of dollars that will be paid out as coupons. The "principal outstanding for one year" is each year's serial obligation, multiplied by the number of years it will be outstanding. The total of "principal outstanding for one year" is the equivalent of a single amount if it were at interest for one year.[2] The average rate of interest cost is then simply the interest cost in dollars divided by the total "principal outstanding for one year." If the bidder offers a premium, it is deducted from the dollar amount of coupons before computing the rate of interest cost. This will be illustrated in later parts.

It should be noted that this form of computation makes no distinction between a dollar of interest paid during the early years of the obligation and a dollar of interest paid in the late years near final maturity. According to a present value basis of computation, of course, the earlier dollar is worth more and correspondingly "costs" more than a later dollar. This lies back of much of the complexity in the coupon structures of many state and local government issues. Most of the sale announcements allow bidders to name the coupon or coupons to be placed in the proposed issue. Some invitations allow the bidders to name only one coupon rate; others permit varying "split coupon" arrangements. Usually only one coupon can be named for each maturity, but in a few cases more than one coupon rate for a given maturity is allowed. While the nonaccrual interest cost computation formula makes no distinction between early coupon dollars and later ones, the market does. In all investment markets, including that for state and local government securities, the conventions of computation are on a "present value" basis. Underwriters, therefore, can realize more from the sale of a given dollar volume of coupons on early maturities (where the discount to present value of the coupon is small) than for a similar volume of coupons on later maturities. Accordingly, there is a general disposition for the underwriters to put high coupons on early issues and lower ones on the longer maturities. The more this is done, the lower the computed interest cost ac-

---

[2] If the amounts in each maturity of an issue are equal and the period to maturity is in whole number digits, then the simple sum of digits formula could be used; i.e., $\dfrac{n(n+1)}{2}$ in this case $\dfrac{10(10+1)}{2} = 55$ times \$1,000 = \$55,000. In practice these assumptions are quite often not true so the more direct even if more laborious calculation is usually performed.

cording to this archaic formula of state and municipal bidding. It is not a real saving to the borrowing governments, only a fictional one. The trouble is that this fiction has even fooled some members of the investment banking community. They speak of spending tedious hours in the price meetings held by syndicates working out coupon structures that will "save the borrowing government's money." Nothing is being saved, of course, and the market is only being made that much more complex.

This is shown in Part 2 of the hypothetical illustration (see Table B-2). For the purpose of this part one added assumption has been made: that of an up-sweeping yield "curve," a straight line in this case. Three different hypothetical cases are presented. In the first

TABLE B-2

Hypothetical Illustration

Part 2. Same assumptions as in Part 1, with added assumptions about prevailing yields and different coupon assumptions

Maturity	Prevailing Yield (Assumed)	CASE 1 Coupon-Yield Interest Cost	CASE 2 2.6 Per Cent Coupon Interest Cost	Price	Coupon (per cent)	CASE 3 Interest Cost	Pri
1957	2.00	20	26	1,005.90	108.0	1,080	2,039
1958	2.10	42	52	1,009.70	0.5	10	968
1959	2.20	66	78	1,011.60	0.5	15	950
1960	2.30	92	104	1,011.40	0.5	20	931
1961	2.40	120	130	1,009.40	0.5	25	911
1962	2.50	150	156	1,005.50	0.5	30	889
1963	2.60	182	182	1,000.00	0.5	35	866
1964	2.70	216	208	992.80	0.5	40	842
1965	2.80	252	234	984.20	0.5	45	818
1966	2.90	290	260	974.10	0.5	50	793
Total		1,430	1,430	10,004.60		1,350	10,010

Interest cost computations:

Case 1: $1,430 ÷ $55,000 = 2.6 per cent (equivalent to "present value" cost).
Case 2: ($1,430—$4.60*) ÷ $55,000 = 2.5916 per cent.
Case 3: ($1,350—$10.90*) ÷ $55,000 = 2.4347 per cent.

* Premium.
Cols. 5 and 9 were taken from yield tables using the assumed coupons of the yields applica in each case.

one a different coupon is put on each maturity and the coupon is made exactly identical to the assumed yield. In other words, these bonds should all sell exactly at par. This should result in as near a true interest cost at present value as any case we present here. In the second case, just one coupon has been attached to the issue, the coupon which is the average interest cost for the entire issue according to the computations of case 1. Here, the price which would be realized for each maturity of bond is shown in column 5 of part 2; the total for this column shows that the issue as a whole would sell for $4.60 more than par. If this $4.60 is deducted from the interest cost as figured in column 4 (which has the same total as column 3 but not the same amounts year-by-year), the resulting computation of interest cost by the conventional formula for awarding bids for state and local government bonds ends up slightly less than that shown in case 1. In other words, with the assumption of an ascending yield curve, a single coupon gives a computed lower average interest cost than a coupon fitted exactly to the yields of the market which is presumably a sort of ideal case in which present value and interest cost both yield the same results.

But the extreme, and of course unreal, case would be that in which the coupon cost was moved into the first year as much as possible and as little as possible was allowed for later years. This grotesque illustration is case 3. Here a coupon of $\frac{1}{2}$ of 1 per cent for the last nine maturities was assumed; the coupon of the first year was loaded to the point necessary to make the whole issue sell for more than par, which amount turned out to be the absurd coupon of 108 per cent per annum. When the computation of interest cost according to the conventional state and local government formula is made, the presumption of lower cost is striking; the margin is much more than that which usually separates the bids of competing buyers.

In practice, of course, the buyers of issues could never go as far as case 3 assumes. The buyers are usually underwriting groups who must sell the obligations to ultimate investors, and ultimate investors have an understandable reluctance for odd and extreme coupons. A security having a coupon of 108 per cent might be salable to a commercial bank with a sophisticated investment department and, what is more important, a sophisticated and understanding board of directors. But there are problems of an even greater character in selling low-coupon long-term bonds even at deep discounts. For one thing, as already pointed out in Chapter 6, only the initial purchaser of these bonds can use the full yield for purposes of getting an exemption from income taxation; subsequent purchasers can use only the coupon. Thus these bonds are peculiarly unmarketable obligations.

But just the same, the effects of manipulated coupon structures on the computed interest cost is material; shrewd investment bankers with sharp pencils have found that it is worthwhile to go to the extra trouble involved in marketing these securities with special coupons; they can win bids by such devices. Much of the energy of the great houses which manage the syndicate accounts that bid for these securities is devoted to just this purpose.

In Part 3 of our hypothetical illustration, we attempt to introduce a note of reality into our computations (Table B-3). In the first place, the other computations assumed a market yield and any premium resulting from the "price" calculated in each case was deducted from the dollar value of the coupons or the interest cost in dollars in full. In other words, we were making no allowance for the margin of the investment banker. In cases 4 and 5 we drop this quite unreal assumption and allow a margin of one dollar a bond. For case 4 we assume a bidding group that can market some of the early maturities at a fairly high coupon, but otherwise they cannot find buyers unless they put on coupons that will "produce" prices not too far from par. The price (which multiplied by the dollar amount in each maturity is called the "production" in underwriting parlance) must yield a little margin over par since the bidding rules in most cases require a bid of par or better and the group must also work out its own margin from the sale price of the obligations. For the purpose of this case we have assumed that the second bidding group (case 5) has somewhat more aggressive salesmen; they figure that they will be able to sell the early maturities at an even higher coupon than was estimated by the first group. But their real secret weapon is assumed to be an advance deal by which they can sell the one longest maturity at a ½ of one per cent coupon. They have found one investor who will buy this long-term, deep-discount bond in spite of its dis-

TABLE B-3

Hypothetical Illustration

Part 3. Same assumptions as in Parts 1 and 2, with still different coupon assumptions and with the further exception that underwriters bidding for issues are assumed to retain a profit of one dollar a bond

	CASE 4			CASE 5		
turities	*Coupon*	*Interest Cost* (Same as Part I)	*Price ("produc-tion")*	*Coupon*	*Interest Cost*	*Price ("produc-tion")*
957	4	40	1,019.70	5	50	1,029.50
958	4	80	1,037.00	5	100	1,056.50
959	4	120	1,052.00	5	150	1,080.90
960	2¼	90	998.10	5	200	1,102.60
961	2¼	112.5	993.00	2½	125	1,004.70
962	2½	150	1,000.00	2½	150	1,000.00
963	2½	175	993.60	2½	175	993.60
964	2½	200	985.70	2½	200	985.70
965	2½	225	976.30	2½	225	976.30
966	2½	250	965.40	½	50	793.00
Total		1,442.5	10,020.80		1,425	10,022.80

Interest cost computations:
Case 4: ($1,442.50−$10.80*) ÷ $55,000 = 2.6031 per cent.
Case 5: ($1,425−$12.80*) ÷ $55,000 = 2.5676 per cent.

Premium less underwriters' profit.

advantages.[3] The intervening coupon was doubtless arrived at during the price meeting of this bidding group at a level which was figured salable and which would "produce" a price above par for the whole issue. Using these assumptions, we find that the interest cost in case 5 is materially below that of case 4.

[3] In practice they probably would have had to offer this one maturity at a yield considerably higher than the market for a more conventional issue. The low-coupon terminal maturities are usually not reoffered publicly, but underwriters report that the effective yield at which these special obligations are sold is usually from 40 to 60 basis points above a comparable maturity sold at par.

INDEX